J. S. Bach's much-performed motets are probably the most sophisticated pieces ever composed in the genre. Daniel Melamed takes a fresh look at Bach's works in the context of the German motet tradition, showing that they are firmly rooted in the conventions of his time. This allows new insights into Bach's contribution to the genre and into the vexing question of instrumental participation in the motets. Professor Melamed argues for Bach's authorship of an early motet wrongly dismissed as inauthentic, and demonstrates that other motets were products of Bach's familiar technique of musical reworking. The chronology of the motets can be substantially revised, and Bach's activities as a motet composer shown to extend over his entire career. An understanding of the eighteenth-century conception of "motet" sheds light on how and why Bach used motet style in his cantatas, Latin works, and oratorios. Finally Bach's study and performance of seventeenth-century motets late in his life, documented in newly discovered and reconstructed sources, played an important role in his exploration of his family's history and of the musical past.

J. S. Bach and the German motet

J. S. Bach
and the
German motet

DANIEL R. MELAMED

Yale University

CAMBRIDGE
UNIVERSITY PRESS

PUBLISHED BY THE PRESS SYNDICATE OF THE UNIVERSITY OF CAMBRIDGE
The Pitt Building, Trumpington Street, Cambridge, United Kingdom

CAMBRIDGE UNIVERSITY PRESS
The Edinburgh Building, Cambridge CB2 2RU, UK
40 West 20th Street, New York NY 10011–4211, USA
477 Williamstown Road, Port Melbourne, VIC 3207, Australia
Ruiz de Alarcón 13, 28014 Madrid, Spain
Dock House, The Waterfront, Cape Town 8001, South Africa

http://www.cambridge.org

First published 1995
First paperback edition 2005

A catalogue record for this book is available from the British Library

Library of Congress cataloguing in publication data
Melamed, Daniel R.
J. S. Bach and the German motet / Daniel R. Melamed.
p.   cm.
Includes bibliographical references (p.   ) and index.
ISBN 0 521 41864 X (hardback)
1. Bach, Johann Sebastian, 1685–1750. Motets.
2. Motet – Germany – 17th century.   3. Motet – Germany – 18th century.
I. Title.
ML410.Bl3M33 1995
782.2'6'092 – dc20   94–5293 CIP MN

ISBN 0 521 41864 X hardback
ISBN 0 521 61976 9 paperback

To the memory of my father,
the scholar

CONTENTS

TABLES

MUSIC EXAMPLES

FIGURES

PREFACE

This book started as my doctoral dissertation, so my acknowledgments must begin with thanks to those who supported it (and me) when I was a graduate student. First comes my adviser, Christoph Wolff, who guided the study and taught wise lessons about turning interesting observations into good ideas. Next, many scholars have given me large amounts of their time and the benefit of their expert advice, especially Kirsten Beißwenger, Robert Hill, Klaus Hofmann, Yoshitake Kobayashi, Michael Marissen, Joshua Rifkin, Hans-Joachim Schulze, Anne Stone, and Peter Wollny, and I thank them all.

The research for this study would not have been possible without the assistance of many libraries and their librarians. I want especially to thank Rudolf Elvers, Joachim Jaenecke, and Hans-Günter Klein of the former Staatsbibliothek Preußischer Kulturbesitz, and Wolfgang Goldhan of the former Deutsche Staatsbibliothek. The staff of the Eda Kuhn Loeb and Isham Memorial Libraries at Harvard University were indefatigable in tracking down and acquiring sources and materials.

I acknowledge here the kind permission given by the following libraries and individuals to reproduce manuscripts, prints, photographs, and architectural features: the Staatsbibliothek zu Berlin/Preußischer Kulturbesitz and the director of its Music Division, Dr. Helmut Hell; the Eda Kuhn Loeb Music Library, Harvard University; the Music Library, Yale University; the Nikolaikirche, Leipzig; and Breitkopf & Härtel, Wiesbaden.

I am grateful for financial support for research and writing provided by a John Knowles Paine Traveling Fellowship from Harvard University, a grant from the Wesley Weyman Fund, a grant from the German Academic Exchange Service, and a year's fellowship from the Mrs. Giles Whiting Foundation. And to all who have been patient with me – especially Penny Souster of the Cambridge University Press – thank you.

ABBREVIATIONS

ABA	Altbachisches Archiv
AmB	Amalien-Bibliothek (now in SBB)
BG	Bach-Gesellschaft, *Johann Sebastian Bachs Werke*
BJ	*Bach-Jahrbuch*
BT	Werner Neumann, ed., *Sämtliche von Johann Sebastian Bach vertonte Texte*
BuxWV	Georg Karstädt, *Thematisch-systematisches Verzeichnis der musikalischen Werke von Dietrich Buxtehude*
BWV	Wolfgang Schmieder, *Thematisch-systematisches Verzeichnis der musikalischen Werke von Johann Sebastian Bach*
DDT	Denkmäler deutscher Tonkunst
Dok	Bach-Archiv Leipzig, *Bach-Dokumente*, vols. 1–3
EDM	Das Erbe deutscher Musik
MGG	*Die Musik in Geschichte und Gegenwart*, ed. Friedrich Blume
NBA [KB]	Johann Sebastian Bach, *Neue Ausgabe sämtlicher Werke* [*Kritischer Bericht*]
New Grove	*The New Grove Dictionary of Music and Musicians*, ed. Stanley Sadie
P, St	SBB Mus. ms. Bach P (score), St (parts)
SA	Sing-Akademie zu Berlin
SBB	Staatsbibliothek zu Berlin/Preußischer Kulturbesitz

Introduction

On a trip to Leipzig a few years ago I had the opportunity of visiting the room where the Thomanerchor rehearses. On the walls are portraits of past Thomascantors, with Johann Sebastian Bach's portrait occupying the place of honor. There was no music in sight, with one exception: on a small table at the front of the room sat neat piles of the scores of Bach's motets, stacked like some kind of bar graph of the choir's work. It seemed particularly fitting that these compositions, which have apparently never left the repertory of the Thomanerchor since their composer's tenure as its director, should be symbolically displayed as the heart of the choir's repertory even today.

The splendid isolation of Bach's motets in the choir's rehearsal room also supplies a telling metaphor for the place of these works in the motet tradition. Bach's motets are among the most often published, performed, and recorded of his vocal works, but the general consensus among specialists and non-specialists alike has long been that they have little to do with the motet tradition in Germany in Bach's time. Writers from Philipp Spitta on have looked elsewhere for clues to the origins of Bach's motets – to organ music, to concerted vocal works – anywhere but to the motet. Bach's motets have been cut off from their context; they sit on a pedestal rather than at the summit of the genre.

The tendency to isolate Bach's motets is well illustrated by their treatment in the long-standard history of the motet, Hugo Leichtentritt's *Geschichte der Motette* (Leipzig, 1908). Leichtentritt presents a chapter called "The German motet from Heinrich Schütz to J. S. Bach," and then one called "The motet since J. S. Bach," but his discussion of Bach's motets themselves occupies exactly one page – about the same as the treatment of those of his ancestors Johann Michael Bach and Johann Christoph Bach, and six pages fewer than are devoted to the motets of Andreas Hammerschmidt. The structure of the book suggests that Bach's motets represent some kind of watershed, but its content is hardly affected by them. Leichtentritt explains that Bach's motets "stand entirely apart in the motet genre," and that in their design they "diverge completely from that which one otherwise calls a motet" (pp. 362f.). Later he writes that Bach was, in fact, of little importance as a motet composer. His incomparably great compositions bear the name "motet" unjustly; they are, he avers, rather "cantatas for chorus" (p. 429).

The reluctance to consider Bach's music in the context of the musical conventions and traditions of his time – Leichtentritt is by no means alone, and the motets were not the only compositions to be so treated – is a little hard to explain. Perhaps the nineteenth-century images of Bach as a musical genius on the one hand and as a religiously inspired composer on the other have left their mark, making us less inclined to seek the roots of Bach's music in such relatively mundane explanations as musical traditions and conventions. Also, we know so much more about Bach than about other composers, especially in the realm of unglamorous genres like the motet, that there is a temptation to measure them and their music against Bach rather than the other way around. In the case of the motets, it is probably true that Bach's are the most sophisticated ever composed, and it is understandable that commentators should be disinclined to try to make sense of them in relation to lesser repertory. There is no real need, because the works stand up magnificently in isolation.

But surely there is much to be gained from looking at Bach's motets in context. At the moment, doing so is problematic. Our control over the history of the motet in early eighteenth-century German-speaking lands is incomplete, so a full study of the repertorial context of Bach's motets is not yet possible. Nonetheless, we can still examine Bach's motets in light of the norms of motet writing of his time, primarily by turning to written sources on the motet and its characteristics. It is clear from a study of these sources that musicians of the time had definite ideas about what a motet was and how it should be constructed, and that they used the term discriminately for certain kinds of compositions. It should come as no surprise that a careful investigation shows that Bach, too, was discriminating in his use of the term.

Perhaps more importantly, if we look at Bach's motets from the point of view of the early eighteenth-century understanding of "motet," it becomes clear that the works he called by that name do, in fact, agree with the contemporary understanding of what a motet was. Bach brought a level of musical sophistication to the motet that is apparently not found in other composers' music, he did enlarge the conception of the motet slightly, and there is little doubt that he borrowed techniques from other musical types. But his fundamental conception of the motet was that of his contemporaries, and the special qualities of his contributions to the genre are all the more striking in light of an understanding of his starting-place: the early eighteenth-century norm of the motet.

The special status awarded to Bach's motets has led to some misconceptions that need to be addressed. If Bach did indeed create his motets entirely apart from the tradition of the late seventeenth and early eighteenth centuries, as was the premise for many years, then the idea that the young Bach composed motets in the mold of his predecessors was essentially unthinkable. And if his motets were the towering works of original genius that admirers made them out to be, then unthinkable, too, was the possibility that parody, arrangement, and reworking of musical materials might have played a role in their creation. The chronology and compositional history of Bach's motets, although still not fully illuminated, turn out on close examination to resemble those of his other works: motet composition spanned Bach's professional career, some of Bach's motets were the product of musical reworking of extant material, and his works in the genre show a change from earlier motets that resemble seventeenth-century models to later compositions that are more modern and innovative.

An understanding of Bach's conception of motet style has other consequences as well. Commentators have long identified motet-like elements in Bach's concerted compositions, especially the cantatas, but for the most part they have not recognized the extent to which the motet-like movements in concerted works reflect the norms of the motet genre. Many of the textual and musical features of motet-like movements in concerted works can be better understood from the perspective of the contemporary motet. This insight puts in our hands a potentially useful analytical and interpretive tool for examining Bach's concerted music.

Motets and motet style also turn out to play an important role in Bach's exploration of the musical past and in his interest in his distinguished musical ancestry. Late in his life, Bach performed a substantial number of late seventeenth-century vocal works, most of them motets. Most of the motets, in turn, were compositions by an older member of the Bach family. Motet style was thus a locus of Bach's exploration of his musical patrimony. Not only does the examination of this repertory and Bach's use of it illuminate his later years and his historical interests, it also gives us a glimpse at the kind of music with which he grew up – a repertory otherwise difficult to identify. It was from this repertory, of course, that Bach learned his craft and the conventions of musical practice that governed his own compositions. Thus, in his last years, Bach explored through the motet his place in the music of his time.

PART ONE

The term and concept "motet"

CHAPTER 1

The term "motet" in the first half of the eighteenth century

It is by now a commonplace that J. S. Bach rarely called his church cantatas "cantatas," referring to them instead as concertos, or church pieces, or principal music for the worship service. Nonetheless, the term cantata has stuck because it is convenient and because there is a clear historical reason for its use: we can draw connections between Bach's concerted sacred vocal works and pieces that are explicitly called "cantatas." These connections are well studied and much discussed, and the position of Bach's compositions in the history of the cantata is reasonably clear. Bach's cantatas have a place in the genre and a connection to the term.

In the repertory of J. S. Bach's sacred vocal works there is another small but important group of pieces that the composer, his students, and his copyists called by the same name used today: the motets. Dozens of works Bach did not call cantatas are now routinely included under the rubric "cantata," but among the motets there is the opposite tendency to doubt Bach's own label – to question whether a piece he labeled "motet" really is one. What is more, his motets are generally considered so superior to those of his contemporaries and predecessors that little thought is given to their connection to the genre or to the early eighteenth-century German understanding of the term.

"Motet" was, in fact, a technical term in the first half of the eighteenth century. It described a particular genre and an associated musical style, and brought with it conventions of text selection, musical construction, and performance practice. If we start with an examination of the general understanding of the word "motet" in Bach's time, we will then be in a position to appreciate what the term meant to Bach, to make sense of when he used it and when not, to understand his cultivation of the musical genre and style it described, and to assess whether he applied it in the same way as did his contemporaries in central Germany. There is ample evidence that his understanding of the term was in fundamental agreement with that of his contemporaries, and a study of the term and Bach's use of it illuminates strong connections between the motet tradition in Germany and Bach's own remarkable motets. A study of the term and the musical concepts behind it also provides valuable insights into Bach's concerted music, and can help refine the concept of motet style as an important analytical tool for that repertory.

Fortunately, the eighteenth-century understanding of the term is well documented in written sources of the time. Not all writers are in complete agreement – there are inevitably individual points of view – but the various discussions nonetheless give a clear view of the scope of the term and of the points of contention over its use and meaning.

Like many other words, "motet" presents several fundamental problems that make its meaning difficult to establish exactly. First, there is the question of exactly what kind of composition the term refers to: a type of piece (a genre), a way of writing (a style), or – later in the eighteenth century – perhaps even a musical form. Second, as eighteenth-century writers themselves occasionally note, several different types of compositions were referred to as "motets." These pieces are musically different enough that some definitions of the term appear to struggle with internal inconsistencies in an attempt to accommodate them. Finally, in different languages the term could refer to different kinds of pieces, making the musical identity of a motet hard to pin down, even in the limited context of German writings and compositions. One needs to understand and keep in mind the various possible meanings of "motet" in deciding what the term signifies in a particular context.

Despite these ambiguities, it is usually not difficult to figure out what a user of the term intended, and there is little question that the term "motet" had a definite meaning. My aim here is to use contemporary writings and definitions of "motet" to establish what musicians in central Germany in the early eighteenth century meant by the term, and to explore the most important musical issues surrounding the motet and motet style.

Johann Gottfried Walther's definition in his *Musicalisches Lexicon* (Leipzig, 1732) makes a good starting-point because it raises most of the issues that eighteenth-century writers apparently found most important, and because it is likely that J. S. Bach was familiar with it. Walther and Bach were cousins, colleagues in Weimar, and correspondents; Bach was also a sales agent for Walther's dictionary.[1] The first part of Walther's definition, which begins by clearly laying out the motet as a musical genre with particular characteristics, is as follows:

> Motetto, plural Motetti [Italian] Motet, plural Motets [French]. Others write: Motteto; still others, Moteto; Latin: Motettus or Mottetus, Motetus, Motectum, Moteta, etc. is properly a musical composition written on a biblical *Spruch*, just to be sung without instruments (basso continuo excepted), richly ornamented with *Fugen* and *Imitationibus*. But the vocal parts can be taken by and strengthened with diverse instruments. Foreigners nowadays extend the meaning of this term Motetto, to a sacred composition whose text is in Latin, consisting of arias and recitatives, and to which various instruments are supplied, with *à parten* melodies by turn; as to be seen, among others, in the first opus of Gio. Batt. Allegri.[2]

---

[1] *Dok* II/260.

[2] Johann Gottfried Walther, *Musicalisches Lexicon* (Leipzig, 1732). The complete original text of Walther's and other motet definitions discussed here will be found in the Appendix.

Motet texts

When Walther describes a motet as being composed "on a biblical *Spruch*," he identifies one of the most important characteristics of the genre and one pursued by many other writers: the nature of its texts. Indeed, Johann Adolph Scheibe begins the long discussion of motets in his *Critischer Musicus* with the question of text selection. This makes sense from a compositional point of view, but also underscores the importance of text type in defining the genre. Nearly every definition of motet cites one or two possible text sources characteristic of motets: biblical *Sprüche* or *dicta*, and chorale verses. (It is taken mostly for granted in eighteenth-century writings that motets are sacred compositions, but Scheibe suggests that secular motets were occasionally undertaken, a practice of which he disapproves.[3])

Spruch texts, which had a particularly strong association with the motet, are the type most frequently cited and discussed in connection with the genre. Friedrich Wilhelm Marpurg also describes a type of motet setting using a chorale alone: "This type results . . . when one introduces the fixed melody of the chorale in augmentation in a specific voice according to the measure of the entering *Glieder* or *Sätze*, or in other somewhat contrasting values against them."[4] Writers often cite a type of motet made from both a chorale and a biblical text, the latter usually sung twice. Friedrich Erhard Niedt describes these pieces as follows: "There is also a kind of motet . . . in which a verse from a chorale or other sacred song is introduced, ordinarily sung by the soprano; the other voices – alto, tenor and bass – sing a *Dictum*, or *Spruch*, from the Bible in figural style in between."[5]

Given the large number of double-choir motets in the repertory, it comes as no surprise that Scheibe praises double-choir motets as best because they are most satisfying to the ear.[6] He offers the following guidelines for the disposition of material among the voices and choirs, a division based on text type:

> If chorale verses are used, one has one choir enter with them, at certain times; the second choir must continue to sing the main *Spruch* of the motet unimpeded. In this case an exchange can also take place, in that one gives the chorale now to one choir, now to the other. But if the motet is for only one choir, the chorale must be sung by one or two voices, and the others must work their way through their principal material steadily and unimpeded.[7]

The combination and simultaneous presentation of two different texts (usually a chorale and a biblical *Spruch*) was also used in other types of compositions such as arias, but was especially associated with the motet.

Scheibe and Niedt each stress the importance of choosing a chorale and biblical text that work together well. Scheibe warns of the many "contradictory and laughable" motets in which they do not.[8] Niedt relates two such examples, one showing a nonsensical combination of chorale and *Spruch* that he attributes to a small-town

---

[3] Johann Adolph Scheibe, *Critischer Musicus*, 2nd edn. (Leipzig, 1745), 179f.
[4] Friedrich Wilhelm Marpurg, *Abhandlung von der Fuge*, 2 vols. (Berlin, 1753–54), 2:132.
[5] Friedrich Erhard Niedt, *Musicalische Handleitung Dritter Theil*, ed. Johann Mattheson (Hamburg, 1717), 34.
[6] *Critischer Musikus*, 181.
[7] *Critischer Musikus*, 181.
[8] *Critischer Musikus*, 179.

cantor, and one intentionally off-color combination perpetrated by an unnamed Thuringian composer at the expense of a member of the clergy and his daughter.[9] The combination of texts was important enough to the motet that it deserved comment when it was mishandled, deliberately or not.

The particular qualities of the motet texts specified by these writers are an important influence on motets' musical characteristics. Chorale texts, for example, bring with them regular meter as well as fixed poetic form, rhyme, and melodic material. Eighteenth-century writers do not discuss in detail the treatment of chorales in motets; presumably, the setting of hymn melodies was sufficiently well discussed in other contexts. The same writers have more to say about biblical prose texts and their contribution to the musical characteristics of motets. From a structural point of view, for example, Scheibe writes that the biblical words chosen for a motet "must be so constructed that one can divide them without difficulty into two, three, or four sections, because that is how long a motet should be."[10] It is significant that Scheibe suggests selecting a text that will yield this structure; a fixed musical organization has come to govern the selection of texts, at least to some extent.

The prosodic qualities of biblical texts were also seen to influence a motet's thematic material. This influence is addressed in Heinrich Bokemeyer's discussion in *Der melodische Vorhof* of the suitability of different kinds of texts for musical treatment, and in Johann Mattheson's commentary on it. Bokemeyer first establishes that poetry is better suited to music because of its inherent meter; prose, because of its varying metrical feet, he argues, does not always lend itself to singing.[11] Bokemeyer goes on to say that some prose texts are better suited than others, particularly emphasizing biblical texts: "In German, most biblical *Sprüche* are well suited to be sung, because the feet are so varied that they provide a pleasant rhythm; if only a few syllables are sung a little longer, and a sensible [composer] deals with them."[12] Mattheson's gloss on this section suggests the kinds of musical setting that are appropriate to such texts: "German *dicta* lend themselves, in my humble opinion, to nothing other than full choruses, fugues, *Motetten-Art*, and recitative."[13] The strong affinity between motets and biblical *dicta* is here explained by the prosody of that kind of text.

Implicit in these comments is the judgment that *Spruch* texts were unsuited to most other kinds of musical treatment, and Bokemeyer and Mattheson were not the only ones to pick on German prose texts in this way. Bach's predecessor in Leipzig, Johann Kuhnau, addressed the difficulty of setting German *dicta* to music by suggesting that if a German text did not lead the composer to a fitting musical idea, the composer should turn to a translation of the text in another language.[14] Mattheson himself suggested Latin, whose metrical feet he presumably found more amenable to musical settings.[15]

---

[9]   *Musicalische Handleitung*, 36f.
[10]   *Critischer musikus*, 179.
[11]   Heinrich Bokemeyer, *Der melodische Vorhof*, in Johann Mattheson, *Critica Musica*, 2 vols. (Hamburg, 1722–25), 2: 301.
[12]   *Der melodische Vorhof*, 2:301f.
[13]   *Der melodische Vorhof*, 2:302. Mattheson also makes the same point on p. 296.
[14]   Johann Kuhnau, *Text zur Leipziger Kirchen-Music* (Leipzig, 1709), transcribed in Bernhard Friedrich Richter, "Eine Abhandlung Joh. Kuhnau's," *Monatshefte für Musik-Geschichte* 34, no. 9 (1902): 150.
[15]   *Der melodische Vorhof*, 2:302.

Despite their enthusiasm for the practice, both Bokemeyer and Mattheson suggest that it is difficult to set metrically irregular biblical prose to music successfully. At the same time, Mattheson praises the interesting musical results that irregular prose texts can produce. These apparently contradictory views arise because the writers are actually referring to two different kinds of musical settings. Poetic texts, with their regular meter, were considered suited to rhythmically and metrically more regular settings of the type found in arias. Metrically irregular prose text, on the other hand, was thought to be best suited to rhythmically free kinds of composition like motets, fugues, and recitatives, in which regularity of textual and musical phrases was not important. (Mattheson's other possibility, "volle Chor," could presumably accommodate both metrically regular and irregular musical settings.) Motet style and the closely related fugue were associated with biblical prose, for which they were well suited because of their freedom from metrical constraints. Bokemeyer shows a bias toward the rhythmically regular styles when he suggests that one should probably have a poet versify biblical texts to make them more suitable for setting[16] – suitable, that is, for metrically regular musical treatments – and Mattheson suggests that Psalm texts are better suited for setting than other biblical texts because they resemble poetry.[17]

Along with prosody, the content and organization of biblical verses were also important in eighteenth-century discussions of their musical treatment. For example, Bokemeyer suggests that certain kinds of texts present two different affects

> in those units that consist of two contrary sentences. E.g., Psalm 20:9 "They are brought down and fallen: but we are risen, and stand upright." Ps. 34:11 "The rich do lack, and suffer hunger: but they that seek the Lord shall not want any good thing." (This point must be more thoroughly investigated, because sometimes contrary affects appear together, as in the last example.)[18]

Mattheson takes strong objection, arguing that such texts do not, in fact, present contradictory affects:

> Excuse me! No contradictory affects appear in the words "The rich . . ." This is simply a contemplation of God's friendliness, and a taking of pleasure in his righteousness, that he lets the rich go hungry, and the God-fearing want for nothing. These antitheses yield good double fugues, because they work toward the same end, although in different terms.[19]

Mattheson suggests that instead of contradictions, such texts embody the rhetorical device of antithesis, in which two strongly contrasting ideas are juxtaposed. Here, in a rare display of specificity about a matter of rhetoric, Mattheson suggests that this rhetorical device is well suited to a particular kind of musical setting: the double fugue. He does not explain the technique in detail, but it is not difficult to guess how it works: each phrase of a text constructed in two parallel segments, such as an antithesis, can be given to one of the two subjects of a double fugue. The clear further implication is that the two textual and musical units can then be presented simultaneously.

---

[16] *Der melodische Vorhof*, 2:302.
[17] *Der melodische Vorhof*, 2:296.
[18] *Der melodische Vorhof*, 2:322f.
[19] *Der melodische Vorhof*, 2:324.

(This technique is later discussed by Heinrich Christoph Koch, who extends it to triple fugues and beyond.[20]) In fact, this practice is well represented in J. S. Bach's motets and motet-like settings of texts containing antitheses (see chapter 8). In this respect and in others, the organization of biblical texts and their prosody had a strong influence on the musical characteristics of the motets with which they were so closely associated in the early eighteenth century.

Voices and instruments in motets

Perhaps the most important musical characteristic Walther cites in his definition of the motet concerns performing forces. A motet is a composition "just to be sung without instruments (basso continuo excepted)," an essential restriction echoed by many other writers. Significantly, although the motet was understood as a vocal genre, nearly every writer also allows for the participation of instruments, whose presence does not make a work any less a motet. There is one important restriction on the role of instruments in motets: they play strictly *colla parte* with the voices, as Mattheson explains in detail:

> The earlier motets consisted of fugues or fugal sections, without instruments, without basso continuo; though in recent times one admits not only basso continuo, but also has that which the voices sing doubled by sundry instruments to play along, and thinks it proper. But the players play not a single note more than, different from, or less than the singers, which is an essential condition of motets.[21]

These and other definitions make clear that the musical substance of a motet is contained in its vocal parts; Mattheson acknowledges that this characteristic extends back to earlier (i.e., sixteenth-century) motets. Nonetheless, despite the restriction on the role of instruments in a motet, their participation figures consistently in definitions of the genre. *Colla parte* participation is cited routinely in eighteenth-century definitions and discussions of the motet. The use of doubling instruments was not merely conceivable or permissible, but was fully compatible with the fundamental conception of "motet."

Few writers have much to say about the purpose of the doubling instruments. Walther says that the instruments strengthen the voices; Scheibe takes a similar position: "The other instruments play regularly with the voices, and not to stand out from them, but only to make them clear."[22] This comment makes clear the subordinate role of instruments in motets. Significantly, it also shows that the participation of doubling instruments was a separate matter from the participation of basso continuo in the performance of a motet, because Scheibe refers to "the other instruments," having already discussed the role of the continuo, which he says should always be present. This view is echoed in Walther's definition, in which he calls a motet a piece "to be sung without instruments (basso continuo excepted)." For Walther as for Scheibe, the continuo group does not count among the "instruments."

---

[20] *Musikalisches Lexikon* (Frankfurt-am-Main, 1802), s.v. "Motette."
[21] Johann Mattheson, *Der vollkommene Capellmeister* (Hamburg, 1739), 75.
[22] *Critischer Musikus*, 182.

Motet definitions distinguish explicitly or implicitly between vocal compositions in which the instruments simply double the voices (motets), and those in which the instruments have independent parts (concertos). Scheibe makes the distinction between motets and concertos clear in discussing the material given to instruments. He warns that if one goes beyond a doubling role for the instruments in a motet, "then one would change the style, and lapse into proper *Kirchenconcerten* or Masses."[23] In other words, the role of instruments in a vocal composition largely determines the work's identity: *colla parte* instruments make a motet, independent instruments a concerto.

Curiously, by the first half of the eighteenth century, the motet was sometimes defined by what it did *not* have – independent instruments – and what any instruments that might be present did *not* do. For example, Daniel Speer defines "Motteti" [sic] as "a choral piece in which the voices do not concertize."[24] Martin Heinrich Fuhrmann described a motet as a piece "in which the voices *fugiren* and *concertiren* not at all or just a little."[25] These negative definitions of the motet – more or less as vocal compositions that are not concertos – show clearly that the vocal concerto had come to be regarded as the normative kind of sacred vocal music against which other types were measured. Negative definitions of "motet," with their explicit or implicit references to the vocal concerto, illustrate the fundamental contrast between the two genres.[26]

Some early eighteenth-century writings address this issue directly. For example, Johann Heinrich Buttstedt complains that "these days one further extends the meaning of the word *Motetti*, so that the motets that are now composed are to be called more concertos than motets."[27] Coming from Buttstedt, this comment is not merely a pedantic gripe about nomenclature; it probably has to be read as his lament for the corruption of the older style (the motet) by a newer one (the concerto). Even so, the fundamental opposition of motet and concerto is clear. Scheibe, too, begins his discussion of the motet by contrasting motet and concerto, but he puts the blame for the demise of the motet even further back, writing that "Ludwig Viadana, an Italian, inventor of the basso continuo, was a great enemy of motets."[28] Scheibe does not intend to proscribe the use of basso continuo in motets; recall that he writes elsewhere that continuo should always be present.[29] Rather, he acknowledges the fundamental difference in musical procedure between the often contrapuntally conceived motet and the vocal concerto with its melody–bass polarization, and blames Viadana's "invention" of the concerto for the motet's downfall.

The relationship between the motet and the concerto plays a role in Walther's assertion that "foreigners nowadays extend the meaning of this term." His statement is echoed and amplified by Mattheson, who observes that "nowadays one extends the

---

[23] *Critischer Musikus*, 182.
[24] Daniel Speer, *Grundrichtiger Unterricht der musikalischen Kunst*, 2nd edn. (Ulm, 1697), 285.
[25] *Musicalischer-Trichter* (Berlin, 1706), 82. This definition also appears in the *Kurtzgefaßtes Musicalisches Lexicon* (Chemnitz, 1737).
[26] One occasionally encounters the hybrid term "motetti concertali," defined by Speer, *Grundrichtiger Unterricht*, 285, as "ein bemeldtes Stuck mit Instrumenten."
[27] Johann Heinrich Buttstedt, *Ut, mi, sol, re, fa, la* (Erfurt, 1716), 86.
[28] *Critischer Musikus*, 177.
[29] *Critischer Musikus*, 181.

meaning of this word further, and composes *Motetti* with instrumental as well as vocal choirs."[30] Mattheson may or may not have been referring here to foreigners, but either way, his and Walther's statements suggest that "motet" could be more broadly construed, especially in languages other than German. Indeed, Sebastian de Brossard, on whose definition Walther's is apparently based, wrote that the term "motet" sometimes referred to all pieces set to Latin texts, whatever the subject of the text.[31] French music prints of the late seventeenth century confirm this broad usage in the French language; for example, Brossard himself used the term in the title of his *Elevations et Motets à II. et III. voix, et à voix seule, deux Dessus de Violon ou deux Flûtes avec la Basse-continue* (Paris, 1698). As Walther implies, in French the term was considerably wider in scope than in German.

In Italian, too, "motet" had come to represent a wide range of sacred compositions, from solo works with basso continuo to pieces with several voices and instruments; this usage is illustrated, for example, in the title of Giovanni Legrenzi's *Motetti sacri a voce sola con tre Strumenti* (Venice, 1692). This Italian usage – referring to pieces that German speakers would probably have called concertos – may have been in the minds of composers, copyists, and writers who occasionally applied the term "motet" to works with independent instruments.

These various national uses of the term help account for the hesitancy of writers, especially those writing in German, to restrict themselves to narrow definitions of a motet's musical characteristics. A restrictive definition might describe nicely the kind of piece German speakers called "motets," but would exclude very different pieces that French and Italian speakers called by the same name. The different linguistic usages also help to explain certain uses of the word in Germany that do not conform to its main definition in the German language; sometimes – including in sources connected with J. S. Bach – the term is apparently used in its French or Italian senses. This explains why the heading "motet" sometimes appears on a composition one would first think of as a concerto. (For example, see chapter 2 on J. S. Bach's use of the term to refer to three concerted works.) In early eighteenth-century German usage, a motet was a vocal work without independent instruments, but the vocal concerto, with its independent writing for instruments, was paradoxically never far from the surface when the term was invoked.

Motet style and motet genre

"Motet" is defined and discussed in early eighteenth-century writings both as type of piece (*Gattung*, genre) and as way of writing (*stylus, Schreib-Art*, style).[32] For example, Mattheson defines a motet as a kind of piece, with certain musical characteristics,[33] whereas Buttstedt invokes the concept of motet style as one of several styles, or ways

---

[30] Johann Mattheson, *Das neu-eröffnete Orchestre* (Hamburg, 1713), 142.
[31] *Dictionaire de Musique*, 2nd edn. (Paris, 1703).
[32] This issue is the focus of the discussion of the eighteenth-century motet in Rolf Dammann, "Geschichte der Begriffsbestimmung Motette," *Archiv für Musikwissenschaft* 16, no. 4 (1959): 367–72.
[33] *Das neu-eröffnete Orchestre*, 141f.

of writing: *Kirchen Stylus*, *Stylus canonicus*, *motecticus*, *phantasticus*, *madrigalescus*, *melismaticus*, *hyporchematicus*, *symphoniacus*, and *dramaticus*.[34] Scheibe calls motet writing a style, part of the larger category of *Kirchen-Stylo* that includes the Mass, but he later presents more a formal scheme than a set of style characteristics, suggesting that he viewed motet as a type of piece – a genre.[35] Both views were useful. The concept of the genre permits the definition of categories into which pieces could be placed, and makes possible the identification of a particular composition as being of one or another type. The concept of musical style, on the other hand, implicitly invokes the compositional process: a style is a way of writing, independent of specific musical context. The motet was viewed both ways.

The view of "motet" as a style has an important consequence: the style could be used not only in motets themselves, but in other contexts as well, most importantly in multi-movement concerted vocal works. For example, Scheibe suggests that a fugal chorus in a cantata is constructed just like a motet, a view that presumes the concept of a transferable motet style.[36] Mattheson, in his discussion of the setting of biblical *dicta*, suggests the possibility of setting them as a "full chorus" or as a recitative (presumably as parts of a multi-movement vocal concerto) and in *Motetten-Art*. This shows that he considered motet style appropriate not only for motets, but also as an option for a particular kind of text in a mixed text-type libretto. Mattheson here makes explicit the possibility of employing motet style in a concerted vocal work. The understanding of "motet" as a style permits the importation of its musical techniques into other kinds of compositions, a possibility fully explored in J. S. Bach's concerted vocal music.

Motet style, the *stile antico*, and counterpoint

"Motet" was both a style and a genre, but there was also another way in which it had a double meaning: the term was applied in the early eighteenth century to two different kinds of pieces, even discounting its broad Italian and French meanings. On the one hand, it describes German-language settings of biblical and chorale texts; on the other, it was understood to refer to pieces in sixteenth-century contrapuntal style. Thus, in some contexts "motet style" was considered synonymous with *stylus antiquus*, *stile antico*, and similar terms.[37]

The exact division between the two repertories is not always clear, largely because they share certain musical features like notation in relatively large note values, limited role of instruments, and a significant use of counterpoint. What is more, from a historical point of view, the neo-Palestrinian contrapuntal style and that of the German motet have common roots in sixteenth-century practice. But by the eighteenth century, the two styles were apparently regarded as distinct, however loosely they may have been labeled. Johann Mattheson was implicitly attempting to reconcile the two

34 *Ut, mi, sol, re, fa, la*, 62f. Mattheson takes up style in his counter-response, *Das beschützte Orchestre* (Hamburg, 1717), 116.
35 *Critischer Musikus*, 168f.
36 *Critischer Musikus*, 162.
37 See Christoph Wolff, *Der Stile antico in der Musik Johann Sebastian Bachs* (Wiesbaden, 1968).

definitions when he mentions both Hammerschmidt and Lassus as exemplary composers of motets.[38] Here, Lassus clearly represents old-fashioned vocal counterpoint, Hammerschmidt a more modern (and almost exclusively German-language) kind of composition. Nonetheless, works by both composers were called "motets."

This twofold meaning of "motet" can help to explain some of the musical characteristics cited by eighteenth-century writers that apply only loosely to one or the other repertories. Because they apparently wished to draw connections between *stile antico* motets and the somewhat more modern German motets, writers often fashioned definitions that would encompass both. This is especially true with respect to the most frequently mentioned musical characteristic of motets, the use of counterpoint and imitation. Nearly every writer cites this feature. Walther's definition describes motets as "richly ornamented with fugues and imitation." Scheibe writes that "in motets one is accustomed to write nothing but fugues and *Contrapuncten*,"[39] and that "for the working out [of a motet], one needs nothing but full-voiced imitations, fugues, and double fugues."[40] According to Mattheson, motets "do not easily admit a solo, but rather begin one fugue after the other in regular succession, and work them out in all voices";[41] motet style "admits of many interweaved artful manners: colorful, decorated with fugues, *Allabreven*, *Contrapuncten*, etc."[42] For Marpurg, counterpoint defines a motet, which he describes as "a piece of church music put together from many small fugues."[43]

The description of motets as contrapuntal pieces does apply to late-seventeenth-century German motets, but only to a limited extent. Contrapuntal technique did remain important in certain kinds of motets, for example, those of Schütz and Hammerschmidt, often constructed using numerous points of imitation. But in the vast majority of the later Thuringian repertory, for example, counterpoint plays a small role; much of the repertory is relentlessly homophonic. It is clear that the definitions of motets as contrapuntal works are designed largely to fit older music – "Palestrina style" motets and their musical progeny. The continuing use of old Latin motets and the later derivatives of this old style kept alive a traditional association of motets and counterpoint, and kept references to counterpoint in motet definitions. In fact, for some writers, the *stylus motecticus* encompassed the *stylus canonicus* – canons – because of the strong association between imitation and the motet.

The status of the motet

For all the veneration accorded to the polyphonic masters of the sixteenth century and their motets, by the eighteenth century the German motet was considered by some to be a provincial and second-class kind of music, associated with less sophisticated

---

[38] *Der vollkommene Capellmeister*, 74.
[39] *Compendium Musices*; manuscript, transcribed in Peter Benary, *Die deutsche Kompositionslehre des 18. Jahrhunderts* (Leipzig, 1961), 79.
[40] *Critischer Musikus*, 183.
[41] *Das neu-eröffnete Orchestre*, 142.
[42] *Der vollkommene Capellmeister*, 75.
[43] *Abhandlung von der Fuge*, 2:132.

churches and towns. This attitude is apparently the reason for Niedt's disdain for the motet: "I leave the explication of motets to the Thuringian yokels, who retain such [motets] from Hammerschmidt's time (just as the farmers' daughters from Altenburg inherited their boots from their ancestors, and the Spanish their short coats)."[44] Niedt considers the motet a Thuringian specialty, and nearly worthy of dismissal. His derogatory tone is confirmed in anecdotes about motets he recounts at the expense of small-town musicians, and he clearly regarded motets as music for churches of limited resources, culture, and musical ability.

The surviving sources of motets from the late seventeenth and early eighteenth centuries, both in manuscripts and in prints, indeed suggest that the motet was particularly cultivated in Thuringia and Saxony. Among the printed sources, the association of motets with central Germany was even more specific: it was embodied in the person and publications of Andreas Hammerschmidt (1611/12–75), whose music was issued in Freiberg, Dresden, and Zittau.[45] The wide circulation of Hammerschmidt's works and the importance of motets in his publications contributed to the apparently widely-held association of the motet with central Germany in general and with him in particular.[46] This association could be cited in a derogatory way; to at least one reactionary commentator writing in 1722, the "Hammer-schmiedische Manier" represented everything old-fashioned in music.[47]

Scheibe saw great value in motets, but the premise of his comments makes clear the low regard in which the motet was held: "The greatest mistake that is still made in the performance of motets is this: that many accomplished singers consider this kind of composition to be *schülerhaft*, and thus scorn them, and regard them as mere trifles."[48] There is probably an implicit comparison being made here between motets and concerted vocal music, to which the motet had long since given way as the most sophisticated kind of church music. Mattheson gives a reason, writing of motets: "Modern times do not admit of these styles in their former contexts. In this motet style, both the understanding of the words (that is, the sense of the text) and the prop-er, natural course of a pleasant melody suffer too much."[49] This sentiment is echoed by Lorenz Mizler in his summary of Mattheson's text: "In our day, [motets] have fallen out of fashion, because in them the text is horribly tortured."[50]

The ideals of music implied here – clarity of text and the presence of a leading melody – are manifestly not goals of motet style. Scheibe takes this as a given: "That in

---

44   *Musicalische Handleitung*, 34.

45   The contents of Hammerschmidt's prints are summarized in Hugo Leichtentritt, ed., *Ausgewählte Werke von Andreas Hammerschmidt*, DDT 40 (Leipzig, 1910).

46   See Fuhrmann, *Musicalischer-Trichter*, 82; Niedt, *Musicalische Handleitung*, 34; Mattheson, *Der vollkommene Capellmeister*, 74; Scheibe, *Critischer Musikus*, 178.

47   Gottfried Ephraim Scheibel, *Zufällige Gedanken von der Kirchenmusik, wie sie heutiges Tages beschaffen* (Frankfurt and Leipzig, 1722), quoted in Arnold Schering, "Über Bachs Parodieverfahren," *BJ* 18 (1921): 53ff.

48   *Critischer Musikus*, 185.

49   *Der vollkommene Capellmeister*, 75.

50   "Zu unsern Zeiten aber sind sie billig abgekommen, weil der Text dadurch gar erschrecklich gemartert wird." Lorenz Mizler von Kolof, *Neu-eröffnete musikalische Bibliothek*, 4 vols. (Leipzig, 1739–54), 2:222.

motets there can, in general, be no regular and dominating main melody can be gleaned from the foregoing remarks. Thus above all one must see to a well-regulated harmonic coherence."[51] In fact, for Mattheson, the lack of a single unifying melody was an essential characteristic of motets. Chiding Buttstedt for missing the most essential feature in his discussion of motets, he writes that a motet "is full of colorful variations, and not restricted to a single theme."[52] This lack of a restriction to a principal and governing melody, though potentially allowing the expression of several affects in one composition, put the current ideals of music out of the reach of the motet. The motet had not kept up with the new standards of melody and text setting; it could offer its long tradition and close association with certain text types, but could not compete with the cantatas cultivated in progressive musical centers.

Early eighteenth-century writings on the motet suggest that the genre had a generally agreed-on set of musical and textual characteristics, but also that it bore the burden of its place in musical history. This burden forced the term "motet" to accommodate musical types and characteristics of both earlier and later music. To eighteenth-century writers in German, the term referred primarily to German-language compositions treating verses from the Bible (*Sprüche*), chorales verses, or both in the same work. But at the same time, definitions of the term often encompassed Palestrina-style compositions inherited from the late sixteenth century. Motets were understood to be sacred vocal compositions in which instruments could participate; in contrast to vocal concertos, the instruments played only *colla parte* (basso continuo was considered standard). Nonetheless, developments of the modern musical world (and the tendency to construe the term more broadly in Italian and French) meant that the term could, under certain circumstances, also refer to pieces using concerted instruments. About some of the most important aspects of the motet there was more general agreement. The particular qualities of biblical prose texts were considered especially appropriate to motet settings, and counterpoint and fugue were considered essential to motets' musical style. Increasing concern for textual clarity and a strong leading melody later in the century contributed to the declining regard in which motets (considered the province of small churches, especially in Thuringia) were held. In the light of the widespread agreement among writers on most points, the term "motet" needs to be seen as a useful technical term, one that pointed clearly to a specific kind of composition and a particular musical style.

[51] *Critischer Musikus*, 183.
[52] *Das beschützte Orchestre*, 120.

CHAPTER 2

J. S. Bach's use of the term "motet"

It is clear from writings of the first half of the eighteenth century that the term "motet" had a circumscribed if not completely unambiguous meaning to those who used and discussed it. The word described a particular kind of sacred vocal composition and brought with it certain expectations about the choice of texts and about the use of vocal and instrumental forces. The term's ambiguity arose from the different meanings it had in different languages, and from the fact that it covered compositions written over a relatively long period.

The range of meanings sketched in the previous chapter represents a general understanding of the term in the early eighteenth century. When we turn our attention to the meaning and significance of "motet" – both as a term and as a musical concept – to J. S. Bach in particular, we are surely justified in measuring his understanding of the word against that held by writers of the time. It should come as no surprise that Bach's understanding of the term was in near complete agreement with that of his contemporaries. To understand "motet" as Bach himself meant it, we need to take a close look at his use of the term in documents and in the compositions (both his own and those of other composers) that he labeled motets.

The term "motet" in documents

The term "motet" appears in several documents in Bach's hand or prepared for his signature. In each, it refers to the older Latin motets and related works that were part of the Leipzig working repertoire. It is clear from this evidence that for Bach, "motet" could refer to older motets of the sort that many writers sought to account for in their definitions of the term.

In 1723, on the back of the title page of "Nun komm, der Heiden Heiland" BWV 61, Bach noted the order of the Leipzig morning service for the first Sunday in Advent, the beginning of the liturgical year.[1] The second item in the list, after the opening prelude, is "Motetta." As has been recognized for some time, the compositions

---

[1] SBB P 45; *Dok* I/178. "Anordnung des GottesDienstes in Leipzig am 1 Advent-Sontag frühe." A later version (?1736) appears in the score of "Nun komm, der Heiden Heiland" BWV 62 (SBB P 877; *Dok* I/181).

performed in this place in the liturgy were the mostly Latin-texted motets found in large printed collections like Erhard Bodenschatz's *Florilegium Portense* (Leipzig, 1603, rev. edn. 1618; 2nd vol. 1621).[2]

Most of the motets in the *Florilegium* call for two four-part choirs, and it was presumably these works to which Bach was referring when he used the word "motet" in his notorious "Short but most necessary draft for a well-appointed church music" ("Kurtzer, iedoch höchstnöthiger Entwurff einer wohlbestallten Kirchen Music") addressed to the Leipzig Town Council. Bach wrote: "Every musical choir should contain at least 3 sopranos, 3 altos, 3 tenors, and as many basses, so that even if one happens to fall ill . . . at least a double-chorus motet may be sung." ("Zu iedweden musicalischen Chor gehören wenigstens 3 Sopranisten, 3 Altisten, 3 Tenoristen, und eben so viel Baßisten, damit, so etwa einer unpaß wird . . . wenigstens ein 2 Chörigte Motette gesungen werden kan.")[3] Whatever else this much-debated sentence might mean, in it Bach was presumably referring to motets like those in the *Florilegium*. It is difficult, in fact, to imagine what other repertory this could refer to, because the motets in the *Florilegium* and similar collections were the only double-choir compositions known to have had any regular place in the liturgy. Later in the same document he enumerates the "Motetten Singer," those not yet qualified to sing figural music but able to sing motets.

These same compositions were at issue in another series of Bach's references to motets, in the so-called "Präfektenstreit." Bach found himself in a protracted dispute with the Thomasschule Rector J. A. Ernesti over the right to appoint prefects (musical assistants), a dispute amply documented in Bach's written complaints, Ernesti's replies, and the decisions of the town council and King.[4] Because the most important duty of the prefects was to conduct motets in place of the cantor, motet singing is mentioned often. In these documents, Bach refers to "the usual motets" ("die gewöhnliche Motette"),[5] a choice of words that suggests that he was almost certainly referring to the same pieces performed as a regular part of the liturgy.

The term "motet" surfaces again in the documents concerning Bach's claim that he was entitled to be paid for certain services held in the University Church, services that included the singing of motets by Thomasschule students. Bach eventually complained in writing to the Elector, and referred to "motets attended to and directed by the Prefects."[6] The complaint by the University to which Bach was responding refers to "the old Latin motets usual for the quarterly ceremonies,"[7] works that were probably similar to (if not identical with) those sung in the civic churches at Sunday

---

[2] See Otto Riemer, "Erhard Bodenschatz und sein Florilegium Portense" (Ph.D. diss., Halle-Wittenberg, 1927). On the use of these motets in Leipzig in Bach's time, see Charles Sanford Terry, *Joh. Seb. Bach Cantata Texts Sacred and Secular* (London, 1926) and Arnold Schering, *Johann Sebastian Bachs Leipziger Kirchenmusik*, 2nd edn. (Leipzig, 1954), 121–29.

[3] *Dok* I/22; transl. Hans T. David and Arthur Mendel, eds., *The Bach Reader*, 2nd edn. (New York, 1966), 121.

[4] *Dok* I/32–35, 39–41.

[5] *Dok* I/33.

[6] *Dok* I/12.

[7] *Dok* I/12.

services. Here, as in the other documents, Bach and his fellow disputants used the term "motet" to refer to pieces in Latin of the type found in the *Florilegium Portense*. These works fall within the definitions of "motet" put forth by writers in the early eighteenth century, although they represent only one of the kinds of pieces covered by the term.

The term "motet" in musical sources

If J. S. Bach used the term "motet" in written documents in only one of its eighteenth-century senses, in musical sources he used it in the others. In autograph musical materials, Bach occasionally used the term "motet" to refer to works with independent instruments; that is, in its Italian and French senses. Most frequently, though, he used "motet" in connection with German-language works without independent instruments – the usual understanding of the term in German. His use of the term was discriminate, and there is every reason to think that we should take the label "motet" seriously when Bach applied it. If we do so, then it becomes clear that Bach's conception of "motet" extended somewhat beyond that discussed by contemporaries to include works that made carefully limited use of partially independent instruments. His use of the term to describe one of his own such compositions points up Bach's modest but important extension of the genre of the motet.

The pieces Bach labeled "motet" in musical sources may be divided into three categories, summarized in table 2–1. The first and largest group comprises settings of biblical texts and chorales for voices only; the second, consisting of two versions of the same work, uses a chorale text and partly independent instruments; and the third contains pieces with mixed textual and musical types and using concerted and obbligato instruments. In addition to these autograph materials, several scores and a set of parts for German motets from Bach's library are also labeled "motet." These sources are listed in table 2–2.

The largest group of compositions that Bach labeled "motet" comprises six pieces without independent instruments, all traditional central-German motets using biblical texts and chorale poetry. Bach was consistent with the label "motet" for this kind of composition; every known musical source of a German motet in his hand is explicitly headed "Motetto" or "Motetta." This is true not only of older works – three of the six are by composers at least a generation older than J. S. Bach – but of his own motets as well. Autograph sources are known only for BWV Anh. 159, BWV 225, and BWV 226, but it is suggestive that almost all of the secondary sources that transmit BWV 227–29 are headed "Motetto."

Most of the autograph items Bach labeled "motet" are scores, but some are performing parts, and they are of particular interest. All known motet performing parts in J. S. Bach's hand are labeled "Motetto": the nineteen parts for Knüpfer's "Erforsche mich, Gott," the continuo part for J. C. Bach's "Der Gerechte, ob er gleich zu zeitlich stirbt," and those original parts for BWV 226 that J. S. Bach started, listed in table 2–3. (See figure 2–1.) The heading "Motetto" on a performing part is important because it probably told the musicians something meaningful about the composition in front of

Table 2–1 *J. S. Bach's use of the term "motet" in autograph musical sources*

Bach's designation	Composition	Source	Date
Compositions without independent instruments			
Motetta à [8 Voci]	"Ich lasse dich nicht" BWV Anh. 159	SBB P 4/1	1712/13
Motetto a doi Cori	"Singet dem Herrn ein neues Lied" BWV 225	SBB P 36	1726/27
Motetta à doi Cori Motetto	"Der Geist hilft unser Schwachheit auf" BWV 226	SBB P 36 SBB St 121	1729 1729
Motetto . . . a 5. Voci 1 Sopr. 1 Alt. 2 Tenori 1 Basso e Continuo	Joh. Chr. Bach, "Der Gerechte, ob er gleich"	[SA]	1743–46
Motetto	Sebastian Knüpfer, "Erforsche mich, Gott"	SBB Mus. ms. 11788	1746/47
Motetto: ab 8 Voc:	Joh. Chr. Bach, "Unsers Herzens Freude"	SBB P 4/2	1746/47
Compositions with partly independent instruments			
Motetto a 4 Voci. due Litui. 1 Cornet. 3 Trombone.	"O Jesu Christ, meins Lebens Licht" BWV 118 (first version)	Private (Scheide)	1736/37
Motetto. à 4 Voci. 2 Litui. 2 Violini, Viola, 3 Oboe e Bassono se piace e Continuo.	"O Jesu Christ, meins Lebens Licht" BWV 118 (second version)	Private (Wilhelm)	1746/47
Compositions with independent instruments			
Mottetto. diviso in quatuor Chori Glückwünschende Kirchen MOTETTO	"Gott ist mein König" BWV 71	SBB St 377 Printed libretto	1708 1708
Motetto. à 4 Trombe. è Tympani. 2 Flaut: Allem: 2 Violini 2 Viole. Violono: Fag. S. A. T et B. e 4 Ripie:	Johann Christoph Schmidt, "Auf Gott hoffe ich"	SBB Mus. ms. 30187	1716
Ψ. 51. Motetto a due Voci, 3 Stromenti e Cont.	G. B. Pergolesi, "Tilge, Höchster, meine Sünden"	SBB Mus. ms. 30199	1746/47

Dates from Yoshitake Kobayashi, "Zur Chronologie der Spätwerke Johann Sebastian Bachs: Kompositions- und Aufführungstätigkeit von 1736 bis 1750," *BJ* 74 (1988): 7–72; Alfred Dürr, *Zur Chronologie der Leipziger Vokalwerke J. S. Bachs*, 2nd edn. (Cassel, 1976).

Table 2–2 *The term "motet" in non-autograph musical sources from J. S. Bach's library*

Designation	Composition	Source
Motetta â 8 Voc: Motetta . . . â 8. Voc.	Joh. Chr. Bach, "Lieber Herr Gott, wecke uns auf"	SBB P 4/2 (score) [SA] (parts)
Motetta . . . à 9.	"JB," "Unser Leben ist ein Schatten"	[SA] (score)
Motetta	Sebastian Knüpfer, "Erforsche mich, Gott"	SBB Mus. ms. autogr. Knüpfer, S. 1 (score)

Table 2–3 *Original parts for BWV 226 (SBB St 121)*

Heading		Copyist of beginning
	Canto Chori primi	Johann Ludwig Krebs
	Alto Chori primi	JLK
	Tenore Chori primi	JLK
	Baßo Chori primi	JLK
	Canto Chori secundi	JLK
	[A II missing]	
	[T II missing]	
	Baßo Chori secundi	JLK
Motetto	Violino 1 del Coro 1	J. S. Bach
Motetto	Violino 2 del Coro 1	JSB
Motetto	Viola del Coro 1	JSB
Motetto	Violoncello del Coro 1	JSB
	Hautbois 1 del Coro 2	C. P. E. Bach
	Hautbois 2 del Coro 2	CPEB
	Taille del Coro 2	CPEB
	Baßono del Coro 2	CPEB
Motetto	Violon e Continuo	JSB
Motetto	Organo	JSB

them. The heading "motet" indicated that the composition was different in construction from the normative vocal/instrumental genre, the vocal concerto. (Cantata parts rarely contain a corresponding label.) This would certainly have been important to the instrumentalists, whose role in a motet was substantially different from that in a concerted movement; the label "motet" warned them of this role. To a lesser extent, this information may have been useful to the singers as well, because the relationship of their parts to those of the instrumentalists in a motet was substantially different than in a concerto.

The second group of pieces that Bach called "motet" consists of the two versions of "O Jesu Christ, meins Lebens Licht" BWV 118, whose independent instrumental parts have raised questions about its genre. Although Bach labeled both versions "Motetto," the work was printed in volume 24 of the Bach-Gesellschaft edition as a cantata, and was thus assigned a number among the cantatas by Schmieder in the BWV. The Neue Bach Ausgabe printed it in the motet volume (though out of BWV

Figure 2–1 Violin 1 part for BWV 226 (SBB St 121) in the hand of J. S. Bach, f. 1

order, at the end of the volume); Hans-Joachim Schulze and Christoph Wolff describe it in the *Bach Compendium* as "border[ing] on the motet," but assign it to a category of vocal concertos that includes BWV 106, 157, and the Cöthen funeral music (BWV deest), all concerted works.[8] Commentators often conclude that BWV 118 falls between the motet and cantata genres.

Nonetheless, Bach clearly marked both autograph scores of the work "Motetto," a term he apparently used carefully and discriminately. In what sense did he mean it in BWV 118? To begin with, the work has a number of important features in common with pieces that eighteenth-century writers called motets, and with other compositions Bach labeled as such. It consists of a single musical unit, it treats a chorale melody as a cantus firmus, and it is contrapuntal, features that agree with eighteenth-century discussions of motets. (See example 2–1.)

The instruments in BWV 118 are the problem, because their partially independent writing seems to contradict the eighteenth-century understanding of the role of instruments in a motet. For the most part, though, the instrumental parts are identical to the vocal parts: when the voices are active, the main group of instruments (trombones and strings, respectively, in the two versions) play *colla parte*. The function of the instruments changes during the framing and articulating ritornellos between chorale phrases. Nonetheless, the material they play in them is restricted mostly to a simple scalar figure and derivations from it, material of little thematic importance. The essence of the piece is in its vocal parts. The mostly *colla parte* role of the instruments – and particularly the use of trombones in the first version – points to the motet as it was understood in the early eighteenth century.[9]

The two lituus parts – apparently meant for horns or trumpets of some kind[10] – are more independent, but not much. Some of their material is identical with the ritornello motive played by the other instruments; the rest consists of a repeating figure that provides harmonic filler with little melodic interest except at cadences. To judge by the absence of a continuo line in the autograph score, the first version of this work was apparently intended for performance without keyboard continuo. In its place, the litui provide the harmonic and rhythmic support that would normally be supplied by basso continuo, and are thus not so much an addition to the texture as a substitute for a missing element.

BWV 118 is thus a composition on a chorale text, dominated by contrapuntal vocal parts, and doubled with *colla parte* instruments (including trombones), all characteristics one would expect in a motet. The work has the added elements of instrumental ritornellos and the participation of two non-*colla-parte* instruments. Bach called this work a "motet," and one can only conclude that his conception of the genre admitted these elaborations. This kind of extended motet – with very similar and limited instrumental participation – surfaces in concerted works in the Bach repertory, just as the more traditional kind does. (See chapter 8.)

---

8 *Bach Compendium. Vokalwerke. Teil III* (Leipzig and Frankfurt, 1988), 828, 902.
9 On the significance of trombones in motet style, see chapter 10.
10 See Thomas G. MacCracken, "Die Verwendung der Blechblasinstrumente bei J. S. Bach unter besonderer Berücksichtigung der Tromba da tirarsi," *BJ* 70 (1984): 77f.

Example 2–1 BWV 118 (first version), mm. 1–29

In addition to the traditional German motets and the two versions of BWV 118, the third group of compositions that Bach labeled "Motetto" consists of three vocal concertos employing voices and fully independent instruments. One is an original composition; the other two are works by other composers. All three are exceptions to Bach's usual use of the term "motet," and in each case – and probably for a specific reason – Bach most likely employed the word in its broad meaning in French or Italian. His use of the word in this sense, though, was secondary to his main understanding of the term. (In addition to the three works discussed below, Bach's Weimar copy of Francesco Conti's "Languet anima mea" is headed "Motetto" on its title page, but this designation is not in Bach's hand.[11] Philipp Spitta also suggested that Bach called "Aus der Tiefen" BWV 131 a motet. The autograph score does not use the term, but the work is referred to as a motet in its catalogue entry by a onetime owner, Aloys Fuchs.[12] It is not out of the question that Fuchs took this designation from a lost title page, but in any event the matter cannot be pursued any further.)

The first vocal concerto Bach labeled "Motetto" is the score he copied in 1716 of Johann Christoph Schmidt's "Auf Gott hoffe ich."[13] "Auf Gott hoffe ich" uses mixed textual and musical types (verses from Psalms 56 and 116 and an aria in free poetry). In labeling this work "Motetto," it is likely that Bach meant the word in its extended French meaning, and possibly he took this designation from his (unknown) source. Laurence Dreyfus has pointed out that many musical features of Schmidt's composition and several aspects of its notation in Bach's score point to French influence: the use of transverse flutes and theorbo, the part designation "Fagotto o Basson," and the notation of the upper viola line in C2 clef, a notation not otherwise encountered in the Bach sources.[14] The musical features, Dreyfus argues, point more to Schmidt's "frenchified" practices at Dresden than to Bach's practices in Weimar. One suspects that the notational peculiarities of the score stem from the model from which Bach copied, including the unexpected heading "Motetto." Bach's use of the term probably does not reflect his own fundamental understanding, but may simply have been taken from his model. Three autograph performing parts for this work also survive; significantly, Bach did not label any of them "motet," in contrast to his consistent later practice in motet performing parts.[15] In the more independent act of preparing parts, Bach reverted to his more normal usage and avoided the term "motet."

The second concerted work that Bach labeled a motet is "Tilge, Höchster, meine Sünden," a parody of Pergolesi's "Stabat mater" for which Bach prepared a short score in 1746/47. The heading on this score reads "Ψ.51. Motetto a due Voci, 3 Stromenti e Cont." Bach labeled the work first as a psalm setting, and then as a motet. The original parts, mostly in a copyist's hand, are headed "Psalm LI."[16]

---

[11] SBB Mus. ms. 30098; parts SBB Mus. ms. 4081.

[12] Philipp Spitta, *Johann Sebastian Bach*, 2 vols. (Leipzig, 1873–80), 2:429. Score in private possession.

[13] SBB Mus. ms. 30187; facsimile of the first page in Laurence Dreyfus, *Bach's Continuo Group: Players and Practices in his Vocal Works* (Cambridge, Mass., 1987), 121.

[14] *Bach's Continuo Group*, 123.

[15] SBB Mus. ms. 19921/1.

[16] *Particell*, SBB Mus. ms. 30199; parts, SBB Mus. ms. 17155/16 (*olim* Mus. ms. anon. 713). On the dating of this material, see Yoshitake Kobayashi, "Zur Chronologie der Spätwerke Johann Sebastian Bachs: Kompositions- und Aufführungstätigkeit von 1736 bis 1750," *BJ* 74 (1988): 57f.

Both the original version and the parody call for two solo voices and independent instruments, and neither is the sort of piece usually called "motet" in German. Emil Platen has suggested that Bach applied the term "motet" in reference to the polyphonic style of the work's opening movement.[17] This is conceivable, but one has to wonder whether Bach instead used the term "Motetto" in its Italian sense for this Italian work, just as he may have used it in its similar French sense for Schmidt's "Auf Gott hoffe ich." Perhaps Bach's model called the work a motet, and he simply took over this designation in his copy. We do not know Bach's model, but there are strong indications that it was some arranged version of Pergolesi's composition, possibly of Dresden origin.[18]

Perhaps most interesting of the three vocal concertos Bach called "Motetto" is his "Gott ist mein König" BWV 71, the only one of the three of his own composition. This work, composed in 1708 for the installation of the new town council in Mühlhausen, presents Bach's earliest known use of the term. The word "Motetto" does not appear on the title page of Bach's autograph score nor on any of the printed or autograph performing parts, but is on the title page of the printed libretto of the work. The extent of Bach's control over the production of the print is unknown, so it is not certain that the use of "Motetto" there rests on his authority, but Bach himself did refer to BWV 71 as a "motet" on his autograph wrapper for the manuscript parts.

But in what sense did he use the word? The text of BWV 71 is of mixed type, employing biblical passages, one chorale, and two free poetic texts. Bach's musical response is also mixed, and includes choruses, arias, and ariosos (but no recitative). Spitta suggested that the predominance of biblical texts and chorales prompted Bach's use of the label "motet" for BWV 71, but concluded that his use of the term for this composition was a sign of its uncertain meaning.[19] Rather than applying it uncertainly, Bach as likely used the label "Motetto" for this piece in its Italian meaning of sacred vocal works in general. The relatively early date of BWV 71 might suggest that Bach used the term differently in 1708 than he did later. If the nearly contemporary "Aus der Tiefen" BWV 131 was indeed originally called a motet (see above), then perhaps this points to Bach's early usage of the term in a broader sense than was his practice later.

Bach's label "Motetto" for BWV 71 may also be connected to some particular musical aspect of this work. BWV 71 is organized in five choirs (trumpets/drums, strings, oboes/bassoon, recorders/cello, voices [solo and ripieno]), a division reflected in the compositional use of the forces, in the layout of Bach's autograph score, and in the wording of the title page. It is often pointed out that this disposition is old-fashioned, and at least one writer has suggested that Bach was following the model he had encountered in Lübeck in Dieterich Buxtehude's music.[20]

---

17 Emil Platen, "Eine Pergolesi-Bearbeitung Bachs," *BJ* 48 (1961): 47 n. 22.

18 On Dresden practice, see Wolfgang Horn, *Die Dresdner Hofkirchenmusik 1720–1745* (Cassel and Stuttgart, 1987), 194ff.

19 "Das Vorherrschen des Bibelworts und Chorals wird Bach veranlaßt haben, der Composition den Namen *Motetto* zu geben, und nicht *Concerto*, eine Bezeichnung, welche er späterhin vorwiegend anwendete . . . Für die Unsicherheit des Motetten-Begriffs in jener Zeit ist diese Bezeichnung ein Beleg; später unterschied Bach die Gattungen genau." J. S. Bach, 1:341f.

20 Christine Fröde (*NBA* I/32.1, vi) suggests the influence of the Lübeck *Abendmusiken*. No definite *Abendmusiken* compositions survive, although the text of "Castrum doloris / Templum honoris" suggests the use of multiple choirs. See Kerala J. Snyder, *Dieterich Buxtehude: Organist in Lübeck* (New York, 1987), 69.

In fact, there is a striking parallel between BWV 71 and Buxtehude's "Benedicam Domino" BuxWV 113, a setting of verses from Ps. 34. This work, known from a set of parts in the Düben collection, is divided into six choirs (strings, trumpets/bass trombone, concertato voices, cornetti/bassoon, trombones, ripieno voices), a division specified on the work's title page. The similarity between this work and BWV 71 is all the more interesting because both compositions are called "Motetto" in their sources. (BuxWV 113 is one of only two of Buxtehude's compositions so designated.[21])

Bach's autograph wrapper for the parts for BWV 71 reads:

Mottetto. diviso in quatour Chori.

> Chora 1mo. â tre Trombe è Tamburi.

> Choro 2do. â doi Violini una Viola è Violone.

> Choro 3zo. â doi Oboe è Bassono.

The wrapper for Buxtehude's composition in the Düben collection reads:

> Motetto
>
> Benedicam Dominum in omni
>
> tempore
>
> a 24
>
> p[er]: 6 Choros.
>
> 1. Chor: doi Violini è Violon
>
> 2. Chor: 4 Clarini Posauna è Bombarde
>
> 3. Chor: doi Soprani, Alto, Tenor è Basso
>
> 4. Chor: doi Cornetti è Fagotto
>
> 5. Chor: tre Tromboni
>
> 6. Chor: Soprano, Alto, Tenor è Basso.
>
> con Continuo
>
> Dieteric Buxtehude [manu propria][22]

In applying the term "Motetto" to BWV 71, Bach may well have been taking up a usage also employed by Buxtehude. The function of BuxWV 113 is not known, so it is difficult to say what elements of the composition made "Motetto" an appropriate designation for it (or even whether the designation was its composer's), but perhaps it was the feature it shares most clearly with BWV 71: division into choirs. Bach's early use of the term "motet" for a concerted vocal work, "Gott ist mein König," may represent his special understanding of an older use of the word.

---

[21] According to Snyder, *Dieterich Buxtehude*. The other is "O clemens, o mitis, o coelestis Pater" BuxWV 82, a setting of biblical prose texts for solo soprano and strings, also known from a Düben source, Uppsala Universitetsbiblioteket 51:18.

[22] Uppsala, Universitetsbiblioteket 50:6, not a Buxtehude autograph despite claims made for it; complete facsimile (Stockholm, 1973), facsimile of wrapper and one part and a modern score in Dietrich Buxtehude, *Werke*, vol. 4 (Hamburg, 1931).

Bach's conception of the motet

The musical characteristics of the compositions that J. S. Bach labeled "motet" show that his conception of the term was largely consistent with general eighteenth-century usage. The majority of his uses of the word in musical sources appears in connection with German-language settings of biblical and chorale texts using no independent instruments, in works both of his own composition and by others. His use of the term in written documents, in contrast, refers to the repertory of older Latin-language motets, works that were also within the scope of the term in the early eighteenth century.

Bach's application of the word "motet" to his composition "O Jesu Christ, meins Lebens Licht" BWV 118 shows further that his understanding of the term – and the musical type – although firmly grounded in generally accepted usage, allowed some expansion of musical resources. In BWV 118 and similar compositions, Bach made carefully circumscribed use of independent instruments. Even in these pieces, his fundamental understanding of "motet" in its accepted meaning in German remains clear in the many features of these pieces that agree with contemporary definitions of "motet."

Finally, Bach applied the word "motet" to two concerted vocal compositions by other composers. In these instances, he was most likely using the word in its extended Italian and French senses, perhaps adopting the term from his sources. He also applied the term to his 1708 composition "Gott ist mein König" BWV 71, a usage that may have reflected the old-fashioned polychoral disposition of the work, or perhaps his earlier understanding of the term.

PART TWO

Bach's motets

CHAPTER 3

Bach's motets and their relation to the genre

The Bach biographer Philipp Spitta, who was familiar with a substantial repertory of motets of the late seventeenth and early eighteenth centuries, held the opinion that the origins of J. S. Bach's motets were to be found less in the motet tradition than in organ and cantata repertory. Given the centrality of Bach's church cantatas and his organ works in Spitta's image of the composer, it is perhaps not surprising that he regarded Bach's motets as having only "an indirect connection with the seventeenth-century motet."[1] This outlook may well be the origin of a continued tendency to treat Bach's motets apart from their seventeenth-century antecedents; at the least, it is symptomatic of that tendency.

There is no doubt that in many ways Bach's motets transcend those of earlier composers and of contemporaries, but they nonetheless retain a strong connection to the genre as it was understood in Bach's time. Despite Spitta's doubts, Bach's motets are indeed in accord with the early eighteenth-century view of "motet" in the essential matters of text type and general musical characteristics. Not surprisingly, Bach's motets also show his innovations and manipulations of the received motet tradition, but these innovations are rooted firmly in the acknowledged basis of the genre. What is more, a fresh look at the canon of Bach's motets makes it clear that as in so many other genres, the composer's first surviving compositions are clearly in the mold of late seventeenth- and early eighteenth-century works. It takes nothing away from Bach's accomplishments as a motet composer to recognize his indebtedness to the motet tradition, especially in his earlier works, and his continued acknowledgment of contemporary understanding of the genre.

Text types

The definitions and discussions of "motet" surveyed in chapter 1 make it clear that text type was one of the most important distinguishing features of the genre. The texts Bach used in his motets (summarized in table 3–1) agree almost entirely with eighteenth-century conventions. They comprise biblical texts (*Sprüche*), chorales (and one chorale-like strophic poem), and combinations of the two. The texts Bach

---

[1] *J. S. Bach*, 2:428.

Table 3–1 *J. S. Bach's motets and their texts*

BWV	Text	Text source
	Biblical texts	
226	"Der Geist hilft unser Schwachheit auf"	Rom. 8:26–27
230	"Lobet den Herrn, alle Heiden"	Ps. 117:1–2
	Chorales/strophic poetry	
118	"O Jesu Christ, meins Lebens Licht"	Chorale (M. Behm, 1610)
229	"Komm, Jesu, komm"	Chorale-like stropic text
	"Drum schließ ich mich in deine Hände"	(P. Thymich, 1684)
	Combined texts	
Anh. 159	"Ich lasse dich nicht"	Gen. 32:27+"mein Jesu"
	"Weil du mein Gott und Vater bist"	Chorale (anon., 16th C.)
	["Warum betrübst du dich, mein Herz"]	
225	"Singet dem Herrn ein neues Lied"	Ps. 149:1–3
	"Wie sich ein Vater erbarmet"	Chorale (J. Gramann, 1530)
	["Nun lob, mein Seel, den Herren"]	
	"Gott nimm dich ferner unser an"	"Arie"
	"Lobet den Herrn in seinen Taten"	Ps. 150:2, 6
227	"Jesu, meine Freude"	Chorale (J. Franck, 1650)
	"Es ist nun nichts Verdammliches"	Rom. 8:1
	"Unter deinen Schirmen"	Chorale
	"Denn das Gesetz des Geistes"	Rom. 8:2
	"Trotz den alten Drachen"	Chorale
	"Ihr aber seid nicht fleischlich"	Rom. 8:9
	"Weg mit allen Schätzen"	Chorale
	"So aber Christus in euch ist"	Rom. 8:10
	"Gute Nacht, o Wesen"	Chorale
	"So nun der Geist"	Rom. 8:11
	"Weicht, ihr Trauergeister"	Chorale
228	"Fürchte dich nicht, ich bin bei dir"	Isa. 41:10
	"Fürchte dich nicht, denn ich habe dich erlöset"	Isa. 43:1
	"Herr, mein Hirt, Brunn aller Freuden"	Chorale (P. Gerhardt, 1653)
	["Warum sollt ich mich denn grämen"]	
Anh. 160/231	"Jauchzet dem Herrn, alle welt"	Ps. 100:1–2
	"Sei Lob und Preis mit Ehren"	Chorale (J. Gramann, 1530)
	["Nun lob, mein Seel, den Herren"]	

employed in his motets also compare in type and proportion to those used in the late seventeenth-century motets by other composers from his music library. These works and their texts are summarized in table 3–2.[2]

Two of J. S. Bach's motets are purely biblical. The first is "Der Geist hilft unser Schwachheit auf" BWV 226, which sets several verses from Romans. The four-voice

[2] The following motets may also be from Bach's library: G. G. Wagner, "Lob und Ehre und Weisheit und Dank" BWV Anh. 162 (biblical text, chorale, "Aria"); J. C. Altnickol, "Nun danket alle Gott" BWV Anh. 164 (chorale); ?Johann Christoph Bach, "Merk auf, mein Herz" BWV Anh 163 (chorale).

Table 3–2 *Motets from J. S. Bach's library and their texts*

Composer	Text	Text source
	Biblical texts	
[Anon]	"Sey nun wieder zufrieden"	Ps. 116:7
Johann Christoph Bach	"Der Gerechte, ob er gleich"	Wisd. of Sol. 7, 10–11, 13–14
Johann Christoph Bach	"Herr, nun läßest du deinen Diener"	Luke 2:29–32
Johann Christoph Bach	"Unsers Herzens Freude hat ein Ende"	Lam. 5:15–16
Sebastian Knüpfer	"Erforsche mich, Gott"	Ps. 139:23–24
	Chorales	
Johann Michael Bach	"Nun hab ich überwunden" ["Christus, der ist mein Leben"]	Chorale (M. Vulpius, 1609)
	Combined texts	
"J. B."	"Unser Leben ist ein Schatten"	Job 8:9
	"Ich bin die Auferstehung"	John 11:25
	"Ich weiß wohl, daß unser Leben" ["Ach, was soll ich Sünder machen"]	Chorale (J. Flitner, 1661)
	"Weil du vom Tod erstanden bist" ["Wenn mein Stündlein vorhanden ist"]	Chorale (Anon., 1569)
	"Ach wie flüchtig, ach wie nichtig"	Chorale (J. Crüger, 1661)
Johann Michael Bach	"Ich weiß, daß mein Erlöser lebt"	Job 19:25–26
	"Christus, der ist mein Leben"	Chorale (M. Vulpius, 1609)
Johann Michael Bach	"Das Blut Jesu Christi"	John 1:7
	"Dein Blut, der edle Saft" ["Wo soll ich fliehen hin"]	Chorale (J. Heermann, 1630)
Johann Michael Bach	"Herr, wenn ich nur dich habe"	Ps. 73:25–26
	"Jesu, du edler Bräutgam wert" ["Ach Gott, wie manches Herzeleid"]	Chorale (M. Moller, 1587)
	Other	
Johann Christoph Bach	"Lieber Herr Gott, wecke uns auf"	Liturgical (Collect)

setting of a stanza of "Komm, heiliger Geist" that appears at the end of the original vocal parts most likely is not part of the motet. (See chapter 5.) The other purely biblical motet is the problematic "Lobet den Herrn, alle Heiden" BWV 230, whose authenticity and status as a motet have long been subject to reservations. Until recently, the work was known only from an early nineteenth-century printed edition; a recently discovered manuscript source has been identified by Yoshitake Kobayashi as a pre-1800 Breitkopf *Verkaufsabschrift*.[3] A preliminary source-critical examination suggests that this copy and the printed edition may well have been made from the same source, but the manuscript's attribution of the work merely to "Signor Bach"

---

[3] Warsaw, University Library, Rps. Mus. 92. Personal communication.

raises the question of which Bach was intended, and thus leaves open the question of authorship. BWV 230's genre has also been subject to question. Its lack of independent instruments probably explains its assignment to the motets, even if it was not originally conceived as one. The work's text, drawn from Psalm 117, is certainly appropriate for a motet, though not exclusively so.

Three of Bach's motets are based on chorales or similar texts. The two versions of BWV 118 set at least one stanza of "O Jesu Christ, meins Lebens Licht," and probably more. Both autograph scores indicate musical repeats, suggesting the singing of more than one stanza. The notation of the repeat in the two versions differs: in the score of the first version, there is a clear *da capo* indication, but no corresponding *fine* or fermata;[4] in the score of the second version, Bach provided explicit repeat signs, and wrote out the concluding ritornello (essentially identical to the one that opens the work) at the end.[5] Presumably, the first version was intended to be performed the same way as the second: an opening ritornello, some number of chorale verses, and then the closing ritornello.

Bach almost certainly intended the singing of more than one stanza of this fifteen-strophe hymn, though this fact has largely been overlooked. The Bach-Gesellschaft edition (which presents only the first version) specifies "Dal segno ad libitum," though without providing any additional text;[6] Max Schneider's edition of the second version indicates Bach's repeat but is silent on the question of what text to use;[7] and the Neue Bach Ausgabe prints all fifteen strophes at the end of the second version, but with no explicit suggestion that more than one verse is to be sung.[8] If the supposition is correct that Bach intended the first version, which uses no stationary instruments, for a funeral procession or the like, then a provision for the singing of multiple verses would certainly make sense.

The text of "Komm, Jesu, komm" BWV 229 comprises two of eleven stanzas of a strophic sacred song whose text is by Paul Thymich of the Thomasschule, who wrote it for the funeral of the Rector Jacob Thomasius (d. 1684). Thymich's text was originally sung to a five-voice setting by the Thomascantor Johann Schelle.[9] Bach's source for the text was apparently the so-called Wagner Hymnal, a copy of which he owned, where the text appears under the rubric "Sterbe-Lieder."[10] Neither in the motet (which sets the first stanza) nor the following aria (which sets the last) did Bach make direct use of Schelle's setting, although the older work was apparently known at the Thomasschule; Hans-Joachim Schulze points out a copy – presumably of this setting – from the school's library.[11] Nonetheless, there is a striking similarity in melody and sequential

---

4 In the collection of W. Scheide, Princeton.
5 In the collection of A. Wilhelm, Basel.
6 BG 24.
7 Veröffentlichung der Neuen Bachgesellschaft 17, no. 1 (Leipzig, 1916).
8 *NBA* III/1, 179.
9 See J. Bachmair, "'Komm, Jesu, komm': Der Textdichter. – Ein unebekanntes Werk von Johann Schelle," *BJ*, 29 (1932): 142–45. Schelle's composition is transcribed in *NBA* III/1 *KB*, 163ff.
10 *Andächtiger Seelen geistliches Brand- und Gantz-Opfer / Das ist: vollständiges Gesangbuch*, 8 vols. (Leipzig, 1697), 8:326–29; heading: "In eigener Melodey." Facsimile *BT*, 374f. On Bach's copy, see *Dok* II/627. Note that the poetic structure of the transcription in *BT*, 224, is corrupt.
11 *Studien zur Bach-Überlieferung im 18. Jahrhundert* (Leipzig, 1984), 134 n. 533.

treatment between Bach's and Schelle's setting of the last lines of the text. If Bach indeed knew Schelle's composition, his reliance on it did not go beyond this similarity; he apparently did not consider Schelle's melody to be inseparably linked to the text. At the most, he may have borrowed some melodic material from the older work.

From the point of view of text type, "Komm, Jesu, komm" is most like a chorale, which it resembles in rhyme, meter, form, and strophic construction. Despite the text's resemblance to a chorale in structure and prosody, Bach did not set it in any usual chorale motet style. The first stanza is treated phrase by phrase in a setting specific to the meaning of the strophe, more resembling a motet setting of a biblical prose text than of a chorale verse. Nonetheless, Bach did not entirely ignore the textual structure; he set the first two phrases of this Barform text to closely parallel music.[12] Paul Brainard points to this parallelism as evidence of Bach's willingness to use the same musical material for different texts, but this feature of the composition is probably better explained as Bach's response to the structure of the poem.[13] The apparent contradiction of textual and musical types – a rhymed metrical text treated phrase by phrase – may be responsible for the bizarre descriptions of the motet in recent times; e.g., comprising a madrigal, fugato and concerted minuet adding up to a trio sonata or a sonata da chiesa without a second slow movement, or comprising a sarabande changing to a multi-voiced arioso.[14]

The second stanza in Bach's setting (verse 11 of the original) is treated in a homophonic four-voice movement labeled "Arie." (See example 3–1.) The significance of the term to Bach has been perhaps too narrowly defined by Marianne Danckwardt, who has cast doubt on the possibility that it had generic significance for Bach.[15] In the context of the motet, it almost certainly did. Although commentators have been puzzled by this term (and by its use in the middle movement of "Singet dem Herrn ein neues Lied" BWV 225), it is particularly appropriate to "Komm, Jesu, komm," whose text is exactly the kind one encounters in homophonic vocal pieces called "arias." One of the late seventeenth- and early eighteenth-century senses of "aria" was a strophic, homophonic composition on a metrical text. (Schelle's setting of "Komm, Jesu, komm" is just such a piece.) One encounters the term frequently in manuscript sources of central German motets, especially at the head of the four-voice settings that often conclude motets. The term is also used in several little strophic pieces from Bach's library, and Mattheson's understanding of the term "aria" allows for such pieces.[16] In BWV 229, Bach treats the first stanza of this aria in a far more elaborate musical setting than is usual for such a text, but the simpler concluding stanza makes clear the text's relationship to its usual kind of treatment.

[12] See Friedhelm Krummacher, "Textauslegung und Satzstruktur in Bachs Motetten," *BJ* 60 (1974): 17f.
[13] "The aria and its ritornello: the question of 'dominance' in Bach," in *Bachiana et alia musicologica: Festschrift Alfred Dürr*, ed. Wolfgang Rehm (Cassel, 1983), 42
[14] Rudolf Gerber, "Über Formstrukturen in Bachs Motetten," *Die Musikforschung* 3 (1950): 186; Ulrich Siegele, "Bemerkungen zu Bachs Motetten," *BJ* 49 (1962): 48 n. 21.
[15] "Zur Aria aus J. S. Bachs Motette 'Komm, Jesu, komm!'" *Archiv für Musikwissenschaft* 44, no. 3 (1987): 195–202.
[16] *Der vollkommene Capellmeister*, 216; see also Fuhrmann, *Musicalischer-Trichter*, 84f.

Example 3–1 BWV 229, "Arie"

It may be significant that the strophic poem used in BWV 229 has its basis in a biblical text: each stanza ends with a quotation or paraphrase of John 14:6 ("Ich bin der Weg, und die Wahrheit, und das Leben"). In Bach's setting, this portion of the text receives disproportionate emphasis, probably in recognition of its special character. It is possible that Bach recognized in the rhymed text of "Komm, Jesu, komm" a ready-made combination of chorale and scriptural texts, both of which were appropriate for motets, and whose combination in motets was a common practice.

Bach's other motets combine chorales and biblical texts. In both BWV 228 and Anh. 159, biblical texts are first presented alone and then in combination with chorale verses that reinforce their theological message. (BWV 228 actually uses two different, closely related biblical texts in its two halves.) This is exactly the method of combination described by eighteenth-century writers on the motet.

BWV 225 and 227 also use both chorales and biblical texts, but in ways not generally found in late seventeenth- and early eighteenth-century motets. In the form in which it is known today, BWV 227 presents stanzas of the chorale "Jesu, meine Freude" in closed movements, in alternation with settings of verses from Romans. There is strong evidence that Bach compiled this work from older material (see chapter 5); in the form in which BWV 227 survives, it employs the text types expected in a motet, but combined in an unusual way, with biblical and chorale texts presented independently.

"Singet dem Herrn ein neues Lied" BWV 225 also combines texts in an unusual way. The two outer sections of BWV 225 use only Psalm verses. A chorale is presented in the middle section in combination with another text, but that text is not the expected biblical passage, but rather a piece of free poetry. Except for the specific nature of the second text, this movement closely resembles traditional double-choir motets that present a chorale together with another text, but the use of free verse in a motet represents an anomaly. (The motet "Lob und Ehre und Weisheit" BWV Anh. 162 by Bach's student G. G. Wagner uses a similar combination in an inner movement.)

The second text, which Bach referred to as "Arie," is as follows:

> Gott, nimm dich ferner unser an,
> Denn ohne dich ist nichts getan
> Mit allen unsern Sachen.
> Drum sei du unser Schirm und [Licht],
> Und trägt uns unsre Hoffnung nicht,
> So wirst du's ferner machen.
> Wohl dem der sich nur steif und fest
> Auf dich und deine Huld verläßt.

The source of this text is unknown; it is possible that it was written expressly for whatever occasion prompted the composition of BWV 225, but that occasion, a matter of endless speculation, is a mystery. Curiously, Bach wrote the word "Schild" in his composing score where the rhyme scheme strongly suggests that a word rhyming with "nicht" is required. Even more puzzling is the fact that the original performing parts give the word "Licht" at this point. By all indications, the parts were made from this score, leaving the question of how the copyist of this section, Johann Andreas Kuhnau, knew to make the change.[17] There must have been some other text source available to him, but none has come to light.

Spitta pointed out that the text has the metrical scheme of the chorale "O Ewigkeit, du Donnerwort," but that is probably just a coincidence.[18] It has also been pointed out that two lines in Bach's setting ("Drum sei du unser Schirm und Licht" and "Wohl dem der sich nur steif und fest") quote the last phrase of the chorale "Mach's mit mir Gott, nach deiner Güt," and that the second of these bears a striking resemblance to the opening lines of another text traditionally sung to the same tune, beginning "Wohl dem! der sich auf seinen Gott / recht kindlich kann verlassen."[19] None of these observations has brought us any closer to identifying the text. Whatever its origin, perhaps Bach thought it similar enough to a chorale to include in a motet. Alternatively, it may represent a commentary on the verse of "Nun lob, mein Seel"; just as chorales often comment on biblical texts in motets, here the free text may have been chosen or written as a gloss on the chorale.

Bach referred to his setting of this text as an "Aria" in a note at the end of this movement in the composing score: "The second verse is like the first, except that the choirs switch, and the first one sings the chorale, the second one the Aria."[20] (This instruction was not realized in the original performing parts.) As in the last section of BWV 229, Bach apparently meant the term "aria" in the sense of settings of strophic poetry. It is possible that this aria text was originally intended to be set separately, perhaps in the manner of the arias that conclude many late seventeenth- and early eighteenth-century motets, but that Bach instead combined it with a chorale within the motet. The central section of BWV 225 may thus represent Bach's integration of the motet and the choral aria. Incidentally, the mysterious "second verse" in Bach's note may well refer not to a second strophe of "Nun lob, mein Seel," as is often assumed, but rather to a further strophe of the aria.

Finally, the pastiche motet "Jauchzet dem Herrn alle Welt" BWV Anh. 160 uses both biblical and chorale texts, in separate movements. The first sets verses from Psalm 100, the second a stanza of the chorale "Nun lob, mein Seel, den Herren." This chorale movement, also part of cantata 28, may also have existed as an independent chorale motet, "Sei Lob und Preis mit Ehren" BWV 231 (see chapter 5).

Bach's somewhat unconventional distribution of texts in motets should not distract us from an important point about his selection of those texts. With the exception of the apparently free poetic text in the central section of BWV 225 (and possibly the text of BWV 229), the texts of Bach's motets conform to eighteenth-century norms. He used biblical and chorale texts, and these two in combination. From the textual point of view, then, Bach's conception of "motet" was in line with that of his contemporaries.

---

[17] See *NBA* III/1 *KB*, 46.

[18] *J. S. Bach*, 2:433.

[19] See S. T. M. Newman, "Bach's motet: 'Singet dem Herrn,'" *Proceedings of the Royal Musical Association 1937–38*, 101.

[20] "Der 2. Vers. ist wie der erste, nur daß die Chöre ümwechseln, und das 1ste Chor den Choral, das 2dere die Aria singe" (SBB P 36).

Musical characteristics

In the most important musical respects, too, Bach's motets agree with the characteristics of the genre as it was understood and discussed by his contemporaries. Counterpoint, so important to early eighteenth-century discussions of motets, plays a significant role in Bach's motets, although sometimes in a manner probably not envisioned by contemporary writers. When late seventeenth- and early eighteenth-century writers speak of the importance of "fugue" in motets, the concept of "fugue" they had in mind was apparently directed more to the kind of imitative polyphony found in sixteenth-century models than to modern tonal fugal procedures. The older type of counterpoint is indeed to be found in Bach's motets, persisting most strongly in imitative cantus-firmus settings of chorales like BWV Anh. 160/231 and 118. (This type is also particularly important among motet-like movements in Bach's church cantatas; see chapter 8.) There are also traces of an old-fashioned kind of imitative counterpoint in BWV 229 as well, which is made up of short musical and textual units, a few of them imitative.

Even in Bach's motets not constructed along the old lines, the strong traditional association between counterpoint and the motet persisted, but rather than using short points of imitation, Bach's motets integrate sophisticated fugal techniques on a larger scale. In BWV 228 and Anh. 159, the accompaniments to the chorale cantus firmi are fugal, replacing the homophonic or loosely imitative material found in the corresponding places in seventeenth- and early eighteenth-century models. BWV 225 contains two large fugues, one of them making up half of the first section of the motet and the other the concluding section. The surviving form of BWV 227 has as its central movement a fugue on a *Spruch* text, and the final section of BWV 226 is a double fugue on such a text. The association between imitative vocal counterpoint and the motet remained strong for Bach, even as he brought more modern contrapuntal writing to bear on the genre.

Despite the importance of fugue in Bach's motets, it is worth recognizing that a large proportion of the musical material in them is essentially homophonic. In fact, the declamatory and textural model for most of the motets (outside the fugal sections) is homophonic and syllabic. Bach's motets go beyond the simple chordal text declamation typical of many seventeenth-century works, especially in his handling of double choirs, but the elaborate counterpoint that distinguishes Bach's motets exists side-by-side with homophonic presentation of text. A surprisingly large proportion of each of the motets consists of extended sequences, not a musical feature expressly mentioned in contemporary discussions of the motet, but one that distinguishes Bach's motet writing from much of his other vocal ensemble writing. (Consider, for example, the long sequential homophonic passages in "Fürchte dich nicht" BWV 228 and "Komm, Jesu, komm" BWV 229.) The animated homophony of much of Bach's motet writing connects these works to the motet repertory of the time.

The performing forces called for in Bach's motets, lacking independent instruments, also conform to the norms of the early eighteenth century. The one exception is "O Jesu Christ, meins Lebens Licht" BWV 118, whose partly independent instruments point to Bach's expanded view of the motet (see chapter 2). *Colla parte* instruments, so important in contemporary discussions, survive for one work ("Der Geist hilft unser Schwachheit auf" BWV 226), and similar parts may well have existed for others. Bach's documented performance practice of other composers' motets strongly suggests that he considered *colla parte* doubling an option in his works as well. (See chapter 6.) This, too, agrees with contemporary views.

Basso continuo parts also survive for BWV 226, as they do for several of the motets of other composers in Bach's working repertory. In addition, the most important source for BWV 228 strongly suggests that the work was conceived with basso continuo; the principal manuscript source contains extra, untexted notes in the bass part of the concluding four-voice section, notes apparently intended for a continuo instrument.[21] The listing for "Ich lasse dich nicht" BWV Anh. 159 in the catalogue of C. P. E. Bach's estate suggests that he probably owned a continuo part (of unknown age) for that work (see chapter 11), and aspects of "Jesu, meine Freude" BWV 227 (discussed in chapter 5) suggest that continuo may have been required for it as well. In the matter of basso continuo, so strongly endorsed by writers on the motet, Bach's motets appear to be in line with contemporary norms.

In sum, in text choice and fundamental musical characteristics, Bach's motets show their indebtedness to seventeenth-century models and their general adherence to the early eighteenth-century concept of "motet." In length, architecture, and contrapuntal innovation they are distinguished from the works of his predecessors, but Bach's innovations in motets are not substantially different from those he made in other genres, especially in other types of sacred compositions. The motets, like the cantatas and oratorios, are rooted in the conventions of the genre and the contemporary understanding of the style.

---

[21]   SBB P 569 (score).

CHAPTER 4

Bach's earlier motets: rethinking authorship and dating

The discussion of Bach's motets and their relationship to the genre presented in the previous chapter obviously depends on a clear definition of the repertory – what Bach wrote and when he wrote it – but defining the canon of Bach's motets and its chronology is a tricky proposition. We must start with a close look at the authorship, transmission, genesis, and dating of certain of Bach's motets, because a great deal of the conventional wisdom about these compositions needs rethinking. To begin with, for reasons discussed in chapter 6, Bach's motets have long been assumed to date from his Leipzig period, 1723 and after. But at least one work that is demonstrably older has been dismissed as inauthentic, and a reexamination suggests that it is, in fact, by the young J. S. Bach. This attribution necessitates a fresh look at another of his motets that may be almost as old. It turns out that we are indeed justified in establishing the concept of Bach's early motets.

"Ich lasse dich nicht" BWV Anh. 159

The earliest source for the eight-voice motet "Ich lasse dich nicht" BWV Anh. 159,[1] partly in the hand of the young J. S. Bach, was transmitted as part of the Altbachisches Archiv, Bach's collection of family vocal music (discussed in chapters 11 and 12). It has never been clear, though, whether Bach composed the piece or just copied another composer's work. Since the nineteenth century the motet has been ascribed both to J. S. Bach and to his father's cousin Johann Christoph Bach (13) (1642–1703). When Franz Wüllner edited the motets for the Bach-Gesellschaft in 1892, he described "Ich lasse dich nicht" as "one of the most beautiful works of German church music," but declared it to be inauthentic, naming Johann Christoph Bach as its composer.[2] Wolfgang Schmieder followed his lead, relegating the motet to the appendix of the BWV, and describing it as "presumably by Johann Christoph Bach." These authorities had a significant influence on the NBA, and in his volume of motets

---

[1] Further detail on the history of this composition can be found in my article "The authorship of the motet *Ich lasse dich nicht* (BWV Anh. 159)," *Journal of the American Musicological Society* 41, no. 3 (1988): 491–526.

[2] BG 39, xxxixf. Numbers associated with Bach family members are based on those in J. S. Bach's genealogy (*Dok* I/184).

for that edition, Konrad Ameln cited Wüllner's opinion that "Ich lasse dich nicht" was the work of Johann Christoph Bach, and omitted it.[3]

Not everyone has been comfortable with the attribution to Johann Christoph Bach. Philipp Spitta, in the first volume of his Bach biography, assigned the motet to Johann Christoph, but in the second volume allowed the possibility that it might be a work of Johann Sebastian, writing that the source evidence did not permit a definite attribution.[4] Although the editor of the Bach-Gesellschaft motet volume thought "Ich lasse dich nicht" inauthentic, the motet was printed nonetheless in an appendix at the insistence of the project's editor-in-chief Wilhelm Rust, who firmly believed the motet to be by J. S. Bach.[5] (Rust was later quoted as saying that he thought it anachronistic to attribute the concluding fugal chorale setting to a composer before Bach's time.[6]) The place of the motet in the choral repertory and its numerous editions and recordings testify to the high general opinion of the work.

The transmission of the motet is puzzling enough that it is easy to see how the confusion arose. There are two eighteenth-century manuscript sources: one lacking an attribution, and one attributing the work to Johann Christoph. There are also two early printed editions, one assigning "Ich lasse dich nicht" to Johann Sebastian (in 1802) and the other to Johann Christoph (in 1823). New information about the provenance of the manuscripts and about the sources used in the production of the prints, together with a careful examination of all the attributions, makes it possible to demonstrate that the assignment of the motet to Johann Christoph Bach was almost certainly a nineteenth-century speculation that must be rejected. To arrive at a new attribution for "Ich lasse dich nicht," we have to turn to a systematic examination of the sources and other evidence of the work's transmission.

The manuscript source attributing "Ich lasse dich nicht" to Johann Christoph Bach is part of the convolute manuscript SBB P 4/2.[7] This copy of the motet is in the hand of the singer Michel, one of Carl Philipp Emanuel Bach's principal copyists in Hamburg. The score bears the name "J. Christoph Bach," but this attribution is in neither Michel's nor C. P. E. Bach's hand. Further, "J. Christoph" and "Bach" appear to have been written at two different times, because the two names do not quite line up horizontally. The score was almost certainly not given an attribution when it was first copied, was later labeled "Bach," and then finally "J. Christoph Bach." The word "Bach" is most likely in the hand of Georg Poelchau, an early owner of the manu-script; "J. Christoph" may also be.[8] In any event, Michel did not put a composer's name on the score when he wrote it out.

The source from which Michel made his copy can be deduced: it was another manuscript also now in Berlin, SBB P 4/1 (see figure 4–1). The lack of substantive variants, the inclusion of redundant accidentals found in P 4/1, and other details

[3] *NBA* III/1 *KB*, 10.
[4] *J. S. Bach*, 1:93f. and 2:981.
[5] BG 39, xl. The motet appears on pp. 157–66.
[6] Bernhard Friedrich Richter, "über die Motetten Seb. Bachs," *BJ* 9 (1912): 1f.
[7] Pp. 11–17. The convolute manuscript was assembled by Georg Poelchau.
[8] BG 11[1], xiiin.

Figure 4–1 Score of BWV Anh. 159 (SBB P 4/1) in the hands of J. S. Bach and Philipp David Kräuter, f. 1

demonstrate the relationship. P 4/1 does not now contain a composer's name, and probably lacked one when Michel copied P 4/2 from it, so he was unable to put an attribution on his copy. P 4/1 is partly in the hand of the young J. S. Bach, dating from between 1708 and 1714 in Georg von Dadelsen's estimation.[9] (A more exact dating was not possible because only a small part of the manuscript is in Bach's hand.) Bach wrote out the first system, and another copyist wrote out most of the rest of the motet, with the exception of the closing measures, which Bach completed.

P 4/1 is in a wrapper in the hand of Siegfried Wilhelm Dehn, the mid-nineteenth-century curator of the Music Collection of the Royal Library in Berlin. The notations on the wrapper clearly indicate that P 4/1 came from the Berlin Sing-Akademie; in fact, this score (and the copy P 4/2) came originally from the Altbachisches Archiv and the estate of Carl Philipp Emanuel Bach. (In its listing in C. P. E. Bach's estate catalogue, the motet is described as a four-voice work, but this is almost certainly a simple error.) P 4/1 followed most of the ABA from C. P. E. Bach's estate to the collection of Georg Poelchau, to Carl Friedrich Zelter and the Sing-Akademie, and finally to the Royal Library in Berlin in 1854. P 4/2 arrived there directly from Poelchau's collection, which the library bought in 1841.[10]

This information about the provenance of the two manuscript scores helps clarify the attributions on them. Neither P 4/1 nor P 4/2 bore an attribution when Carl Philipp Emanuel Bach owned them; that is why the motet is listed without a composer's name in his estate catalogue. C. P. E. Bach believed at least that "Ich lasse dich nicht" was by a Bach family member – the motet was kept with the ABA – but apparently he did not know which one. This would explain why Poelchau originally wrote just "Bach" on P 4/2, following the catalogue. When and why "J. Christoph" was added remains open for the moment, but the score read "J. Christoph Bach" when it was purchased by the Royal Library. When the library later purchased P 4/1 from the Sing-Akademie, the two scores were reunited. The librarian Dehn put Johann Christoph Bach's name on his new wrapper for the anonymous P 4/1, taking his cue from P 4/2, which was already catalogued that way. The name "Johann Christoph Bach" on Dehn's wrapper for P 4/1 thus derives from Poelchau and P 4/2, and has no independent authority.

The next question, obviously, is where this attribution came from. The earliest datable assignment of "Ich lasse dich nicht" to Johann Christoph Bach was made in the third volume of a printed edition (Leipzig, *c.* 1821–23; see figure 4–2)[11] by Johann Friedrich Naue, a prominent Halle musician who was the founder of that city's music festival and Sing-Akademie. The three volumes that make up the edition contain nine motets attributed to Johann Christoph and Johann Michael Bach, of which "Ich lasse dich nicht" is the last.

[9] Georg von Dadelsen, *Beiträge zur Chronologie der Werke Johann Sebastian Bachs*, Tübinger Bach-Studien, nos. 4/5 (Trossingen, 1958), 74.
[10] See Klaus Engler, "Georg Poelchau und seine Musikaliensammlung: Ein Beitrag zur Überlieferung bachscher Musik in der ersten Hälfte des 19. Jahrhunderts" (Ph.D. diss., Tübingen, 1984).
[11] *Neun Motetten für Singchöre von Johann Christoph Bach und Johann Michael Bach Ites [IItes/IIItes] Heft. Kirchenmusik verschiedener Zeiten und Völker, gesammelt von F. Naue. No I [II/III] Leipzig bei Fried: Hofmeister.* Dates of publication from Friedrich Hofmeister, *Handbuch der Musikalischen Literatur . . . Vierter [Fünfter, Sechster] Nachtrag* (Leipzig, 1821–23).

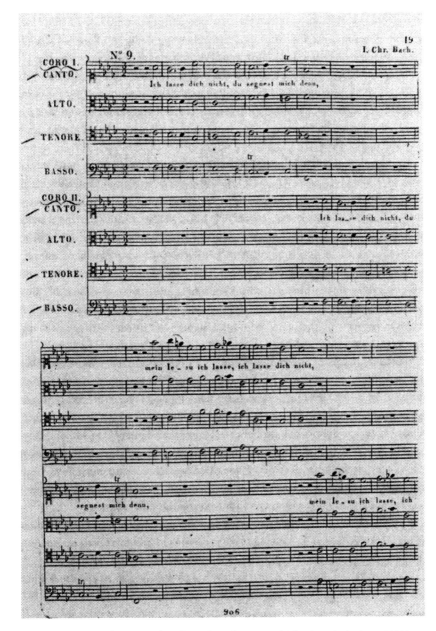

Figure 4–2 BWV Anh. 159 in the edition by Johann Friedrich Naue (Leipzig, *c.* 1823)

Several pieces of evidence strongly suggest that Naue's sources were the ABA copies then in Poelchau's or Zelter's possession. Naue was Zelter's student and a member of the Sing-Akademie, and maintained a correspondence with Zelter after he returned to Halle.[12] Georg Poelchau himself confirmed in an entry in the catalogue of

---

[12] On Naue and his activities in Halle, see Walter Serauky, *Musikgeschichte der Stadt Halle*, vol. ii, part 2 (Halle, 1942), 410ff. Naue's name appeared in the lists of participants in Sing-Akademie rehearsals in 1810, summarized in *Zur Geschichte der Sing-Akademie in Berlin nebst . . . einem alphabetischen Verzeichniss aller Personen, die ihr als Mitglieder angehört haben* (Berlin, 1843).

his collection that Naue's edition had been based in the ABA.[13] Finally, Naue's publication was nothing less than a complete edition of the nine ABA motets, eight of which are unica. The one motet from the ABA that existed in other sources is "Ich lasse dich nicht," as we shall see later, but it is highly unlikely that Naue obtained this work from a different source than the other eight. Naue's source was almost certainly the unattributed ABA copy, P 4/1 (and perhaps also P 4/2), and his edition thus has no independence from those sources. This hypothesis is supported by the readings in Naue's edition and P 4/1.

Naue's attribution of "Ich lasse dich nicht" to Johann Christoph Bach did not come from P 4/1, which was anonymous; in fact, it did not come from Zelter or the Sing-Akademie at all. Rehearsal records show that "Ich lasse dich nicht" was sung there as a work of J. S. Bach at least as late as 1828,[14] if not well after – that is, after Naue had published it under Johann Christoph's name. In fact, there is no evidence that the motet was ever assigned to Johann Christoph Bach at the Sing-Akademie during this time. Naue's assignment of "Ich lasse dich nicht" to Johann Christoph Bach did not derive from his source, but was almost certainly speculative, a guess based on the work's inclusion in the ABA and perhaps also on a stylistic judgment. Naue made two other speculations in the same edition, assigning to Johann Michael Bach one anonymous motet and one labeled simply "JB" in the ABA sources.[15]

Poelchau's assignment of the work in P 4/2 probably stems from Naue. When Poelchau purchased the ABA, he could write only "Bach" on P 4/2, based on the entry in the C. P. E. Bach estate catalogue without a first name. He later acquired a copy of Naue's edition, and most likely added "J. Christoph" in P 4/2 on its authority. We have already seen how this attribution was propagated in P 4/1, and all subsequent ascriptions of "Ich lasse dich nicht" to Johann Christoph Bach apparently derive from these copies and ultimately from Naue. Because Naue's attribution was by all indications a speculation – required because his source was anonymous – it must be discarded, leaving us for the moment with no attribution for the motet.

The oldest copy, 4/1, has more to tell us. The participation of Bach's student Philipp David Kräuter in its copying make it possible to date it to between mid-April 1712 and late September 1713, the period Kräuter was with Bach.[16] Bach started the score as a fair copy in a regular, neat hand, with ruled barlines, and using two different-sized rastra to allow for the change from eight voices to four halfway through. The copying job was continued by Kräuter, and Bach resumed work at the very end of the piece, squeezing in the last passage. By the end, the score no longer has the look of a fair copy, but it was clearly started as such.

---

[13] SBB Mus. ms. theor. Kat. 51, f. 9.

[14] Georg Schünemann, "Die Bachpflege der Berliner Singakademie," *BJ* 25 (1928): 138–71, cites numerous rehearsals of "Ich lasse dich nicht" starting in 1808.

[15] "Sey nun wieder zufrieden" and "Unser Leben ist ein Schatten." See chapter 11.

[16] Kräuter's hand identifed by Yoshitake Kobayashi, personal communication. On Kräuter's time with Bach, see *Dok* II/58, 58a, 53a–c; Franz Krautwurst, "Anmerkungen zu den Augsburger Bach-Dokumenten," in *Festschrift Martin Ruhnke*, ed. Institut für Musikwissenschaft der Universität Erlangen-Nürnberg (Neuhausen-Stuttgart, 1986), 176–84; and Schulze, *Studien zur Bach-Überlieferung*, 156f.

Kräuter's copying errors show that he and Bach copied P 4/1 from a score, and a detail of Kräuter's work suggests that that score may have been in Bach's hand. In copying a metrical change halfway through the motet, Kräuter attempted one distinctive time signature ¢ (in the Soprano I part) made with two strokes, a shape that closely resembles the form found in Bach's hand. Kräuter was very likely trying to imitate it from a model in Bach's hand in front of him. If this model was Bach's composing score, that would make "Ich lasse dich nicht" J. S. Bach's composition.

The lack of a composer's name on P 4/1 has long been a problem. Bach's heading reads "Motetta à" and presumably originally continued "8 Voci" or perhaps "doi Cori." (The top of the first page is torn.) It is possible that there was once a composer's name in the section of the page that is now missing, but not necessarily. The autograph score of the Hunt Cantata "Was mir behagt, ist nur die muntre Jagd" BWV 208 (SBB P 42), a score contemporary with P 4/1, has a very similar heading; it reads "Cantata â 4 Voci. 2 Corni di Caccia 2 Violini una Viola è Cont." It, too, lacks the composer's name, and clearly never had one in its heading. It is thus possible that P 4/1 never had anyone's name on it, so the lack of a name cannot be fairly taken as evidence against J. S. Bach's authorship.

Bach is known to have shared the copying of his own compositions with Weimar assistants. He shared the copying of the score of "Nun komm der Heiden Heiland" BWV 61 (SBB P 45) in December 1714, and of the score of "Barmherziges Herze der ewigen Liebe" BWV 185 (SBB P 59) in 1715. In each instance, an unidentified copyist ("Anon. Weimar 2" and "Anon. Weimar 1," respectively) started, and Bach finished the job. The copying of "Ich lasse dich nicht" together with Kräuter is entirely consistent with this practice. We cannot be sure from source evidence that "Ich lasse dich nicht" is a composition of J. S. Bach, but the evidence of the preparation of the score certainly suggests that he may well have been its composer, which would make BWV Anh. 159 Bach's earliest known contribution to the motet genre, dating from *c.* 1712/13 or before.

We can turn to other kinds of evidence for confirmation. First, there is an early source that does attribute "Ich lasse dich nicht" to J. S. Bach: an edition published in the first of two volumes by Breitkopf and Härtel in 1802–3 containing the motets BWV 225–29 and "Ich lasse dich nicht."[17] (See figure 4–3.) Various evidence suggests that this edition was made from Leipzig sources that derived ultimately from J. S. Bach's own materials, and that document an eighteenth-century tradition of the performance of "Ich lasse dich nicht" there under J. S. Bach's name.

The strongest suggestion of a Leipzig origin of the sources for the print concerns its editor. He is generally thought to have been Johann Gottfried Schicht (1753–1823), who had studied under the Thomascantor Johann Adam Hiller while a student at the University of Leipzig. He succeeded Hiller as director of the Gewandhaus concerts, founded the Leipzig Sing-Akademie, served as University music director, and eventually became Thomascantor himself in 1810.[18] Schicht's editorship of the motets is difficult to document, but an entry in Gerber's *Neues Lexikon* credits him with editing

---

[17] *Joh. Seb. Bach's Motetten in Partitur Erster Heft [Zweites Heft] . . . Leipzig bey Breitkopf und Härtel* [1802/3].
[18] Gaynor G. Jones, *New Grove,* s.v. "Schicht, Johann Gottfried."

Figure 4–3 BWV Anh. 159 in the edition by Johann Gottfried Schicht (Leipzig, 1802)

the motets and two other volumes of Bach's music. Most of the entry is in Schicht's own words, and the list of Schicht's editions follows a catalogue of his own compositions provided (according to Gerber) by Schicht. It is thus highly probable that Schicht himself confirmed his editorship of Bach's motets.[19]

[19] Ernst Ludwig Gerber, *Neues historisch-biographisches Lexikon der Tonkünstler*, 4 vols. (Leipzig, 1812–14).

Schicht would have had access to a variety of Leipzig sources on which to base the edition and the ascription to J. S. Bach. One source of potential interest was the collection of motet partbooks of the Thomasschule. These are now lost, and the surviving descriptions of them do not list "Ich lasse dich nicht" among their contents.[20] It is clear, though, that these partbooks were recopied often; just because "Ich lasse dich nicht" did not survive in them into the late nineteenth century does not mean that it was never there. Schicht also owned another copy of the motet attributing the work to J. S. Bach. This manuscript, now lost, was in the former Royal and University Library in Königsberg. We do not know from where Schicht copied it, but descriptions of it make clear that it was not based on the printed edition. Its existence and attribution suggest that Schicht had a source of "Ich lasse dich nicht" that attributed the work to J. S. Bach.[21]

There are several other pieces of evidence supporting an early Leipzig attribution of the motet to J. S. Bach. First, it appears that Schicht had more motets attributed to J. S. Bach available to him than the six he published, and it may be significant that the other five motets in his edition (BWV 225–29) are the most securely attributable to Bach in other sources, whereas several other works of doubtful authenticity were omitted. "Ich lasse dich nicht" was apparently deemed to fall into the more secure category. Second, an early Leipzig tradition of the motet as Bach's work is suggested by a report by Friedrich Rochlitz that he had participated in performances of Bach's motets, apparently including "Ich lasse dich nicht," while he was a Thomasschule student from 1781 to 1788.[22] Third, that the work was familiar to Leipzig musicians before the publication of the Breitkopf and Härtel edition is also strongly suggested by the review of its first volume in the *Allgemeine musikalische Zeitung*, a Leipzig publication, which raised no objection to the inclusion of "Ich lasse dich nicht" under Bach's name.[23] These various pieces of evidence suggest that "Ich lasse dich nicht" was known in Leipzig sources, possibly even from the Thomasschule, attributing the work to J. S. Bach. The attribution of "Ich lasse dich nicht" to J. S. Bach from the Leipzig line of transmission lends support to the evidence of the Weimar score.

J. S. Bach's authorship is strongly supported by stylistic evidence. First, "Ich lasse dich nicht" can be differentiated from Johann Christoph Bach's motets. Naue's speculative attribution of the motet to him does not stand up, because "Ich lasse dich nicht" does not closely resemble any of Johann Christoph Bach's other surviving works in the genre. All of Johann Christoph's motets employ a great deal more text than does "Ich lasse dich nicht," and, in the eight-voice pieces, make less varied use of the resource of the two choirs. All of Johann Christoph's motets use quickly-changing motivic material and textures; in comparison, "Ich lasse dich nicht" uses a carefully limited amount of

---

[20] BG 39, xvi.

[21] Shelf number 13583. See Joseph Müller, *Die musikalischen Schätze der Königlichen- und Universitäts-Bibliothek zu Königsberg in Preussen* (Bonn, 1870), 93; *Versteigerungs-Katalog der von dem verstorbenen Herrn J. G. Schicht . . . hinterlassenen Musikaliensammlung* (Leipzig, [1832]), 25; BG 39, xxxix.

[22] *Dok* III/716; "über den Geschmack an Sebastian Bachs Kompositionen, besonders für das Klavier," *Allgemeine musikalische Zeitung* 5, no. 31 (27 April 1803): 509–22; *Für Freunde der Tonkunst* (Leipzig, 1824; 2nd edn. 1830), 228f.

[23] Unsigned review, *Allgemeine musikalische Zeitung* 5, no. 20 (9 February 1803): 333–35, possibly by Friedrich Rochlitz.

musical material over a relatively long span. The concluding section of one motet, "Lieber Herr Gott, wecke uns auf," is contrapuntally elaborate, as is that of "Ich lasse dich nicht," but is much less thorough in working out its material, and is, of course, a different kind of composition, lacking the chorale found in "Ich lasse dich nicht."

Johann Christoph Bach's one known chorale motet, "Fürchte dich nicht," is structurally similar to "Ich lasse dich nicht," but clearly differentiated from it in musical style (see example 4–1). In this work, a *Spruch* text is presented in the first part, and a chorale appears in long notes in the soprano in the second over statements of the biblical text. The accompanying parts in the second section use a variety of material, including a reprise of the first section, in mostly homophonic textures, with a few short points of imitation. This structure is standard in the chorale motet repertory of the late seventeenth and early eighteenth centuries, and agrees closely with contemporary descriptions of motet construction.

As a rule, though, the accompaniment to the chorale in the second section of these works is homophonic, with an occasional point of imitation. I know of only two exceptions in the repertory in which the chorale cantus firmus is supported by extensive fugal material: "Ich lasse dich nicht," and J. S. Bach's "Fürchte dich nicht" BWV 228. The close relationship between the two compositions supports J. S. Bach's authorship of "Ich lasse dich nicht." In BWV 228 (example 4–2), the lower voices form a double fugue whose two subjects are inversions of each other, one chromatic, the other diatonic; each subject carries a phrase of the text. Most of the remainder of the material in the fugue is made up of sequential repetitions of a neighbor-note *figura corta*. In "Ich lasse dich nicht" (example 4–3), there are also two contrapuntal subjects, each carrying a phrase of the text, used in alternation rather than in combination. The rhythm of the *figura corta* is also essential to the first fugal subject. Although none of the fugal episodes is long, each is distinct, using a different order of voice entry or different rhythmic distance of imitation.

Both BWV 228 and "Ich lasse dich nicht" show the structural outline of the traditional chorale motet, but the contrapuntal concentration in the last sections is unique to them, supporting the attribution of "Ich lasse dich nicht" to J. S. Bach. Bach's application of sophisticated counterpoint represents his contribution to the old form and his personal stamp on it.

The chorale settings in "Ich lasse dich nicht" and "Fürchte dich nicht" are also both extraordinarily economical in their use of musical material. As noted above, the two fugue subjects in BWV 228 are related by free inversion; in addition, the ascending form may be derived from a motive in the chorale cantus firmus, "Warum sollt ich mich denn grämen." In "Ich lasse dich nicht," the first fugal subject is related to the chorale melody used against it, and shares with the chorale a narrow ambitus of a tonic-to-dominant perfect fifth. This is also the ambitus of the opening motive of the motet, and this motive, like the fugal subject, is based on a stepwise descent to the tonic. The striking resemblance of the chorale settings in "Ich lasse dich nicht" and "Fürchte dich nicht," both in formal construction and in deployment of musical material, further strengthens the attribution of "Ich lasse dich nicht" to J. S. Bach.

54

Example 4–1 Johann Christoph Bach, "Fürchte dich nicht," mm. 39–57

Joshua Rifkin has suggested that a composition by another member of the Bach family is similarly contrapuntal and that it throws the attribution of "Ich lasse dich nicht" to J. S. Bach into question.[24] The work is the eight-voice motet "Nun hab ich überwunden" by Johann Michael Bach from the Altbachisches Archiv, which Rifkin claims has essentially the same form as "Ich lasse dich nicht." Although Johann Michael's

---

[24] "Sounds like Bach," BBC broadcast script, program 1 (unpublished, 1993).

Example 4–2 BWV 228, mm. 77–86

motet does begin with an eight-part homophonic section and close with a four-part, more contrapuntal one, it is a piece of a different sort. "Nun hab ich überwunden" is a pure chorale work, treating two stanzas of a hymn, one in each half. Rifkin's claim that the second section (with a chorale cantus firmus) has "precisely the same fugal underpinning" as in "Ich lasse dich nicht" is at worst wrong – each chorale phrase receives support from a new contrapuntal subject, rather than from recurring material – and at best is a poor comparison, because this is a different kind of motet, presenting no biblical text. Imitative cantus firmus treatments of chorale melodies are as old as the Lutheran hymns themselves, and the appearance of the technique in Johann Michael's motet is not at all surprising or unusual. The contrapuntal sophistication of "Ich lasse dich nicht" and "Fürchte dich nicht" is unusual for motets of their type: those that combine biblical and chorale texts.

The type of chorale setting found in "Ich lasse dich nicht" and "Fürchte dich nicht" – a cantus firmus over counterpoint based on one or two subjects set to a biblical text – is found in one other early Bach vocal work. The comparable movement is the ninth of "Ich hatte viel Bekümmernis" BWV 21, a setting of two stanzas of the chorale "Wer nur den lieben Gott läßt walten," presented in long notes, the first stanza in the tenor and the second in the soprano. (See example 4–4.) The first stanza of the chorale is accompanied by a fugal treatment of a single phrase of biblical text ("Sei nun wieder zufrieden, meine Seele"), sung to a single motive and its inversion. When the chorale melody is repeated in the soprano, the accompaniment is similar, adding a new but related motive and a second phrase of text. (These motives may also be chorale-derived.) It has been proposed that this chorale setting was the concluding

Example 4–3 BWV Anh. 159, mm. 84–96

Example 4–4 BWV 21/9, mm. 1–24

movement of the earliest version of BWV 21, most likely dating from before a performance in Weimar in June 1714 and possibly also before one that may have taken place in Halle in December 1713.[25] This movement may thus be roughly contemporary with "Ich lasse dich nicht."

The attribution of "Ich lasse dich nicht" to J. S. Bach has several implications. The considerable consequences for the chronology of the composer's motets are discussed in chapter 6. Another consequence concerns, of all things, Bach's exposure to French orchestral music. In 1885, Robert Eitner pointed out in passing that the opening melodic material of "Ich lasse dich nicht" bore a striking resemblance to a Gavotte en Rondeau from the prologue of the opera *Armide* (1686) by Jean-Baptiste Lully.[26] (See example 4–5.) The resemblance goes beyond the obvious melodic parallel; the two works share a characteristic 6–4–2 harmonization of the second pitch of the melody. The similarity is close enough that one must wonder whether Bach modeled the opening of "Ich lasse dich nicht" on Lully's composition, and if so, how he came to know it.

In fact, there is a ready possibility at hand in Weimar. We know from testimony of Bach's student Kräuter (the copyist of "Ich lasse dich nicht") that the Weimar Prince Johann Ernst brought or sent back from Holland a great deal of interesting new music

25 *NBA* I/16 *KB*. On this movement's motet-like character see chapter 8.
26 Robert Eitner, "Mitteilungen," *Monatshefte für Musik-Geschichte* 17 (1885): 72.

Example 4–5 BWV Anh. 159 (mm. 1–5) and J. B. Lully, Gavotte from *Armide*, mm. 1–4

in 1713.[27] It is fairly certain that the music included the 1711 edition of Vivaldi's Op. 3 concertos published in Amsterdam by Estienne Roger, and most of the scholarly attention paid to this testimony has been to Italian concerto repertory and to the transcriptions and arrangements Bach made of it. But it is worth noting that Kräuter wrote that the Prince was expected to bring back not only Italian but also French music. The question of what French music might have come from Amsterdam has never been answered, but there are candidates in publications from the house of Roger, publisher of Vivaldi's concertos. In particular, Roger published a series of excerpts from the operas of Lully, including a collection of instrumental pieces from *Armide* issued in parts sometime between 1708 and 1712. This collection, arranged for four-part ensemble, includes the gavotte that resembles the opening of "Ich lasse dich nicht."[28] Bach could thus easily have come to know Lully's composition around those years.

It is difficult to know whether the resemblance of the motet and Lully's gavotte and the suggestive date and place of Roger's publication of music from *Armide* amount to a credible chain of evidence or merely represent a coincidence. The influence of French orchestral music on Bach is too little explored, and a German motet is probably the last place one would expect to find that influence manifested. Nonetheless, if there is indeed a connection between the motet and Lully's composition, that would further narrow the likely date of composition of "Ich lasse dich nicht" to between the earliest date the Prince is believed to have shipped music to Weimar and Kräuter's departure for Augsburg, that is, to the summer of 1713.

"Fürchte dich nicht" BWV 228

No original source material survives for "Fürchte dich nicht" BWV 228 and largely as a result, the motet's origins have remained obscure. Spitta did not specify a date for it beyond his general assignment of the motets to the period 1723–34. The first to assign

---

27 *Dok* II/58a.

28 *Overture, Chaconne & Tous les autres Airs à jouer de l'Opera Armide*. See François Lesure, *Bibliographie des éditions musicales publiées par Estienne Roger et Michel-Charles Le Cène (Amsterdam 1696–1743)* (Paris, 1969); Herbert Schneider, *Chronologisch-thematisches Verzeichnis sämtlicher Werke von Jean-Baptiste Lully (LWV)* (Tutzing, 1981), LWV 71/9.

an exact date was Bernhard Friedrich Richter, who turned to circumstantial evidence of memorial sermons preached in the Nikolaikirche by the Superintendent Salomon Deyling. Richter proposed that "Fürchte dich nicht" had been composed for a service for one Susanna Sophia Winkler held on 4 February 1726.[29]

According to the chronicler Sicul, Deyling preached that day on the text Isaiah 43:1–5, but this text and that of BWV 228 correspond only loosely. In the motet, Bach used two different texts from Isaiah (41:10 and 43:1), both beginning with the words "Fürchte dich nicht," a phrase he used as a kind of motto in the composition. Only the second of these is part of the Winkler funeral text. Richter explained this discrepancy by proposing that the motet was conceived back-to-front. He speculated that Bach first composed or planned the second section, a chorale cantus firmus supported by a biblical verse from the Winkler text, and then, left with only three words ("Fürchte dich nicht") remaining to serve as the first half of the motet, added an earlier verse from Isaiah, which gave him the opportunity of writing an eight-voice first half.[30] At best, there is no evidence to support this hypothesis, and it certainly postulates a peculiar compositional approach to the motet. Ameln accepted this line of argument in the NBA, and with it the assignment of BWV 228 to the Winkler memorial service and the year 1726. It is admittedly conceivable that Bach performed the piece in that year, but there is no evidence that it was composed then.

A date for BWV 228 must be sought in another fashion, and we can turn to stylistic evidence and a consideration of the work's relationship to motet composition of the time. As discussed above, this motet is based a traditional structural plan, just as "Ich lasse dich nicht" BWV Anh. 159 is. Among Bach's motets, these two, which share an interrelationship of musical ideas and a striking economy of motivic material, adhere most closely to the norms of motet writing in the early eighteenth century. It thus seems reasonable to propose that BWV 228 is among Bach's earlier motets, and that it can be dated on the basis of style to early in Bach's career. Given the work's close ties to "Ich lasse dich nicht," "Fürchte dich nicht" very likely dates to his Weimar period. Although it may not be quite as old as "Ich lasse dich nicht," the old-fashioned construction of "Fürchte dich nicht" and its other similarities to the early motet together with its strong stylistic contrast to the motets demonstrably from the Leipzig period suggest this early date.

That BWV 228 predates Bach's move to Leipzig is also suggested by the version of the chorale "Warum sollt ich mich denn grämen" he used in it. Example 4–6 gives the melodies from Bach's three settings of the tune. The relationship among them is not simple, but the version found in BWV 228 stands apart from that of BWV 248/33 and 422. BWV 248/33 is from the Christmas Oratorio, dating from 1734; BWV 422, which is melodically closely related, is transmitted in Johann Ludwig Dietel's chorale manuscript from the mid-1730s, although its ultimate source is obscure.[31] If the version in BWV 248/33 and 422 indeed represents Bach's Leipzig form of this tune, then the

---

29 Richter, "Über die Motetten Seb. Bachs," 11. The event is cited in C. E. Sicul, *Annalium Lipsiensium* (1728), quoted in *NBA* III/1 *KB*, 140.

30 Richter, "Über die Motetten Seb. Bachs," 11.

31 Musikbibliothek der Stadt Leipzig Ms. R 18, no. 117. See Hans-Joachim Schulze, "'150 Stück von

Example 4–6 Versions of "Warum sollt ich mich denn grämen"

version in BWV 228 probably predates it, suggesting that BWV 228 was composed before Bach moved to Leipzig.[32]

A Weimar-era origin of "Fürchte dich nicht" is made all the more plausible by a striking parallel between the chorale section of that work and a movement Bach almost certainly composed in Weimar. The last movement of "Christen, ätzet diesen Tag" BWV 63 contains a section built on the same material: a descending chromatic line in quarter notes, an ascending sequence in the rhythm of the *figura corta*, and a motive based on repercussive eighth-note text declamation (see example 4–7). Whether BWV 63, whose original parts suggest a date of *c.* 1714/15, is exactly contemporary with "Fürchte dich nicht" is an open question, but this kind of vocal writing was clearly part of Bach's Weimar style.

Various writers have suggested that BWV 228 may be the earliest of Bach's eight-voice motets.[33] It is likely that Bach composed it after "Ich lasse dich nicht," but probably during his time in Weimar. Without original sources or documentary evidence, we cannot be sure of its exact date of composition, but it is among the most traditional of the composer's motets, and so is probably among his earlier compositions in the genre. A date of *c.* 1715 seems most likely for "Fürchte dich nicht," making it one of two motets Bach probably composed in his years in Weimar.

den Bachischen Erben': Zur Überlieferung der vierstimmigen Choräle Johann Sebastian Bachs," *BJ* 69 (1983): 81–100.

[32] See Alfred Dürr, "Melodievarianten in Johann Sebastian Bachs Kirchenliedbearbeitungen," in *Das protestantische Kirchenlied im 16. und 17. Jahrhundert*, ed. Alfred Dürr and Walther Killy (Wiesbaden, 1986), 154.

[33] Siegele, "Bemerkungen zu Bachs Motetten," 44; Krummacher, "Textauslegung und Satzstruktur in Bachs Motetten," 41.

Example 4–7 BWV 63/7, mm. 50–57

CHAPTER 5

Bach's later motets: rethinking compositional history

The preceding chapter discussed two motets by Bach probably dating from his years in Weimar or before, one whose authenticity has been in doubt and one for which an early date has not been widely considered before. Two other motets, works whose Leipzig origin has long been considered settled, also bear reexamination. A critical look at "Der Geist hilft unser Schwachheit auf" BWV 226 and "Jesu, meine Freude" BWV 227 raises serious questions about the way in which these compositions came to be. There is considerable evidence that neither work, in the form that we now know it, was composed from scratch, but rather that each was assembled or reworked in part from extant material. Thus, although a Leipzig date is probably correct for the form in which we know these works, they have a more complicated genesis than has been generally acknowledged. A third pastiche motet, probably of Bach's assembly, also shows signs of having been arranged from extant music.

"Der Geist hilft unser Schwachheit auf" BWV 226

The origin of "Der Geist hilft unser Schwachheit auf" BWV 226 has long been regarded as secure, largely because we are in possession of Bach's composing score, on which he noted the work's purpose. There is some debate over the specific event at which the motet was performed, but we can be certain that it was heard in connection with the death of the Thomasschule Rector Johann Heinrich Ernesti, who was buried on 20 October 1729.[1] In addition, a nearly complete set of original parts survives, datable to the same period and clearly documenting a performance.

The situation is problematic nevertheless, largely because Bach's score contains both his rough composing hand and his fair-copy script. Some pages of the document are compositional, but other portions of score clearly are not. In addition, there is evidence that the concluding chorale was adapted from another work. These observations, together with other details, have led to the gradual recognition that BWV 226 was compiled in part from extant musical material. A close examination of the sources and

---

[1] See Martin Geck, "Zur Datierung, Verwendung und Aufführungspraxis von Bachs Motetten," in *Eine Sammlung von Aufsätze*, ed. Rudolf Eller and Hans-Joachim Schulze, Bach-Studien, no. 5 (1975), 63f.; and Werner Neumann, "Eine Leipziger Bach-Gedenkstätte: über die Beziehungen der Familien Bach und Bose," *BJ* 56 (1970): 26 n. 29.

careful analysis makes it possible to trace, to some extent, the assembly of the motet in the form in which it survives.

We can start by asking what kind of document Bach's autograph represents. The score, SBB P 36, consists of two gathered bifolia containing mm. 1–145 and a single bifolium containing mm. 146–216, all ruled with 8 + 8 staves per page; these are followed by a single bifolium ruled with 21 or 22 staves per page with no division, containing mm. 217–44, a blank page, and an inverted fragment of another composition. Robert Marshall has pointed out that beginning around the time of this score, Bach returned to his practice of using a fascicle structure for fair and revision copies, in contrast to a structure consisting of individual bifolia more consistently characteristic of his composing scores. Thus the structure of P 36 – at least its beginning – suggests that it is not a compositional document, but rather had its origins as a copy of some other source.[2]

Much of P 36 is calligraphic, but it does contain many corrections, even in the calligraphic portions, that might represent either compositional decisions or revisions to an extant work. This raises the question of whether it is indeed a revision copy or just a near-calligraphic composing score, which Marshall showed Bach to be capable of producing. One hint might come in Bach's preparation of the paper for the score, which is laid out in calligraphic fashion, with exactly the number of staves required for two eight-voice systems per page and with extra space separating the systems. This is the kind of careful preparation typical of Bach's revision and fair copies and not of his composing scores, and suggests that P 36 is indeed a revision copy. (It must be admitted that a motet score might well represent an exception; unlike a cantata score, in which the number of staves in use might change from page to page, the score of a motet requires a constant number of staves. Thus it would have been possible for Bach to lay out his pages calligraphically for this kind of piece even in the score of a newly composed work.)

For the conclusion of the motet, Bach used a bifolium apparently discarded from an abandoned cantata score.[3] Martin Geck proposed that Bach had originally planned a two-section motet, but decided to add a third section (mm. 124–45) after he had already ruled the paper, and thus required this extra sheet.[4] This explanation is doubtful, because Bach was presumably composing a fixed text chosen for Ernesti's funeral; he would clearly have known how much text he was expected to set, and would first have devised an overall plan for the work. What is more, there was presumably nothing stopping him from ruling one more sheet calligraphically for the end of the motet. It is more likely that Bach realized toward the end of the last page of the third bifolium that he would need only a few more systems to complete the piece, and so used a piece of scrap paper rather than commit a fresh piece. Geck's hypothesis also does not jibe with his own argument that the final fugue was a parody of an extant composition, because in that case Bach would have known exactly how much paper he needed to finish had he been adapting an extant piece.

---

[2] Robert L. Marshall, *The Compositional Process of J. S. Bach*, 2 vols. (Princeton, 1972), 1: 63.
[3] BWV Anh. 2. See Marshall, *Compositional Process*, vol. 2, sketch no. 148.
[4] "Datierung, Verwendung und Aufführungspraxis," 64f.

P 36 is a combination of several score types: some of it is calligraphic, and some of it is in Bach's working hand; some of it represents a revision copy, and some a composing score. In general, the beginning of the score is characterized by handwriting and structure typical of revision copies, whereas later parts of the score show clearer evidence of fresh composition. The clear implication is that "Der Geist hilft unser Schwachheit auf" is in part a revision of older material and in part newly composed. This makes it necessary to examine each musical section of the motet individually, because each probably had a slightly different origin.

1. *"Der Geist hilft unser Schwachheit auf"* (mm. 1–123)

Two kinds of evidence suggest that the present form of the first section is not the original. The first concerns the calligraphic nature of this score. The editor of BWV 226 for the NBA suggested that Bach copied the calligraphic opening of this score from a draft, but that is not consistent with what is known of the mature Bach's working methods.[5] More plausible is Geck's suggestion that the neat score showed that Bach had prepared it from a model.[6] It would be most interesting to know what that model was, and what kinds of revisions Bach made to it. Some of the corrections and other features of the score shed some light on this question, and point to a revision of the relationship of the two choirs to each other, and to the section's origin in a work not for double choir.

The most striking correction appears on the calligraphic first page (see figure 5–1). At the end of the first system, Bach made an erasure in all parts in Choir I; the last note of that system has been altered in the top three voices; and the custodes in SI and AI originally pointed to c" and f', respectively, which are not the notes of the next measure. In the next system, an entire measure is canceled; it originally contained whole-measure rests in Choir I; SII had a duplication of m. 10; and the three lowest staves were apparently empty.

Ameln, the NBA editor, suggested that the erasures at the end of the first system were eighth-note rests.[7] Under this hypothesis, the rests in mm. 8–9 in Choir I would correspond to those in Choir II in mm. 1–2. Together with the full-measure rests in the canceled measure in Choir I, this would suggest that the homophonic statement of "Der Geist hilft" in Choir I was an afterthought, intended to connect the two statements of the opening material. Ameln's interpretation of the erasure is difficult to accept. The involvement of all staff lines and spaces in all four parts in the erasure in Choir I suggests that much more than eighth-rests stood there. It is more likely that the erased character was a repeat sign extending through the four voices of Choir I. This hypothesis agrees with the corrections of the notes and custodes that follow, which appear to point to the material in Choir I at m. 17. This is important because mm. 9–16 are a written-out repeat of mm. 1–8 with the two choirs exchanged. The correction suggests that

---

[5] *NBA* III/1 *KB*, 71.
[6] "Datierung, Verwendung und Aufführungspraxis," 63f.
[7] *NBA* III/1 *KB*, 65.

Figure 5–1 Autograph score of BWV 226 (SBB P 36), f. 1

Bach first intended a literal repeat of mm. 1–8, but then decided to write it out instead and exchange the roles of the two choirs. It is conceivable, of course, that this kind of error could have arisen from Bach's accidentally having skipped mm. 9–16 in his copying, but this is extremely unlikely.

What this says about Bach's model is not entirely clear. Presumably, his model had a repeat sign after m. 8, or perhaps there was no repeat – indicated or written out – in the original, and the material now at m. 17 followed immediately. There is no question that the repetition of this material is an important feature of "Der Geist hilft unser Schwachheit auf," for the repeat appears again when the same musical material is reiterated a few measures later. One must wonder, too, whether Bach's decision to swap the choirs in the repeat was the only change he made – whether the model was identical except that it had a literal repeat. Perhaps instead the model was for some ensemble other than eight-voice double choir, and these revisions represent Bach's adaptation of the music to new forces.

Other corrections in this section of Bach's autograph also point to revisions affecting the relationship of the two choirs. In mm. 17–18, the statement of "der Geist hilft" in Choir II was revised; m. 17 in SII and AII originally contained whole- measure rests, and the first two beats of m. 18 in those two parts were originally eighth-note rests. In those two parts at least, then, the supporting homophonic statement of "der Geist hilft" was a later addition. It is possible, for example, that the statement in TII and BII was in the model, and that this passage shows Bach's redistribution of material among the voices.

Most of the other corrections in this section of the motet are subtler and do not point so clearly to a revision of a model or to the model's disposition. But several analytical features of the section and some supporting details of the manuscript score may offer some suggestions about the model Bach was revising. These analytical observations represent the second kind of evidence that Bach was revising a model when he wrote out the score of the first section of "Der Geist hilft unser Schwachheit auf."

The first analytical indication of the origin of this section in an extant composition lies in the way the two choirs are used, in particular the lack of independence of the two bass parts. In the opening phrase and its subsequent restatements, BI and BII join together at the cadence (mm. 5–7, 13–16, etc.). In another passage they double a part exactly (mm. 33ff.), and they occasionally have different texts and phrasing on identical pitches (mm. 55). This lack of independence – encountered to some degree in many double choir motets – points to a more general feature of the first section of "Der Geist hilft unser Schwachheit auf." Especially in the opening material and its several reprises, the relationship of the two choirs is peculiar, representing neither antiphonal writing nor unified 8-part textures. For example, the work opens with what is sometimes described as a brief statement by the first choir (mm. 1–2) answered by the second (mm. 3–4), and concluding with a combined cadence (see example 5-1). But this is equally well regarded as an imitative SI/SII pair supported by an accompaniment split between the two choirs, not a normal use of a double chorus. From a formal point of view, too, the principal material of the movement is handled in an unusual manner: the short imitative duet between the two sopranos is repeated by the two alto voices (mm. 17ff.), tenor voices (mm. 69ff.) and basses (mm. 77ff.).

Several writers have cited these features as evidence of Bach's sophistication in double-choir writing, particularly the accompaniment of various segments of the text

Example 5–1 BWV 226, mm. 1–24

with homophonic statements of the phrase "Der Geist hilft." Friedhelm Krummacher even attached chronological significance to the writing in the piece, suggesting that the subtlety of the double-choir writing in BWV 226 marks it as the latest of Bach's eight-voice motets.[8] It is possible that these features – the often-unified bass parts, extensive use of duets, and blurring of the functions of the two choirs – represent Bach's creative use of an eight-voice double chorus. But in light of the evidence that BWV 226 was based on a model, it seems just as likely that they betray his reworking of an older composition with a different scoring.

The conversion of a model into a composition for eight voices is a practice that is documented in the Bach circle. The cantata movement "Nun ist das Heil und die Kraft" BWV 50, long considered a fragment of Bach's only double-choir church cantata, is most likely an arrangement of a lost five-voice model. The double-choir version may have been the work of Bach's student Carl Gotthelf Gerlach, music director of the Leipzig Neukirche.[9] Bach himself was probably responsible for the conversion of the first section of the pastiche motet "Jauchzet dem Herrn, alle Welt" BWV Anh. 160 into a double-choir piece.[10] In both these works, the arrangements are presumed to have had the same texts as their models, both of which were originally compositions for chorus.

8   "Mehrchörigkeit und thematischer Satz bei Johann Sebastian Bach," *Schütz-Jahrbuch* 1981: 44. See also Christoph Wolff, "Bachs doppelchörige Motetten," *Bachfest-Buch* 44 (Heidelberg, 1969): 96–98.
9   William Scheide, "'Nun ist das Heil und die Kraft' BWV 50: Doppelchörigkeit, Datierung und Bestimmung," *BJ* 68 (1982): 81–96.
10 Klaus Hofmann, "Zur Echtheit der Motette 'Jauchzet dem Herrn, alle Welt' BWV Anh. 160," in *Bachiana et alia musicologica. Festschrift Alfred Dürr*, ed. Wolfgang Rehm (Cassel, 1983), 126–40. See also below.

The possible original scoring and text of the model for BWV 226 are less clear. An origin in a fewer-voiced motet is possible; a five-voice original (SSATB) would agree with the scoring that may underlie the second section of the motet ("Sondern der Geist selbst"; see below). It is also possible that the model was not a motet at all. Indeed, the phrase structure of the first section of BWV 226 is uncharacteristic for a motet. As has often been pointed out, the section is organized in regular four- and eight-measure phrases, atypical for Bach's motet settings of biblical prose. The first half of the text ("Der Geist hilft unser Schwachheit auf") is indeed metrically regular – unusually so for a biblical text – and can be scanned in loose iambs, but its second half ("denn wir wissen nicht, was wir beten sollen") is much less regular. The apparent conflict between textual type and phrase structure could indicate that Bach conceived this music for a different, metrical text, or perhaps for this text but in a musical context in which regular phrasing was more appropriate. The formal and stylistic features of this section have led commentators to attach a bewildering variety of labels to it, and to seek analogies in every musical genre except the motet. Gerber described the first section as "madrigalian" and "prelude-like," and reads a Barform, a formal analysis adopted in part by Krummacher; Siegele sees a combination with dance-like techniques.[11] An origin in a different kind of composition, although by no means certain, would help explain some of the unusual features of the opening.

The regular phrasing, extensive use of duet texture, and the melodic character and ornamentation of the duet voices raise the possibility that Bach may have based the first section of BWV 226 on a vocal duet. The hypothetical model could have comprised the opening imitative duet material and its recurrences in other voices, and the two soprano parts in the antiphonal sections ("denn wir wissen nicht"). (See example 5–2.) An origin in a duet would help explain both the prevalence of duet textures and the close relationship of the two bass voices, which would be derived from the same original continuo line. It may be significant in this regard that the two duet voices and conflated bass parts are harmonically nearly complete in themselves. In reworking a duet as a double-choir piece, Bach would have needed only to split the original duet material and continuo line between the two choruses, and to supply filler in the other parts. The simple homophonic character of most of the non-duet material would have made it possible for Bach to produce a relatively clean score, because almost all of the fundamental compositional decisions would already have been made.

The possible origin of the opening of BWV 226 in a duet is not as crazy as it may sound, because the reworking of vocal duets into choruses is a well-documented practice. For example, many of the choruses in George Frideric Handel's *Messiah* originated in the composer's Italian duets, and several choruses in his oratorio *Theodora* were based on duets by Giovanni Clari. More to the point, this practice is documented in Bach's output as well: the duet "Wer mich liebet, der wird mein Wort halten" BWV 59/1 became the four-voice movement BWV 74/1 with the same text, and the duet "Nimm auch, großer Fürst, uns auf" BWV 173a/8 was reworked into the chorus "Rühre, Höchster, unsern Geist" BWV 173/6.

[11] Gerber, "Über Formstrukturen in Bachs Motetten," 183; Krummacher, "Textauslegung und Satzstruktur in Bachs Motetten," 27; Siegele, "Bemerkungen zu Bachs Motetten," 47f.

Example 5–2 A hypothetical duet model for BWV 226

Perhaps most relevant to BWV 226 are the several versions of the third movement of the Easter Oratorio. Both in musical style and in the process of its transformation, this movement shows a striking similarity to BWV 226. The duet BWV 249/3 has a complex history. With the text "Entfliehet, verschwindet," it was originally part of Bach's 1725 birthday cantata for Weissenfels (the "Schäferkantate" BWV 249a). It was parodied ("Kommt, gehet und eilet") as part of an Easter cantata (BWV deest) of the same year, and as another birthday cantata BWV 249b the following year ("Verjaget, zerstreuet"). Bach reworked the Easter cantata as an oratorio (BWV 249, "Kommt, eilet und laufet") in the late 1730s, and in the 1740s rescored the oratorio version of the duet as a four-part chorus.[12]

Like the opening of "Der Geist hilft unser Schwachheit auf," BWV 249/3 is in 3/8 meter, features an imitative duet (here between tenor and bass), and has regular four- and eight-measure phrases. (See example 5–3.) In transforming the duet into a chorus, Bach preserved the original duet almost completely, assigning it mostly to soprano and alto, but also occasionally to tenor and bass (mm. 56ff.). In mm. 84ff., the duet material is distributed among alto, tenor, and bass, and at the closing cadence (mm. 94ff.) the lower duet part is restored to its original bass register for harmonic reasons. Bach filled in the other parts largely with homophonic statements of "Kommt, eilet!" or "Kommt, eilet / und laufet!" It is not difficult to imagine a similar process of adaptation and the addition of statements of "Der Geist hilft" in BWV 226.

All of the texts that Bach used with the music of BWV 249/3 refer to hurried motion, reflected in swift sixteenth-note activity and an imitative texture. This affect is also found in other duets from Bach's cantatas, for example "Entziehe dich eilends, mein Herze, der Welt" BWV 124/5, which shares meter, texture, regular phrasing, and textual reference to flight. This text, like that of BWV 249/3 (in all its forms), is in anapestic meter, perhaps the inspiration for the use of triple musical meter. Given the

---

[12] *NBA II/7 KB*; Kobayashi, "Chronologie der Spätwerke," 53.

Example 5–3 Duet and chorus versions of BWV 249/3, mm. 24–48

association between texts in this poetic meter, the use of 3/8 musical meter, and regular phrasing, one wonders whether a hypothetical model for the opening section of BWV 226 might have been composed to such a text. This would help explain the unusual use of regular phrasing for a setting of a biblical prose text. It is also possible that the present text was that of the model, and that Bach's use of regular phrasing was simply a compositional choice made for entirely musical reasons.[13]

Whatever the model may have been, some further details of the autograph score suggest Bach's adaptation procedure. As discussed above, the score of "Der Geist hilft unser Schwachheit auf" mixes calligraphic and compositional features. This mixture appears not just in the motet as a whole but in the first section as well. The manuscript clearly takes on the character of composing score from about mm. 105–10 to the end of the section. According to the hypothesis that this piece was reworked from a model, the change in handwriting would indicate that at this point Bach abandoned his model and freely composed the end of the section.

The change in script comes at a structurally significant place in the movement, which falls into the structure A(m. 1)–B(m. 41)–A'(m. 69)–B'(m. 93). The change in handwriting from fair copy to composing score occurs almost exactly at the moment when B' departs from B (mm. 108ff.). At this point Bach leads the section to a cadence in D minor, a harmonic destination that leaves this B♭ major section of the motet tonally open. (See example 5–4.) If Bach was working from a model that was tonally closed, this is the spot at which modifications to the original would have been necessary to arrive at a new harmonic goal.

By this hypothesis, Bach was now freely composing in eight parts, and the music of this section shows some surprising features. The periodic phrasing that has governed until this point disappears, and the musical material used bears little relation to what has gone before. Perhaps most importantly, there is real eight-voice writing here: the bass parts are independent, as are the other voices. Bach appears to have newly composed these measures, in contrast to his revision of a model for the music that precedes them. Freed from his model, he turned to true eight-part writing.

2. "Sondern der Geist selbst" (mm. 124–45)

The next section of BWV 226 ("Sondern der Geist selbst") is in a much rougher hand than the first, suggesting that it was newly composed. (See figure 5–2.) Nevertheless, details of Bach's autograph score and several analytical features make it possible that this section, too, is a reworking of extant material.

Most of this section is in Bach's working script, suggesting fresh composition on these pages, but the imitative entries of the subject are consistently in a much neater hand than the other material. Bach apparently first laid out the contrapuntal entrances in a calligraphic hand, and then filled in the supporting voices. (There is a complicating factor here. In the first six imitative entrances, Bach initially omitted the word "selbst" in the text phrase "sondern der Geist selbst vertritt uns," and was forced to recast the rhythmic shape of his subject to accommodate it, as has been recognized for some time.[14]

---

[13] See Krummacher, "Mehrchörigkeit und thematischer Satz," 45f.
[14] *NBA* III/1 *KB*, 65.

Example 5–4 BWV 226, mm. 108–136

Figure 5–2 Autograph score of BWV 226 (SBB P 36), ff. 3'–4 (detail)

There are any number of reasons this might have happened. Before we take this as evidence that the subject was conceived for a different text, we should note that some Bibles omit the word "selbst" in this phrase. Whatever the explanation, Bach's insertion of the word and his adjustment of the musical subject to accommodate it should not distract us from the initial calligraphic character of the entrances of the subject.)

Marshall has shown that in writing a choral fugue Bach sometimes first wrote out the statements of subjects and answers, and then returned to write countersubjects, but the contrast in script types found in BWV 226 is not common.[15] The strong contrast in the character of Bach's handwriting between the imitative entrances and the other parts suggests that Bach already knew the layout of the imitative entrances and their rhythmic relationship well enough to enter them in a calligraphic script. This suggests that he may have been working from a model, and that the compositional activity in the motet comprised the distribution of the extant material among the eight voices, and the writing of accompanimental parts. There may even be clues here to the nature of the model. For one, the section begins with the new time signature **C** in the six lower parts, but with **C** in SI and AI. Perhaps the model was in cut time, and Bach initially copied the original time signature before deciding to change it to common time.

From an analytical point of view, the section once again makes unusual use of the eight voices. The text is presented in a series of harmonically irregular contrapuntal entrances supported at the beginning by free counterpoint in the three lower voices of Choir I (see example 5–4, mm. 124ff.). By the time all voices have entered, there are only five real parts; alto, tenor, and bass of the two choirs are combined. As in the first section of the motet, the question is whether the unusual use of the resources of a double choir represents an artifact of Bach's reworking of a composition that originally had a different disposition. It is impossible to say with certainty, but given that the work was apparently copied from a model, it is surely possible that the unusual musical features resulted from the adaptation of work for some other forces than eight-part double chorus. The original scoring of the hypothetical model is difficult to determine. A duet texture like that possible for the first section of the motet is not out of the question, nor is a model in five voices, especially given the five-part texture into which the section settles.

Mention should be made here of one notational peculiarity. In copying this section in the vocal parts, Johann Ludwig Krebs added small vertical strokes over certain notes, strokes that have found their way into the NBA score of BWV 226 looking suspiciously like accent marks (see figure 5–3). These marks are not found in Bach's autograph score. Their significance is made clear by the way they were copied in the doubling instrumental parts, which J. S. and C. P. E. Bach demonstrably copied from the vocal parts. In copying the string parts that double Choir I, J. S. Bach omitted the strokes; in copying the woodwind parts that double Choir II, C. P. E. Bach omitted almost all of them, changing the quarter-notes marked by the strokes to two tied eighth-notes. His change makes the significance of the marks clear: they were

---

[15] *Compositional Process*, 1:133ff.

Figure 5–3 Soprano I part for BWV 226 (St 121) in the hands of Johann Ludwig Krebs and J. S. Bach, f. 1'

added by Krebs to clarify the rhythmic organization of the syncopated subject for the performers. They are thus similar to the strokes J. S. Bach himself occasionally used in performing parts.[16] They are not accent marks, and do not belong in a modern score of the motet.

3. *"Der aber die Herzen forschet"* (mm. 146–244)

To understand the genesis of the fugue "Der aber die Herzen forschet," we need first to characterize the portion of Bach's autograph that contains it. Martin Geck has described it as a "Quasi-Reinschrift," pointing to the relatively clean state of much of the score, and to corrections purportedly concentrated in the text underlay. Because of the character of the manuscript, he suggests that this final fugue was a parody of some lost original.[17] The characterization of the score as a fair copy is difficult to accept; in fact, the score shows clear evidence of compositional activity, including many "diminution corrections," which Marshall has shown to be typical of composing scores of movements in large note values.[18] The corrections of various kinds are numerous and occur in significant places, and together suggest that this part of the score is a composing document.

The impression of a fair copy comes from the neat opening passage, from the use of a sheet of calligraphically ruled paper (like that used for the first sections of the motet) and from the relatively clean appearance of the four lower voices on each system (see figure 5–4). The two choirs join together in this movement, but Bach wrote out all eight parts nonetheless, for reasons that are far from clear. He did his composing in Choir I, where the majority of corrections appear, and then copied the results into Choir II, which is in essence a fair copy. Afterwards, he made further revisions that are reflected in both choirs. So although the section begins nearly calligraphically and Choir II is essentially a fair copy of Choir I, the corrections strongly suggest that this is a composing score.

Geck further claimed that changes in the text underlay in the movement also suggest that it is a parody.[19] I cannot agree that there are particularly large numbers of text corrections in this movement. The most extensive text revision is in the soprano, mm. 193ff. The corrections in this passage – both musical and textual – were made in several layers, and many of them were made in both SI and SII, showing that they were made after Bach had copied Choir II from Choir I. The extensive reworking of this passage suggests not parody but rather composition, as does other evidence from the score.

As further evidence of a parody, Geck has suggested that the second section of the fugue, "denn er vertritt die Heiligen" (mm. 178ff.) presents both its theme and countersubject with the same text, a procedure he regarded as atypical. (See example 5–5.) This analysis is strained. When A enters with the second fugal subject of the section (half-note theme "denn er vertritt," m. 178), Bach did not wish to present it

---

[16] For example in Palestrina, *Missa sine nomine*, and Knüpfer, "Erforsche mich, Gott" (see chapter 13).
[17] "Datierung, Verwendung und Aufführungspraxis," 64f.
[18] Marshall, *Compositional Process*, 1:173.
[19] Geck, "Datierung, Verwendung und Aufführungspraxis," 64.

Example 5–5 BWV 226, mm. 178–186

unaccompanied, a practice against which eighteenth-century writers warn and which Bach himself typically avoided.[20] Bach accompanied the initial A entrance with the second half of the subject; whether one calls this a true countersubject does not really matter. Bach's treatment of the fugue subject is in fact typical of his practice: he has avoided an unaccompanied fugal entrance in an upper voice. Nothing in the construction of this passage suggests parody.

Finally, Geck cites the perfunctory treatment of the last text phrase ("nach dem, das Gott gefället") as evidence of a parody. There is no doubt that the last phrase of text gets short shrift, but the delaying of the last textual unit occurs in at least one other of Bach's movements in motet style, BWV 68/5, thought to be newly composed for its text. The delaying of the last text unit cannot be reliably interpreted as demonstrating parody. In sum, there is no good evidence that this section of BWV 226 is a parody of an extant composition. It was apparently newly composed for the motet.

4. "Concluding" chorale

In the original performing parts – but not in the score – these sections of the motet are followed by a four-part harmonization of the melody "Komm, heiliger Geist," underlaid with its third stanza, "Du heilige Brunst." There was plenty of room for the

---

[20] See the discussion in connection with BWV 227 below.

Figure 5–4 Autograph score of BWV 226 (SBB P 36), f. 5

chorale in the score, but Bach provided only the notation "Choral seqt." This raises questions about the chorale: its relationship to the body of the motet, its origin, the appearance of its sources, and its role in the motet's assembly.

We can profitably begin with an examination of the part-copying process. The first two sections of the motet (mm. 1–145, corresponding to the first fascicle of the score) were copied by Johann Ludwig Krebs in all surviving parts, and presumably in the two missing parts as well. Mm. 146ff. (the fugue and chorale) were copied by several different people; their work is outlined in table 5–1.

Table 5–1 *Copyists of original vocal and continuo parts for BWV 226 (SBB St 121)*

m.	SI	AI	TI	BI	SII	[AII]	[TII]	BII	Violone e Continuo	Organo (fig., transp.)
1ff.	JLK	JLK	JLK	JLK	JLK	[?JLK]	[?JLK]	JLK	JSB	JSB
146ff.	JSB	JLK	JSB	JSB	AMB	[?JSB]	[?]	Anon.	CPEB	JSB

JSB = Johann Sebastian Bach   AMB = Anna Magdalena Bach
CPEB = Carl Philipp Emanuel Bach   JLK = Johann Ludwig Krebs

After Krebs had copied the first section of the motet, Bach himself apparently copied mm. 146ff. into one set of parts (SI, [AII], TI, BI). Even in the absence of the AII part, this hypothesis is borne out by the notation "Allabreve" that appears at m. 146 in the parts but not in the score; it was almost certainly added by Bach as he copied one set of parts and then transferred to the other by the several copyists who used Bach's set as a model. Because "Allabreve" appears in the AI part copied by Krebs, it suggests that the lost AII part also contained this entry, supporting the hypothesis that Bach copied this section of the lost part. (The bass parts do diverge briefly in m. 243. This divergence is not reflected in the original parts; both BI and BII have the BII reading. Bach himself accidentally entered the BII reading in the BI part, and that reading was copied in turn into BII.) Because Choirs I and II are identical from m. 146 on, Bach then turned the simple task of duplicating this section in the other four parts to assistants.

It is not clear why Bach undertook the copying of the fugue, but he did reserve for himself the more difficult copying in the motet. This is reflected in the violone and organ parts, in which he did all the complex tasks. He wrote the entire organ part, whose preparation required the conflation of a single continuo part from the two vocal basses in the double choir section, transposition (*Chorton* notation), and figuring. In the untransposed violone part, Bach copied through m. 145, up to which point the bass parts had to be combined, but left to Carl Philipp Emanuel the routine copying of the last section.

With this picture of the part-copying process in mind, we can return to the copying of the four-part chorale at the end of the vocal parts. One has to wonder why Bach undertook the extremely simple task of copying a routine four-part chorale harmonization, a task that could easily have been left to even the most inexperienced copyist.[21] The puzzle is even greater because Bach copied only the music and not the text of the chorale in the three surviving parts containing this section in his hand. Given that Bach undertook the more complicated tasks throughout the production of parts for BWV 226, he may similarly have undertaken the copying of the music of the concluding chorale because it required some sort of special attention.

Because Bach did not bother to write out the chorale in the autograph score of the motet, we can fairly safely assume that there was another source for it. In fact, it seems likely that the chorale was lifted from some other work.[22] This harmonization is not part of any other surviving composition, but it does appear in Johann Ludwig Dietel's chorale manuscript,[23] and the placement of slurs in Dietel's score suggests that he may well have copied it from the parts for Choir II of the motet. The same harmonization also appears in the two early printed collections of Bach's chorales.[24] The chorale is in G major in both prints, but in B♭ major in the motet and in Dietel's manuscript. The tessitura of the vocal parts in the B♭ major version is unusually high (S: f'–g"; A: c–d" T: e–f'; B: B♭–d), and it seems plausible that the B♭ major version is a transposition of an original version in G major, the usual key for this tune.[25]

Perhaps, then, the special attention required by the chorale that called for Bach's own copying of it into the parts was the transposition of the piece from a source in G major. Among the parts in which Bach entered the chorale, there is one copying error that might betray transposition: in TI, third measure from the end, Bach initially wrote the last two notes a step too low, then corrected them. Given that the hypothetical transposition was by a third, this would have been a difficult error to make, and more likely represents a slip of the pen than a transposition mistake. Nonetheless, the distribution of copying labor and the high tessitura of the vocal parts in the chorale suggest that the chorale was taken from some extant work.

Whatever the origin of the chorale may have been, there remains an important question about its connection to the motet. The notation "Choral seqt" at the end of the fugue has probably been misinterpreted. In the NBA, for example, Bach's remark is presented as a performance direction, apparently indicating the immediate performance of the chorale at the end of the biblical portion of the motet and giving the impression that the harmonization represents a "concluding chorale" in the manner of many of Bach's cantatas. As has often been noted, J. S. and C. P. E. Bach omitted the chorale from the instrumental parts that double the biblical portions of the motet. Bach's regular practice was apparently always to double chorale harmonizations with available instruments, so the absence of the chorale from the instrumental parts suggests that the

---

[21]   On the production and copying of chorales, see Marshall, *Compositional Process*, 1:69ff.

[22]   Ameln, *NBA* III/1 *KB*, 71; Klaus Häfner, "Der Picander-Jahrgang," *BJ* 61 (1975): 105 n. 88, proposes an origin in a cantata on a libretto by Picander. See also Siegele, "Bemerkungen zu Bachs Motetten," 47 n. 20.

[23]   Musikbibliothek der Stadt Leipzig Ms. R 18, no. 16. See Schulze, "'150 Stück von den Bachischen Erben.'"

[24]   Berlin and Leipzig, 1765–69, vol. i, no. 73; Leipzig, 1784–87, vol. i, no. 69.

[25]   Cf. BWV 59/3=175/7 in G major; BWV 172/5 in F major *Chorton*/G major *Cammerton*; BWV 652 in G Major; but also BWV 651 in F major.

chorale was not meant immediately to follow the biblical portion of the motet. Perhaps it was performed in a different location such as Ernesti's graveside.

In any event, Bach's remark "Choral seqt" was almost certainly not a performance instruction – he did not copy it into the parts – but was rather intended as a reminder for the copying process. The presentation of this instruction as a performance direction has led to the universal practice of concluding BWV 226 with the singing of this chorale, to the point that the motet has come to seem incomplete without it. This probably misrepresents the motet, because the chorale is not part of the work; "Der Geist hilft unser Schwachheit auf" is a purely biblical motet. Bach did go to the trouble of putting the chorale in the same key as the motet, but it is probable that the biblical sections of BWV 226 were meant to stand on their own.

The picture that emerges from the sources for BWV 226 and from analysis is of a work partly newly composed and partly compiled from extant material. Bach was undoubtedly under considerable time pressure to provide a motet befitting the late Rector of the Thomasschule. Ernesti died on 16 October, and his burial, at which the motet was performed, was held four days later on the twentieth. Before he could begin composing, Bach needed to be informed of the text chosen for the occasion, and thus probably had only a few days in which to compose the motet, copy parts, and prepare the performance. Perhaps this helps explain why he turned in part to extant material, creating an elaborate double-choir motet for the occasion on short notice. The version of "Der Geist hilft unser Schwachheit auf" we know certainly dates from 1729, but some of the material in it – whether originally part of another motet or of some other kind of composition – is older.

"Jesu, meine Freude" BWV 227

No original material survives for "Jesu, meine Freude" BWV 227, making it impossible to determine its origin and genesis from source evidence, and Spitta's hypothesis of its Leipzig origin has generally held sway. Bernhard Friedrich Richter was the first to date the work, assigning it to a Nikolaikirche memorial service for the wife of the Leipzig Postmaster Kees in July 1723, at which the sermon text was Romans 8:11 ("So nun der Geist"), a text that appears in the tenth of the eleven movements of Bach's motet.[26] Despite the funeral text's less-than-central role in the motet and the lack of any corroborating evidence, Richter's date of 1723 has been nearly universally accepted for the composition of BWV 227.

In 1982, Martin Petzoldt found a copy of the order of service for the Kees funeral, which mentions neither the motet nor the chorale "Jesu, meine Freude."[27] It is reported elsewhere that the burial, another possible occasion for the performance of the motet, took place in silence. Petzoldt has nonetheless attempted to rescue the connection with Kees and the date 1723, proposing a performance at the house of

[26] Richter, "Über die Motetten Seb. Bachs," 9.
[27] Martin Petzoldt, "Überlegungen zur theologischen und geistigen Integration Bachs in Leipzig 1723," *Beiträge zur Bachforschung* 1 (Leipzig, 1982): 49.

mourning before the conveyance of the deceased's body to the church.[28] He demonstrates a complex network of theological relationships between the texts from Romans used in the motet, the chorale "Jesu, meine Freude," nearby Sunday Epistles, and the sermon preached for Kees, arguing that these relationships connect BWV 227 with her funeral. The connections Petzoldt cites may be theologically sound, but several are irrelevant to the issue of dating because they concern only the relationship of texts in the motet to each other, and do not connect the motet and its texts to the Kees funeral. The lack of correspondence between the funeral text and the motet remains a serious problem; in all, the 1723 date and connection with Kees must be considered speculative.

Friedrich Smend was the first to discuss the imposing symmetrical architecture of "Jesu, meine Freude,"[29] and his linking of the symmetrical structure of BWV 227 with that of the St. John and St. Matthew Passions BWV 245 and 244 has helped support a date in the 1720s for the motet. Subsequent analyses – some astonishingly farfetched – have attempted to show musical relationships between the biblical sections and the chorale settings with which they alternate.[30] These considerations of the motet's architecture and musical organicism have led to the assumption that BWV 227 was composed as a unit, but there is substantial evidence that the eleven-movement motet is a compilation. The work contains material probably from Bach's Weimar years, some of indeterminate age, and some from the Leipzig period either newly composed or recycled from extant compositions.

The first suggestion that BWV 227 was compiled lies in the number of voices used in each movement. "Jesu, meine Freude" is fundamentally a five-voice composition, and includes two five-voice chorales, but it is peculiar that the motet begins and ends with four-part harmonizations. The many changes in scoring in the motet are understandable for the sake of musical variety, but beginning and ending with four-part chorales seems to contradict the essential five-voice nature of the piece. It is unlikely that Bach would have written an entirely new composition this way. The four-part harmonizations may well have a different origin than the other movements.

The next suggestion of the work's heterogeneous origin concerns the chorale melody "Jesu, meine Freude." One would expect to find only superficial variants in the chorale melody: passing tones, dotted figures, anticipations, and the like. These are indeed encountered in BWV 227, but so is a substantive variant. BWV 227/9 uses a different version of the tune "Jesu, meine Freude" from that found in the other chorale movements of the motet.[31] The variant appears in the second phrase (see example 5–6 and table 5–2); the fifth phrase has the same variant, distributed somewhat differently.

Petzoldt and Ameln attempt to explain the chorale variants by the text-expressive and theological demands of each strophe, and by Bach's interest in creating musical

---

[28] Martin Petzoldt, "J. S. Bach's Bearbeitungen des Liedes 'Jesu, meine Freude' von Johann Franck," *Musik und Kirche* 55, no. 5 (1985): 213–25.

[29] Friedrich Smend, "Bach's Matthäus-Passion," *BJ* 25 (1928): 36ff.

[30] See, for example, the Lorenzian analysis by Wilhelm Leutge, "Bachs Motette 'Jesu, meine Freude,'" *Musik und Kirche* 4, no. 3 (1932): 97–113.

[31] These variants are discussed by Dürr, "Melodievarianten in Johann Sebastian Bachs Kirchenliedbearbeitungen," 153.

Table 5–2 *Distribution of variant versions of "Jesu, meine Freude"*

BWV	Melody version	Date
227/1–3–5–7–11	**A**	
81/7	A	1724[a]
358	A	bef.1735[b]
227/9	**B**	
1105	B	bef. 1713[c]
12/6	B	1714[d]
610	B	1713/14[e]
713	B	?1708–17[f]
64/8	B	1723[a]
87/7	B	1725[a]
753	Free treatment – version unclear	

[a] See Alfred Dürr, *Zur Chronologie der Leipziger Vokalwerke J. S. Bachs.*, 2nd edn. (Cassel, 1976).
[b] See Hans-Joachim Schulze, "'150 Stück von den Bachischen Erben': Zur Überlieferung der vierstimmigen Choräle Johann Sebastian Bachs," *BJ* 69 (1983): 81-100.
[c] See Christoph Wolff, *The Neumeister Collection of Chorale Preludes from the Bach Circle* (New Haven, 1986).
[d] See Alfred Dürr, *Studien über die frühen Kantaten Johann Sebastian Bach*, 2nd edn. (Wiesbaden, 1977).
[e] See Peter Williams, *The Organ Music of J. S. Bach*, vol. ii (Cambridge, 1983).
[f] The dating of this work is problematic. See Ulrich Meyer, "Zur Einordnung von J. S. Bachs einzeln überlieferten Orgelchorälen," *BJ* 60 (1974): 85; and Williams, *The Organ Music of J. S. Bach*, vol. ii, 252n.

Example 5–6 Versions of "Jesu, meine Freude"

variety.[32] Ameln hinted that some of the settings in BWV 227 might be older than the date of composition 1723 he adopted from Richter, but dismissed this as unlikely. Both authors steer clear of the possibility that the variants indicate the presence of more than one compositional layer, preferring to imagine Bach composing the motet as a unified, organic whole, adopting different versions of the chorale for different movements and texts. It is far more likely that the variant tune in BWV 227/9 indicates that the movement was written at a different time than the other chorale settings in the motet.

The version used in BWV 227/9 may also give a hint of its age. The form found in most of BWV 227 (A) is the one Bach used only in Leipzig, whereas the form used in 227/9 (B) is found in pre-Leipzig works. The ninth movement of "Jesu, meine Freude" may well be a Weimar-period or earlier composition; in any event, it was apparently not contemporary with the other motet movements.[33]

[32] Petzoldt, "J. S. Bach's Bearbeitungen des Liedes 'Jesu, meine Freude'"; *NBA* III/1 *KB*, 105.
[33] Werner Breig independently arrived at the same conclusion. "Grundzüge einer Geschichte von Bachs vierstimmigem Choralsatz," part 1, *Archiv für Musikwissenschaft* 45, no. 3 (1988): 183ff.

Another aspect of BWV 227/9 may suggest its origin. Many commentators have pointed to its instrumental character and ritornello-like form, and have worked hard to explain its key of A minor, the only exception to the E minor chorale movements in the motet.[34] Given its style and form, it is quite possible that the movement was originally an instrumental or vocal/instrumental setting of the chorale melody. In fact, it has been pointed out that a passage from the fifth movement of the motet bears a striking relationship to one of Bach's organ settings of "Jesu, meine Freude" (BWV 713);[35] a similar relationship to a lost composition is not out of the question for the ninth movement.

The continuo-like tenor line of BWV 227/9 (the lowest part) is often pointed out, but it has not been noted that the line is carefully worked out so that it does not descend below the pitch C (see example 5–7). This is often the lowest note in Bach's Weimar tenor parts,[36] but would also be the lowest possible pitch in a *bassetto* movement using a viola on the bottom-most part. It is not clear whether BWV 227/9 is a vocal work written in the manner of an instrumental or vocal/instrumental chorale setting, or whether the movement may have had its origin in the reworking of such a composition. The latter is a possibility not to be ignored.

There are further suggestions that BWV 227 was assembled. The first and last biblical movements, BWV 227/2 and 227/10, are based on the same material, and their relationship is a pillar of observations on the motet's symmetry. But the sometimes awkward text declamation in BWV 227/10 suggests that the music of this movement was conceived for BWV 227/2 and then reworked for BWV 227/10. Given the evidence suggesting that the motet was assembled from extant movements, this reworking takes on a new significance. One wonders whether the model, BWV 227/2, was an older composition – perhaps a motet setting of a *Spruch* text – that Bach incorporated into the new motet and reworked to form the penultimate movement.

The central fugue of BWV 227 also presents features that may point to an origin outside the motet. The fugue begins unaccompanied in the tenor, without the support of other parts or continuo. Johann Adolph Scheibe specifically warns against unsupported fugal entrances in motets:

> At the entrance of the main subject the countersubject should already appear in another voice. Otherwise, the monophony sounds too empty and too simple, especially when no instruments are used, and in no way pleases the ear.[37]

Example 5–7 BWV 227/9, Tenor, mm. 22–35

---

[34] Petzoldt, "J. S. Bach's Bearbeitungen des Liedes 'Jesu, meine Freude,'" 216f.; Alfred Lorenz, "Homophone Grossrhythmik in Bachs Polyphonie," *Die Musik* 22, no. 4 (1930): 245–53; Siegele, "Bemerkungen zu Bachs Motetten," 39ff.

[35] Ulrich Meyer, "Zur Einordnung von J. S. Bachs einzeln überlieferten Orgelchorälen," *BJ* 60 (1974): 85; Peter Williams, *The Organ Music of J. S. Bach*, vol. ii (Cambridge, 1983), 251f.

[36] See Alfred Dürr, *Studien über die frühen Kantaten Johann Sebastian Bachs*, 2nd edn. (Wiesbaden, 1977), 240.

[37] *Critischer Musikus*, 180f.

Bach observed this principle in his motets in all but bass entrances. He generally accompanied an opening fugal entry with a second voice in stretto, with a countersubject, or with free material: BWV 225, mm. 75ff. (but not mm. 255ff., a bass entrance); BWV 226, mm. 124ff. and mm. 178 ff.; BWV 228, mm. 77ff.; BWV 229, mm. 64ff. The unaccompanied fugal opening of BWV 227/6 may once have had continuo support. Perhaps there was once a continuo part for the motet, or maybe the movement was once part of a concerted work. In his motet-like cantata movements, Bach usually supported the first entrance of the subject with an independent basso continuo part, but there are three exceptions, all pre-Leipzig pieces, in which the continuo doubles the entering tenor voice (BWV 4/5, 71/3, and 182/7), and we should consider the possibility that BWV 227/6 originated in such an early composition.

There are other features of the motet that can be interpreted as remnants of the assembly of the work from extant material, if not unambiguously so. The fugue BWV 227/6 arguably has a four-part, not a five-part, exposition despite the use of five voices; it has many four-voice passages, and a number of vocal lines doubled in thirds. Might these features point to the reworking of a four-voice model? This movement reaches a strong cadence in G major, the key in which it began, then presents an additional homophonic section with new text ("Wer aber Christi Geist nicht hat . . ."), which cadences in B minor, preparing the return of E minor in the chorale movement that follows. BWV 227/8, in C major, behaves similarly, closing on a phrygian cadence on E. Does this construction betray an effort to unify a work constructed from extant, tonally closed movements?

Hans-Joachim Schulze has demonstrated that the form in which we know BWV 227 was part of Bach's repertory by 1735. Three of its chorales appear in Johann Ludwig Dietel's chorale manuscript, Leipzig R 18: BWV 227/7 (no. 21), BWV 227/1 (no. 31), and BWV 227/3 (no. 32; lacks SII).[38] The predominance of the Leipzig version of the melody "Jesu, meine Freude" suggests that much of the work originated during Bach's time there. Certainly the style of the chorale harmonizations suggests a date after Bach's first Leipzig years. But the motet also contains a version of the melody that probably dates from much earlier in Bach's career (in BWV 227/9), and the first *Spruch* setting BWV 227/2 would not be stylistically out of place in Bach's Weimar years. The form in which the motet is known today remains a monument of Bach's interest in creating large, symmetrical musical structures, but in its character as an assembled work, it more resembles the Credo of the Mass in B minor BWV 232 (assembled largely from extant movements) than it does the Passions BWV 244 and 245 to which it is often compared.

"Jauchzet dem Herrn, alle Welt" BWV Anh. 160 / "Sei Lob und Preis mit Ehren" BWV 231

Bach's cantus firmus setting of the chorale melody "Nun lob, mein Seel, den Herren" appears in three different guises: as the second movement of his 1725 cantata for the Sunday after Christmas "Gottlob! Nun geht das Jahr zum Ende" BWV 28, as an

---

[38] "'150 Stück von den Bachischen Erben,'" 91.

independently transmitted movement referred to as BWV 231, and as the second section of a composite motet "Jauchzet dem Herrn, alle Welt" BWV Anh. 160 attributed to Bach in some sources. There is evidence to suggest that the movement predates its use in the 1725 cantata, although its earlier form is unknown. The piece provides an important link between Bach's motets and his motet-like movements in concerted works, and the pastiche motet of which it is a part is another example of Bach's assembly of a motet from extant musical material.

The source closest to J. S. Bach is the autograph score of the cantata BWV 28, where the piece appears as the second movement. The cantata version uses the first stanza of the chorale "Nun lob, mein Seel, den Herren" and has a partly independent basso continuo part. (See example 5–8.) This motet-like movement, of a type common in Bach's concerted vocal music, uses a text entirely appropriate for a motet and is constructed musically like one. Unusually for motet-like movements, though, its notation in the autograph score of BWV 28 is remarkably clean, suggesting that it may be older than the rest of the cantata, as Robert Marshall first pointed out; the notation suggests that the score of this movement is a fair or revision copy.[39]

Marshall speculated that the model for this cantata movement may have had a different text, suggesting that several revisions of long note values into several shorter ones might point to the accommodation of a new text. This is not altogether convincing. The two examples he gives (mm. 10, 12) are in passages that carry the first line of "Nun lob, mein Seel, den Herren." All of the verses of this chorale have the same number of syllables in their first lines, so no changes would have been necessary on text-declamatory grounds, assuming that the original text (if there was one) was one of these verses.

The score of this movement is also unusual in that, exceptionally, Bach wrote out the *colla parte* instrumental lines on their own staves. Marshall speculates that Bach may have done so for reasons connected with a possible change in instrumentation, but this is not a particularly convincing explanation either. Marshall is almost certainly right that BWV 28/2 was based on a model of some sort, but Bach's autograph score unfortunately tells us little about the nature of that model.

"Nun lob, mein Seel, den Herren" is one of the chorale tunes most often encountered in German motets of the early eighteenth century, so it is not surprising that the other two versions of the composition are both motets. The first, consisting of the movement alone, differs from the cantata version in that it has no independent continuo part – much of the continuo material is absorbed into the vocal bass – and uses the last stanza of the chorale ("Sei Lob und Preis mit Ehren"). The most important source of this version, listed by Schmieder as BWV 231, is the Amalienbibliothek motet manuscript SBB AmB 116, which together with its companion manuscripts contains motets by other Bach family members and may well have had a direct connection to J. S. Bach. (There are other Amalienbibliothek sources of the motet, but they apparently derive from AmB 116.[40])

[39] SBB P 92. Marshall, *Compositional Process*, 1:19, 29, and 174.
[40] See Klaus Hofmann's edition of the work (Neuhausen-Stuttgart, 1978). On the Amalienbibliothek manuscripts, see chapter 11.

Example 5–8 BWV 28/2, mm. 1–25

AmB 116 is of high quality, but it is difficult to know whether its transmission of "Sei Lob und Preis mit Ehren" as an individual composition has anything to do with Bach's practice or conception of the work. Indeed, several of Bach's cantata movements – including several motet-like movements – are transmitted individually without any suggestion that Bach himself ever used them independently. We should thus not automatically assume that the appearance of this work in AmB 116 documents its status as an independent motet.

In fact, Klaus Hofmann has argued that BWV 231 never really existed as an independent composition, but that this motet version of the movement was extracted from a composite motet of Bach's creation, "Jauchzet dem Herrn, alle Welt" BWV Anh. 160, the third place from which the movement is known.[41] This work, whose principal source is a score in the hand of Bach's student and son-in-law Altnickol,[42] was apparently assembled from smaller musical units. The first section of BWV Anh. 160 is an eight-voice double choir setting of Psalm 100:1–2, an entirely characteristic motet text (see example 5–9). The composer of this piece is unknown – possibly

Example 5–9 BWV Anh. 160, mm. 1–14

41 Hofmann, "Zur Echtheit der Motette 'Jauchzet dem Herrn, alle Welt.'" Cf. also his "Alter Stil in Bachs Kirchenmusik. Zu der Choralbearbeitung BWV 28/2," in *Alte Musik als ästhetische Gegenwart. Bach Händel Schütz. Bericht über den internationalen musikwissenschaftlichen Kongreß Stuttgart 1985,* 2 vols., ed. Dietrich Berke and Dorothee Hanemann (Cassel, 1987), 1:164–69.
42 SBB P 37.

Telemann, the sources suggest – but Hofmann has argued convincingly that its second part, which presents a fugue, was originally scored for four voices, and that J. S. Bach was probably responsible for its arrangement for double choir. The work shows a close musical relationship to two compositions of J. S. Bach. One, as Hofmann points out, is the motet "Singet dem Herrn ein neues Lied" BWV 225, the structure of whose first section is similar: an antiphonal opening followed by an accompanied fugue. The other is a motet-like cantata movement, BWV 24/3, similar in meter, opening motivic gesture, and texture, presenting an antiphonal treatment giving way to a less equal relationship (see example 5–10). The often unidiomatic vocal writing in much of BWV Anh. 160 may point to an origin in a concerted work resembling BWV 24/3.

The third movement of BWV Anh. 160, an arrangement from a cantata by Telemann, was probably added after Bach's death. The second movement is essentially identical with BWV 231, the continuo-less motet version transmitted in AmB 116. It is unfortunately not possible to say whether the sources transmitting this movement alone derive from sources of BWV Anh. 160 or from some other source; that is, it is unclear whether Bach created the motet version of BWV 28/2 expressly for use in BWV Anh. 160. Hofmann has suggested that he did, and that BWV 231 is simply an extract from the composite motet. Either way, the existence of both a cantata version and a motet version of this composition shows clearly that motets and motet-like movements in concerted works were indeed closely related.

Example 5–10 BWV 24/3, mm. 1–11

At the same time, there were differences between motet style as Bach used it in his motets and as he used it in cantatas; one of the principal differences between BWV 28/2 and BWV 231/Anh. 160, for example, lies in the elimination of the partly independent continuo part in the motet. (See example 5–11.) Its removal is all the more striking in the light of Hofmann's demonstration that the opening section of BWV Anh. 160 may also have lost its independent continuo part. These revisions, if they really are Bach's, may suggest that he preferred the fundamental bass line in a motet to be part of the vocal material, whereas that was not as great a concern in concerted works. Bach's surviving performing material suggests that he performed double-choir motets with a *basso seguente* part absorbing both vocal bass parts. In contrast, a large number of the motet-like movements from the cantatas have partly independent continuo parts, perhaps pointing to an essential difference between motets proper and motet style as Bach used it in concerted works.

Bach's apparent assembly of various musical units in BWV Anh. 160 provides further evidence of his willingness to rework materials in motets, just as he did in "Der Geist hilft unser Schwachheit auf" BWV 226 and "Jesu, meine Freude" BWV 227. The apparent freedom with which he used the same material both in a cantata and in a motet in BWV Anh. 160 and its related compositions should remind us that he may have done the same in other composite motets as well. In all, the legacy of Bach's motet composition in Leipzig may lie in large measure in the reworking, assembly, and arrangement of extant musical materials.

Example 5–11 BWV 231/Anh. 160, mm. 1–25

CHAPTER 6

Chronology, style, and performance practice of Bach's motets

The chronology of Bach's motets

Few generalizations about J. S. Bach's vocal music have been so unquestioningly accepted as one concerning his motets that can best be called the "Leipzig premise." This is the assumption that the motets represent a small but unified canon of original, organic compositions dating from the years Bach was Thomascantor in Leipzig, 1723–50. The widespread and continued acceptance of this premise has contributed to the dismissal of at least one motet as inauthentic, has been largely responsible for the assignment of insupportable Leipzig dates to several motets, and has caused observers to overlook important evidence concerning the complex origins of several motets.

If we look closely at the roots of the Leipzig premise and the evidence that supposedly underlies it, we will understand that it is misleading in at least two respects. First, one motet previously considered inauthentic dates from before Bach's Leipzig period, and there are strong suggestions that another also stems from that time. These compositions challenge the chronological assumption of the Leipzig premise, that all of Bach's motets date from his Leipzig years. Second, even among the motets that can be securely dated to Bach's Leipzig years, two are most likely assemblies and revisions of extant material, a state of affairs hardly contemplated in the traditional view of Bach's motets. In light of these points, we must substantially revise the chronology of Bach's motets to encompass the whole of his career, and recognize that some works of the Leipzig years have their origin in older material.

The Leipzig premise got its start because Bach's motets are difficult to date. Several are transmitted in late or peripheral sources, so source-critical methods are of limited value in establishing when Bach composed them. What is more, the motets' function is poorly documented, eliminating the possibility of dating them by external criteria. In contrast, Bach's weekly church cantatas are transmitted largely in datable original scores and performing parts, and their chronology and role in the liturgy – at least in Leipzig – are well understood.

Also in contrast to the cantatas, there has been an unbroken tradition of performance of the motets at the Leipzig Thomasschule since Bach's time. This tradition clearly influenced the motet volume of the Bach-Gesellschaft edition (vol. 39, edited by Franz Wüllner), which relied heavily on sources from the Thomasschule. The survival of these Leipzig sources, the testimony of Johann Friedrich Rochlitz and other Leipzig figures, and the early publication of the motets by the Leipzig house of Breitkopf & Härtel (1802–3), have combined to make the pieces conceptually inseparable from that city.

The first to codify the Leipzig premise was the Bach biographer Philipp Spitta, who relied on several stylistic and historical arguments for his assignment of the motets to Bach's Leipzig years.[1] Despite Spitta's familiarity with an important body of seventeenth-century motets, he saw little connection between them and J. S. Bach's motets. He instead regarded Bach's motets as derived from his cantatas; the almost inevitable implication was that the motets were roughly contemporary with or even younger than the concerted pieces. His belief that the motets had been used as substitutes for the Sunday cantatas further suggested that they must have been composed around the same time.

Spitta also regarded Bach's motet style as a derivative of his organ music, implying that the motets were written after a substantial fraction of the organ compositions, i.e., later rather than earlier in Bach's life. For Spitta, the proposed relationship between Bach's motets and his organ music also explained why chorales were so important in the motets: it was a consequence of their central role in the organ repertory. This, in turn, may also have hinted at a connection with Bach's chorale cantatas, which were late works in Spitta's chronology. Spitta's presumed Leipzig dates for the motets were apparently supported by evidence from Bach's own hand that "Der Geist hilft unser Schwachheit auf" BWV 226 was composed in 1729. Spitta believed that the other motets shared that work's stamp of maturity, suggesting in the absence of documentary evidence that the others were roughly contemporary.

Spitta realized that Bach must have had contact with motet style as a young man, and there were two motets that he considered candidates to be early compositions of J. S. Bach. He regarded "Unser Wandel ist im Himmel" BWV Anh. 165 as possibly a Weimar composition, and admitted that "Ich lasse dich nicht" BWV Anh. 159 might also have been an early Bach work. But these works did not carry much weight because Spitta had grave doubts about their authenticity, and he settled on the years 1723–34 for the probable composition of the motets.

The two tributaries of the Leipzig premise – the long-standing association of the motets with the Thomasschule and Spitta's historical view – found their confluence in an influential 1912 essay by Bernhard Friedrich Richter.[2] Richter, son of a Thomas-cantor and himself a member of the Thomasschule faculty, had a strong bias toward Leipzig.[3] His essay on Bach's motets is dedicated to the Thomanerchor, and consists in large part of anecdotes concerning the choir's rehearsal and performance of these works.

Richter rejected Spitta's theory that the motets were substitutes for the Sunday cantatas. Proceeding largely on evidence of practice at the Thomasschule well after Bach's death, and backed up by what was known with certainty about BWV 226, he

---

[1] *J. S. Bach*, 2:426–43.
[2] "Über die Motetten Seb. Bachs."
[3] See Franz Gehring and David Charlton, *New Grove*, s.v. "Richter, Ernst Friedrich," which includes information on his son Bernhard Friedrich.

proposed that most of the motets were intended for funerals or memorial services. It went without saying that Leipzig was the place to look for evidence, and Richter proposed specific services for which he believed several of Bach's motets had been composed. This approach was appealing because it offered both dates and functions for the motets, and Richter showed both diligence and ingenuity in identifying funerals at which he suggested the motets might have been performed. Unfortunately, Richter's speculations do not stand up to scrutiny, but they nonetheless became virtually entrenched, having been adopted to a large extent by Schmieder in the BWV and by the NBA.

Along with the arguments favoring a Leipzig origin of the motets, there were also forces at work that seemed to rule out the possibility that Bach composed some of his motets before 1723. First, we are relatively ignorant about the liturgical requirements of the composer's pre-Leipzig jobs. There is little documentation outside Leipzig to suggest either specific or general occasions for which the motets might have been used. At the least, this has discouraged speculation about Bach's composition and performance of motets before he moved to Leipzig.

The possibility that some of Bach's motets predate 1723 has also been stifled by a peculiar theory that all of Bach's motets have necessarily survived. This idea was first put in writing by Richter, who found it unlikely that early motets existed and were then lost. He believed that it was more probable that we possess the whole of Bach's output in the genre.[4] Konrad Ameln, the editor of the NBA motet volume, joined this opinion, supporting it by reference to the use of individual cantata movements as motets at the Thomasschule and elsewhere after Bach's death. Had there been more "true" motets available, so went his argument, musicians would have been less likely to turn to these pieces. Simple logic related this theory to the problem of chronology:

All known motets are from Leipzig;

All motets are known;

Therefore all motets are from Leipzig.

The dubious premises of this syllogism rely on the repertory preserved in Leipzig sources and on the thesis that what does not survive never existed at all.

Ironically, the new chronology of Bach's vocal works based on systematic source study has worked tacitly in favor of the old dates for the motets. The new chronology affirmed what had been accepted for some time: that "Singet dem Herrn ein neues Lied" BWV 225 and "Der Geist hilft unser Schwachheit auf" BWV 226, known in original sources, dated from Bach's years in Leipzig. The new chronology did eliminate a number of speculative hypotheses about the exact date and purpose of BWV 225, but there was never any doubt that it was a Leipzig work. The source-critical and liturgical evidence on which the new chronologies depended did not say much about the other motets, whose sources do not directly reveal a great deal about their dates of composition and whose liturgical functions remain obscure. The motets remained Leipzig pieces, at least by default.

---

[4] "Über die Motetten Seb. Bachs," 5.

The chronological component of the Leipzig premise is immediately challenged by the reattribution of "Ich lasse dich nicht" BWV Anh. 159 to J. S. Bach and its secure dating to 1712/13 or before. The work had been previously ascribed to the Eisenach Johann Christoph Bach (13), a generation older, but it can be demonstrated that this attribution was an early nineteenth-century speculation that has been propagated by the Berlin Library, the BG, Schmieder, and the NBA. Documentary and stylistic evidence point to the young J. S. Bach as composer. The partially autograph score transmitting the work dates from Weimar in 1712/13, so the motet must be at least that old. In fact, the age of the score has contributed to the rejection of the motet as inauthentic; if it were by Bach, it would have to have been an early composition, an impossibility under the Leipzig premise.

The early origin of BWV Anh. 159 opens up the possibility that other motets predate 1723, realized in the date of *c.* 1715 or earlier proposed for "Fürchte dich nicht" BWV 228 by virtue of its traditional construction and close structural parallels to "Ich lasse dich nicht." The similarity of part of the motet to a movement of the cantata "Christen, ätzet diesen Tag" BWV 63 of *c.* 1715, supports a Weimar date. The secure dating of "Ich lasse dich nicht" to Bach's pre-Leipzig period and the likelihood of an early date for "Fürchte dich nicht" cast immediate doubt on the Leipzig premise.

Documentary and stylistic evidence suggest that the surviving versions of "Der Geist hilft unser Schwachheit auf" BWV 226 and "Jesu, meine Freude" BWV 227 were assembled in Leipzig, but the material that underlies them is of indeterminate age, and may represent lost Leipzig or pre-Leipzig motets. These examples, combined with the two works that are definitely or probably early undercut the image of the motets as newly composed works dating from 1723 or after. We are left with the chronology given in table 6–1.

"Jesu, meine Freude" BWV 227 must have been in the form in which it is now known by *c.* 1735, the date of a student copy of its chorales, and was probably assembled after 1723, given the predominance of a form of the chorale melody Bach used in Leipzig. "Komm, Jesu, komm" BWV 229 must have been composed by 1731/32 (the date of a student copy of the work), as Hans-Joachim Schulze has shown, but its exact date is unknown.[5] Its text was of Leipzig origin, but was published in 1682 and 1697, so it is at least conceivable that Bach knew it before 1723 and that the motet dates from before then. "Lobet den Herrn, alle Heiden" BWV 230 remains undatable; the problems of its authenticity and genre also still loom large.

The datable works alone show that Bach's motets span nearly his entire career, from "Ich lasse dich nicht" BWV Anh. 159 in Weimar or earlier to the revision of "O Jesu Christ, meins Lebens Licht" BWV 118 near the end of his life. (Motet style also plays an important role in Bach's concerted works, again beginning with the earliest layers of his output and extending into the 1740s.) Far from the image suggested by the Leipzig premise, we need to see Bach as a continuous cultivator of the motet and motet style. It is also important to recognize that Bach was apparently willing to revise, rework, and recycle material in his motets, just as he was in his cantatas, oratorios and Masses.

---

[5] Schulze, *Studien zur Bach-Überlieferung*, 130ff.

Table 6–1 *Chronology of J. S. Bach's motets*

Composition	Date	Evidence for date
"Ich lasse dich nicht" BWV Anh. 159	1712/13 or earlier	Original score
"Fürchte dich nicht" BWV 228	*c.* 1715	Stylistic similarity to BWV Anh. 159; chorale version
"Jauchzet dem Herrn, alle Welt" BWV Anh. 160 (Composite work)	Chorale mvt. before late Dec. 1725	Chorale mvt. appears in score of BWV 28 in Bach's hand
"Singet dem Herrn ein neues Lied" BWV 225	1726/27	Original score, parts
"Der Geist hilft unser Schwachheit auf" BWV 226[a]	1729	Original score; funeral
"Jesu, meine Freude" BWV 227[a]	*c.* 1723–*c.* 1735	Student copy of chorales; chorale version
"Komm, Jesu, komm" BWV 229	before 1731/32	Student copy
"O Jesu Christ, meins Lebens Licht" BWV 118 (1st ver.)	1736/37	Original score
"O Jesu Christ, meins Lebens Licht" BWV 118 (2nd ver.)	1746/47	Original score
"Lobet den Herrn, alle Heiden" BWV 230	undatable (motet?)	

[a] reworkings or compilations based on older material

Chronology and style

The understanding that Bach's motets are spread chronologically over most of his composing career puts us in a position to examine his output in the genre in a new light. The first thing that emerges from a chronological look at Bach's motet output is, not surprisingly, that Bach's earliest motets most closely resemble works by other composers of the late seventeenth and early eighteenth centuries and the normative motets described by writers. The first sections of BWV Anh. 159 and BWV 228, the oldest works, present a biblical *Spruch* text in a predominantly homophonic and syllabically declaimed texture; their second sections place a cantus firmus chorale in the uppermost voice supported by statements of the *Spruch*. This is clearly in the mold of earlier models, and in agreement with descriptions of the motet by contemporaries.

At the same time, even these early motets show a degree of musical sophistication largely unknown in older compositions. For example, in both BWV 228 and BWV Anh. 159, Bach treats his *Spruch* text in an exhaustive, even developmental manner; the texts are broken up into strikingly small units. BWV Anh. 159 has an extremely short text, and Bach's writing of an extended motet on so little text is in itself a testament to the musical sophistication of the relatively young composer. In BWV

228, a syllabic declamatory model underlies the first section, but Bach enlivens this model with characteristically active partwriting. Perhaps most striking in these two compositions is the contrapuntal complexity of the works' imitative sections, to a degree not found in works of other composers. The contrapuntal sophistication of Bach's earlier motets is taken another step further in his later motets. In several of these works, biblical texts are presented in extended fugues, as opposed to short points of imitation. The most elaborate of these is found in the first section of BWV 225.

Bach's later motets integrate techniques adopted from other genres and suggest an expansion of scope and musical ambition. BWV 225 and 227 are long, and are constructed as an assembly of several closed, musically independent sections. The texts of these motets, although drawing for the most part on the same types as the earlier works, are less traditionally deployed. For example, in BWV 227, biblical and chorale texts are presented in alternation; in BWV 225, biblical movements frame the presentation of a chorale text in combination with another text. BWV 225 also shows the apparent integration of the "aria" textual and musical type into the motet. The setting of such a text in the inexactly datable BWV 229 may also document Bach's integration of this text type into the motet.

Just as Spitta suggested a century ago, many of these new features in the motets probably point to Bach's importation of techniques from other genres, especially the cantata. The motets do not show the range of text types and corresponding range of musical styles found in the cantatas; nonetheless, the use of a series of closed movements probably points to the influence of multi-movement forms like the cantata. Instrumental music may also have played a role; for example, Christoph Wolff has compared the structure of BWV 225 to that of an Italian instrumental concerto.[6] Whatever its origin, the technique of composing a motet in individual movements is a characteristic of Bach's later motet style.

An honest assessment of the evidence concerning the function of Bach's motets and the occasions on which they were performed leaves most of the motets unassigned. BWV 226 is documented as a funeral piece; BWV 229 uses a text apparently used for funerals in Leipzig. But despite the attempts of Richter and others to assign the motets to specific occasions, the function of the other motets is unclear. The surviving central-German motet repertory shows a heavy concentration of works for the Christmas season, especially settings of the chorales "Nun lob, mein Seel, den Herren" and "Vom Himmel hoch da komm ich her," and the apparently strong association between motet style and this season may well have made its influence felt in Bach's music. Two of Bach's motets set verses from "Nun lob, mein Seel" (BWV 225 and 231/Anh. 160), and it may be significant that the chorale setting in BWV 231/Anh. 160 shows up in a cantata for the Sunday after Christmas. Further, when somebody added yet another movement to the composite motet BWV Anh. 160, they drew on an arrangement of a Christmas cantata by Telemann. Spitta suggested that the motets were used as replacement for cantatas, and this led him to propose that BWV 225 was such a piece for

---

[6] *New Grove*, s.v. "Motet"

New Year's Day.[7] His reasoning can no longer be supported, but the result is still worth considering: a possible connection between certain of Bach's motets and the Christmas season.

Performance practice of Bach's motets

The use of doubling instruments in performances of J. S. Bach's motets is a greatly disputed issue.[8] The material considered in this study – eighteenth-century written sources on the motet, Bach's performing material for his own motets and those of other composers, and his use of instruments in motet-like cantata movements – provides potentially valuable information on early eighteenth-century practice in general, and on Bach's practice in particular. Taken together, these sources point to accompanied performance as a significant part of Bach's performance practice of motets.

As discussed in chapter 1, the use of *colla parte* instruments and basso continuo in motet performances was considered a normal aspect of the genre in the first half of the eighteenth century. Given that Bach's motets fall fundamentally within the parameters of the genre as it was understood in his time, there is no reason to think that his motets differed from the works of his contemporaries in the range of performance practices that was appropriate for them. From the evidence of written sources, *colla parte* doubling must be considered a normal part of the early eighteenth-century concept of the motet, and an appropriate performance practice of Bach's motets.

An examination of the motet-like movements in Bach's cantatas reveals that almost all of them use doubling instruments (see chapter 10). On occasion, Bach even augmented the *Instrumentarium* of a cantata with trombones expressly to double motet-like movements. To the extent that Bach's practice in the cantatas can be related to the performance of his motets, it suggests that they, too, were regularly performed with doubling instruments.

Whether the two practices really were related is problematic; the performance context of the motets and cantatas may well have been different, and there is no guarantee that the practice in the cantatas exactly represents that used for the motets. Wilhelm Ehmann simply declared the two kinds of pieces to be comparable, but the question needs to be approached more circumspectly.[9] The evidence presented in chapter 8 demonstrates the close relationship between Bach's motet-like cantata movements and the eighteenth-century concept of "motet" in matters of text choice and essential musical characteristics, and suggests that the two kinds of pieces are, in fact, closely comparable. Bach's use of doubling instruments almost without exception in his motet-like cantata movements shows that his conception of motet style allowed – or even required – doubling instruments. The close relationship of motet-like cantata movements to the motets suggests that instrumental doubling was appropriate to the latter as well.

---

[7] *J. S. Bach*, 2:433.

[8] The various arguments are summarized by Schulze, *Studien zur Bach-Überlieferung*, 174ff.

[9] "Die Stilwelt seines Werkes kennt nur eine großartige Geschlossenheit. Was den Kantatensätzen recht ist, muß den Motettensätzen billig sein. Wer wollte hier mit zweierlei Maß messen?" Wilhelm Ehmann, "Aufführungspraxis der Bachschen Motetten," in *Kongress-Bericht: Gesellschaft für Musikforschung Lüneburg 1950*, ed. H. Albrecht et al. (Cassel, 1950), 121–23.

Valuable as the written testimony and comparative cantata material may be, perhaps the best evidence of Bach's performance practice of motets lies in his surviving performing material for motets both of his own composition and by other composers. The original performing material for BWV 226 (SBB St 121) includes a set of instrumental parts (strings doubling one choir, woodwinds the other) and basso continuo. The absence of similar material for the other motets has been offered as an argument that Bach's practice in this work was exceptional, but there is no way to know the extent of losses, and it is difficult to see that this argument holds water. The only other original motet performing material that survives is a set of vocal parts for "Singet dem Herrn ein neues Lied" BWV 225 (SBB St 122). It has been claimed that this set is necessarily complete, and – lacking instrumental parts – documents the motet's performance without instruments. Besides being logically indefensible, this view is challenged by the existence of a fragmentary duplicate vocal bass part that may represent further lost original material. It seems almost perverse to take the survival of instrumental parts for BWV 226 as evidence against instrumental doubling. We might as well take the material at face value, as a document of Bach's accompanied performance of his motets.

As discussed in chapter 13, Bach's performing material for an eight-voice motet by Sebastian Knüpfer has recently been identified. Like the parts for BWV 226, the set includes *colla parte* instrumental doubling material using strings with one choir and woodwinds (or substitute trombones) with the other. In addition, continuo parts for violone, organ, and harpsichord survive. J. S. Bach is also known to have performed several motets from the Altbachisches Archiv, discussed in chapter 12. His performing material for Johann Christoph Bach's motet [4][10] "Lieber Herr Gott, wecke uns auf" includes a set of instrumental doubling parts in the same disposition as in BWV 226 and the Knüpfer motet (strings and woodwinds), together with continuo material. Bach also performed Johann Christoph Bach's five-voice motet [3] "Der Gerechte, ob er gleich zu zeitlich stirbt," but only vocal and organ parts are known. The oldest layer of the ABA from Bach's library includes doubling parts for two motets: cornetti and trombones for Johann Michael Bach's [10] "Das Blut Jesu Christi," and unidentified instruments for the anonymous [18] "Sey nun wieder zufrieden," but it is not known whether Bach made use of them.

These examples suggest that Bach did, in fact, double voices with instruments in motets. The evidence is especially strong for double-choir works, for which he used contrasting groups of matched instruments for the two ensembles. This practice is supported by evidence from the anonymous Mass BWV Anh. 167 from Bach's library, whose two choirs are doubled by winds and strings.[11] Bach's practice in single-choir motets is less well documented; his performing material for Palestrina's stylistically related *Missa sine nomine* does include parts for *colla parte* cornetti and trombones, but we do not have doubling material for other single-choir works.

---

10 Bracketed numbers refer to the ABA listing in chapter 11.
11 SBB P 659, *c.* 1738/39. No performing material is known. See Kobayashi, "Chronologie der Spätwerke," 42.

In all the double choir motets by other composers Bach performed with strings and woodwinds (the two by Johann Christoph Bach and Sebastian Knüpfer's "Erforsche mich, Gott"), the doubling instrumental parts occasionally call for notes below those playable on the instruments for which they are written. This feature is also encountered in the original performing material for Bach's cantatas, including motet-like movements. Apparently, the occasional excursion of a doubling part outside an instrument's range was not a matter of concern,[12] and that it was not confirms a fundamental point about Bach's understanding of the role of instruments in this type of piece: in a motet (or motet-like cantata movement), the instruments play *colla parte*, and are strictly subordinate to the voices. The players of these parts – who would have been aware of their role from the musical style of a composition and from Bach's label "Motetto" at head of their parts – presumably either transposed the offending notes up an octave, or simply omitted them. Bach's failure to regard this as a problem points clearly to his conception of such instrumental parts as support for the voices, and subject to practical modifications where necessary.

We can also infer something about instrumental practice in motets from the fact that Bach's understanding of the term "motet" also included pieces like "O Jesu Christ, meins Lebens Licht" BWV 118, with limited roles for independent instruments. It seems unlikely that Bach would have considered such pieces motets if the participation of instruments in some capacity (normally *colla parte*, of course) were not a regular feature of motet performances. In sum, the evidence from eighteenth-century testimony, Bach's orchestration of motet-like cantata movements, and his own surviving motet-performing materials show clearly that instrumental doubling was a regular practice. The incomplete survival of materials and the likelihood of several different acceptable performance practices makes it impossible to specify Bach's practice exactly. But it is clear that instrumental participation was not exceptional by any means, but was rather an essential part of Bach's conception of the motet.

---

[12] For examples, see the discussions of individual instruments in Ulrich Prinz, "Studien zum Instrumentarium Johann Sebastian Bachs mit besonderer Berücksichtigung der Kantaten" (Ph.D. diss., Tübingen, 1979).

PART THREE

Motet style in Bach's concerted compositions

CHAPTER 7

The concept of the motet-like
movement

J. S. Bach's motets demonstrate his cultivation of the received tradition of the motet *genre*. But Bach also made use of motet *style* in his concerted church music, transplanting the features of motets into cantatas, Latin works, and oratorios. Motet style was an important compositional choice that was available for certain kinds of texts in a concerted setting of a mixed text-type libretto or Latin liturgical text. A close study of his use of motet style can provide valuable insight into those concerted works and also into Bach's motets proper (especially in the realm of performance practice), because the motet-like movements from concerted works can be shown to reflect the same stylistic ideas as the independent motets.

The concept of the motet-like movement is a regular feature of typologies and analyses of Bach's vocal music. It has proved to be a useful label for certain kinds of pieces, but has sometimes been applied without careful consideration of its historical and stylistic significance. This is especially true with respect to the German-language motet repertory, in which writers have often been less than rigorous in applying the label "motet-like."[1] One serious obstacle to a clear view of Bach's use of motet style has been the lack of appropriate criteria for identifying motet-like movements. As a result, the repertories considered by studies that invoke the concept have been too restricted or overly inclusive, and the analytical approaches used and stylistic conclusions reached have not served the study of motet style well.

For example, Emil Platen, who examined Bach's chorale settings for chorus, addressed motet style as a subset of the larger category of chorale settings.[2] Eighteenth-century discussions of the motet strongly suggest that we are justified in approaching the matter the other way around; that is, in recognizing chorale settings for vocal ensemble as a subset of the larger category of the motet. Platen uses a single musical criterion for a motet, one that proves to be limiting: the presence of "free or imitative polyphonic partwriting together with and between cantus firmus phrases."[3] This is well suited to many motet-like chorale settings, but has little (if anything) to do with other

---

[1] An exception is Alfred Dürr, *Die Kantaten von Johann Sebastian Bach* (Cassel, 1971).
[2] Emil Platen, "Untersuchungen zur Struktur der chorischen Choralbearbeitung Johann Sebastian Bachs" (Ph.D. diss., Bonn, 1959).
[3] "Struktur der chorischen Choralbearbeitung," 13.

kinds of motet-like movements. Further, Platen's subtypes – simple motet-like settings, those with obbligato instruments, and those with both obbligato instruments and instrumental interludes – are appropriate categories of Bach's adaptations of motet style, but they are not of great use in relating Bach's motet-like movements to the norms of motet style as they were understood in the eighteenth century.[4]

If the scope of Platen's study is too narrow to serve as the basis for an examination of motet style, then Werner Neumann's classic study of Bach's choral fugues casts its net too wide.[5] Motet style is of little importance to Neumann's larger argument. He briefly considers the motet, defining it in terms of a construction in musical units corresponding to successive text phrases,[6] but the concept of the motet is subordinate to the idea of "fugue." Although he does examine many movements that can be considered motet-like, he excludes many others that are motets because of the way they use fugal techniques.

Norman Rubin demonstrated some time ago that there are analytical problems with "fugue" as a category in the analysis of Bach's vocal music.[7] The inadequacy of "fugue" as a movement type is underscored in Neumann's own examination of the relationship between textual content and structure on the one hand and thematic type and movement construction on the other in Bach's fugal movements. Having identified a raft of text types that Bach set as fugues (biblical texts, madrigalian poetry, chorales, Latin liturgical texts, etc.), he is unable to draw any conclusions about the kinds of texts Bach set as choral fugues. Further, he expressly dismisses the possibility of unraveling the relationship between text content and the fugal type, writing that "the question of what sort of textual content Bach considered appropriate to be given fugal (and canonic) form delves so deeply into the mystery of the creative act, that an unambiguous answer is hardly possible."[8]

Given the repertory delineated by Neumann's category "fugue," it is indeed difficult to draw conclusions about either the type or the content of texts Bach set as fugues. The problem lies precisely with the choice of the repertory, and in the use of "fugue" for a typology of movements. That concept draws in too many different kinds of pieces. If we instead examine a group of pieces selected on the basis of a historical view of "motet," we can find much greater consistency in Bach's use of certain techniques in many of these movements, and much clearer suggestions of why he used motet style when he did. (Whether these insights indeed take us any closer to the mystery of the creative process remains an open question.)

Christoph Wolff's study of the role of the *stile antico* in Bach's music also implicitly invokes motet style, and touches on most of the movements that can be considered

[4] "Struktur der chorischen Choralbearbeitung," 15.
[5] Werner Neumann, *J. S. Bachs Chorfuge*, 2nd edn. (Leipzig, 1950).
[6] Neumann, *Chorfuge*, 8.
[7] Norman Rubin, "'Fugue' as a delimiting concept in Bach's choruses: a gloss on Werner Neumann's 'J. S. Bachs Chorfuge,'" in *Studies in Renaissance and Baroque Music in Honor of Arthur Mendel*, ed. Robert L. Marshall (Hackensack, 1974), 195–208.
[8] "Die Frage, welche Textinhalte Bach überhaupt für fugische (und kanonische) Formgebung geeignet hielt, reicht so tief in das Irrationale des Schöpfungsaktes hinein, daß kaum eine eindeutige Antwort möglich ist." *Chorfuge*, 91 n. 221.

motet-like.[9] In addition to his category of strict *stile antico* compositions, Wolff defines a group of pieces he calls "Allabreve-Sätze," a group that has much in common with works in Palestrina style but that is musically differentiated from it in important compositional respects.[10] This category of *allabreve* movements includes most of the motet-like pieces considered here, but excludes certain closely related movements that Bach did not notate in large values. Wolff also interprets the significance of these movements differently. He considers their musical style to represent a modern vocal manifestation of the *stile antico* – an adaptation of Palestrina style. From a historical perspective Wolff's view makes sense, and some of the movements in the category "Allabreve-Sätze" may indeed represent Bach's conscious adaptation of the older polyphonic style. But these pieces are also representatives of the German-language motet. There is little doubt that the roots of this genre are to be found in sixteenth-century motets and their early seventeenth-century successors, but in the late seventeenth and early eighteenth centuries the German motet had apparently had its own identity. Bach and his contemporaries would probably have identified these movements first as motets, and so we are justified in considering them as such.

There are looser uses of the term "motet-like" as well. For example, Michael Märker has suggested that certain concerted vocal movements in 3/2 meter (e.g., BWV 196/4) represent a use of "motettisch-homophone Doppelchörigkeit."[11] There is no question that this movement and similar pieces like BWV 12/2 and 37/1 are old-fashioned, but there is little justification for calling them motet-like. We need a stricter and more historically grounded understanding of motet style and of the concept of the motet-like movement. In this study, motet-like pieces will be considered to be vocal ensemble movements without independent instrumental parts (basso continuo excepted) from concerted sacred works – that is, movements that agree with contemporary understanding of the term "motet." The movements that meet these criteria show a strong unity of text type and of musical procedure, and are clearly related in these respects to the motet as it was understood in Bach's time. An examination of these pieces sheds light not only on the movements themselves and on Bach's compositional choices in the larger works of which they are a part, but on his conception of motet style as well.

---

[9] *Der Stile antico*, esp. 119ff.

[10] *Der Stile antico*, 126ff.

[11] Michael Märker, "Der Stile antico und die frühen Kantaten Johann Sebastian Bachs," in *Johann Sebastian Bachs Traditionsraum*, ed. Reinhard Szeskus, Bach-Studien, no. 9 (Leipzig, 1986), 72–77. See also Wolff, *Der Stile antico*, 19 n. 12.

CHAPTER 8

Motet style in Bach's church cantatas

Movements in pure motet style

The clearest illustration of motet style as Bach used it in concerted works comes in church cantata movements that show motet style in its purest form. An appreciation of these relatively strict works can then lead to a look at cantata movements that are not exclusively dependent on motet style, but that combine motet technique with others. Table 8–1 lists the pure motet-like pieces in the cantatas.

Perhaps the most striking feature of motet-like cantata movements is the narrow range of textual types found in them. Bach used motet style in his church cantatas exclusively for biblical texts, for chorales, and in one movement (BWV 21/9) for a combination of the two; no free ("madrigalian") poetry appears. In other words, Bach employed motet style only for texts that eighteenth-century writers considered appropriate for independent motets.

The particular biblical texts for which Bach chose motet style, transcribed in table 8–2, are dominated by pithy scriptural statements known as *Sprüche* or *dicta*, described by eighteenth-century writers as the staple source of motet texts. Many of the movements that use motet style less strictly (see below) also have texts of this type. A few cantata librettos even carry the label; in the printed libretti of BWV 68 and 108 by Christiane Mariane von Ziegler, the texts of the motet-like movements – as well as the biblical texts set in other styles – are expressly labeled "Dictum."[1] Bach did not set every biblical text as a motet, but the appearance of a *Spruch* in a cantata libretto must immediately have suggested to Bach the possibility of a setting in motet style. (One important category of biblical texts set in a different style comprises first-person words of Jesus, which Bach often set in aria style as a bass solo.)

One factor that may have suggested motet style to Bach for certain *Spruch* texts is their frequent lack of a distinctive affect or concrete textual image. Motet style, like the *stile antico*, is essentially affect-neutral, at least compared to the many other styles available to the early eighteenth-century composer, and is particularly well suited to abstract *Spruch* texts. In the absence of the opportunity for a clear correspondence between the meaning of a biblical text and the musical character of its setting, or even between the text's affect and that of the musical setting, Bach could turn to motet style.

---

[1] Facsimiles in *BT*, 360, 363.

Table 8–1 *Motet-like movements in J. S. Bach's church cantatas*

BWV	Text	Text source
	Biblical texts	
29/2	"Wir danken dir, Gott, wir danken dir"	Ps. 75:2
64/1	"Sehet, welch eine Liebe hat uns der Vater erzeiget"	1 John 3:1
68/5	"Wer an ihn gläubet, der wird nicht gerichtet"	John 3:18
71/3	"Dein Alter sei wie deine Jugend"	Deut. 33:25/Gen. 21:22
108/4	"Wenn aber jener, der Geist der Wahrheit, kommen wird"	John 16:13
144/1	"Nimm, was dein ist, und gehe hin"	Matt. 20:14
179/1	"Siehe zu, daß deine Gottesfurcht nicht Heuchelei sei"	Sir. 1:34
	Chorales	
2/1	"Ach Gott, vom Himmel sieh darein"	(M. Luther)
4/5	"Es war ein wunderlicher Krieg" ["Christ lag in Todes Banden"]	(M. Luther)
14/1	"Wär Gott nicht mit uns diese Zeit"	(M. Luther)
28/2	"Nun lob, mein Seel, den Herren"	(J. Gramann, 1530)
38/1	"Aus tiefer Not schrei ich zu dir"	(M. Luther)
80/1	"Ein feste Burg ist unser Gott"	(M. Luther)
121/1	"Christum wir sollen loben schon"	(M. Luther)
182/7	"Jesu, deine Passion" ["Jesu Leiden, Pein und Tod"]	(P. Stockmann, 1663)
	Combined texts	
21/9	"Sei nun wieder zufrieden, meine Seele"/ "Was helfen uns die schweren Sorgen" ["Wer nur den lieben Gott läßt walten"]	Ps. 116:7/ (G. Neumark, 1657)

Table 8–2 *Biblical texts from motet-like church cantata movements*

BWV	Text
29/2	"Wir danken dir, Gott, wir danken dir, und verkündigen deine Wunder." (Ps. 75:2)
64/1	"Sehet, welch eine Liebe hat uns der Vater erzeiget, daß wir Gottes Kinder heißen." (1 John 3:1)
68/5	"Wer an ihn gläubet, der wird nicht gerichtet; wer aber nicht gläubet, der ist schon gerichtet; denn er gläubet nicht an den Namen des eingebornen Sohnes Gottes." (John 3:18)
71/3	"Dein Alter sei wie deine Jugend, und Gott ist mit dir in allem, das du tust." (Deut. 33:25 + Gen. 21:22)
108/4	"Wenn aber jener, der Geist der Wahrheit, kommen wird, der wird euch in alle Wahrheit leiten. Denn er wird nicht von ihm selber reden, sondern was er hören wird, das wird er reden; und was zukünftig ist, wird er verkündigen." (John 16:13)
144/1	"Nimm, was dein ist, und gehe hin." (Matt. 20:14)
179/1	"Siehe zu, daß deine Gottesfurcht nicht Heuchelei sei, und diene Gott nicht mit falschem Herzen." (Sir. 1:34)

The other texts that Bach set in motet style are chorales. As with biblical texts, motet style was only one of numerous possibilities for the treatment of a chorale in a cantata. Bach's choice of motet style in a particular movement is usually difficult to explain, but one pattern does emerge: almost all the chorales for which Bach chose motet style are from the oldest layer of the repertory. Six of the eight are by Martin Luther himself, and a seventh is nearly as old. The only seventeenth-century chorale setting in motet style (BWV 182/7) is stylistically more modern than the other motet-like chorale movements.

That Bach used motet style for the oldest and most venerable chorale melodies suggests that the style held important historical associations for him. The contrapuntal cantus firmus treatment characteristic of most of these settings (see below) rests on a long and distinguished musical tradition, although the older repertory of such settings with which Bach may have been familiar is largely unknown.[2] Whatever his models may have been – extremely old settings or their seventeenth-century progeny – Bach's choice of motet style for a chorale was clearly influenced by the historical significance of certain texts and melodies, or at least by their age.

In one motet-like cantata movement, BWV 21/9, Bach combined a *Spruch* and a chorale: a Psalm verse and two stanzas of the seventeenth-century hymn "Wer nur den lieben Gott läßt walten." The textual types and their carefully considered complementary relationship point to the techniques of the motet; BWV 21/9 is a classic motet in the manner of the early eighteenth century, and bears some striking resemblances to Bach's own "Ich lasse dich nicht" BWV Anh. 159, probably nearly contemporary. BWV 21/9 was apparently the last movement of older material incorporated into the cantata "Ich hatte viel Bekümmernis" BWV 21, probably part of a layer built around the choral Psalm settings BWV 21/2, 6 and 9.[3] Bach used motet style as a way of incorporating both a third Psalm excerpt and a chorale in the final movement. BWV 21/9, like the other cantata movements in motet style, uses texts that would have been suitable for an independent motet.

The musical features of Bach's motet-like cantata movements are as characteristic as their texts. In motet-like cantata movements, *allabreve* time signatures and large note values dominate. As it does in works in the *stile antico*, this notation carries strong historical associations,[4] and these associations were apparently significant to Bach. Not only did Bach use large note values in most of his motet-like cantata movements, he also consistently retained the archaic, large-value notation in his performing material for motets by older composers, including S. Knüpfer, "Erforsche mich, Gott" and Johann Christoph Bach, [3] "Der Gerechte, ob er gleich zu zeitlich stirbt." What is more, J. S. Bach's earliest known motet, "Ich lasse dich nicht" BWV Anh. 159, is notated in 3/2. Bach also occasionally used more modern time signatures in his motet-like cantata movements, for example, 3/8 in BWV 14/1, but larger note values predominate among these pieces.

2   Cf. Friedhelm Krummacher, "Die Tradition in Bachs vokalen Choralbearbeitungen," in *Bach-Interpretationen: Walter Blankenburg zum 65. Geburtstag*, ed. Martin Geck (Göttingen, 1969), 29–56.
3   *NBA* I/16 *KB*, 129ff.
4   See Christoph Wolff, *Der Stile antico*, 38ff.

Whatever type of text Bach employed, counterpoint plays an essential role in his motet-like cantata movements. Biblical texts usually receive fugal treatments (see example 8–1); often, each phrase of such a text will receive its own fugue, and these are occasionally combined as a double fugue. Bach's consistent use of counterpoint represents his adherence to a tradition cited by eighteenth-century writers (discussed in chapter 1) linking counterpoint with motet style. Bach's use of fugue in settings of biblical texts (in place of the *stile antico* counterpoint of ancient models) represents his application of a modern technique to an old genre. This substitution is nowhere clearer than in his settings of texts of several phrases, in which each phrase of text is given its own fugue, e.g., BWV 108/4. The structure of the Palestrina-style motet and its successors – contrapuntal settings of successive text phrases – is realized in the fugal language of Bach's time.

One of the most important distinctions between the counterpoint used in sixteenth-century motets and that found in Bach's music lies in the different relationship between music and text in each. Whereas the older technique employs a series of points of imitation on short motives (not necessarily related to each other), Bach's motet-like biblical settings in cantatas take as their basic principle the thorough contrapuntal working out of a declamatory theme encompassing all or a substantial segment of the text.

Within this general plan, Bach deployed the biblical texts of his motet-like cantata movements in several different ways. Short texts (BWV 144/1, 105/1, 76/1) are set as a single unit, the whole text set to the entire fugue subject. (I include here movements with sections in motet style, discussed below.) Most of the texts too long to be treated as a whole but still of moderate length are divided, often with the second part of the text set to a fugal countersubject (BWV 64/1, 179/1, 22/1, 24/3, 71/3). BWV 71/3 is a four-voice permutation fugue whose first two thematic units correspond to the two phrases of the bipartite text, and the other two to repetitions of these phrases. In BWV 29/2, the two text phrases and their contrasting settings are used in alternation, and are kept mostly separate. (This movement departs from strict motet style in the use of partly independent trumpets and drums. It should be noted, though, that the independent material carried by the trumpets is limited to the two imitative entrances at mm. 62ff., which briefly create a six-voice texture. Even these entrances do not remain independent for long; in mm. 69ff., trumpets 1 and 2 double alto at the octave and soprano, respectively. Similarly, the first two trumpet parts double tenor and alto at the octave in m.82ff. The other trumpet 1 entrances [mm. 30 and 52] double the soprano, and the third trumpet and drums add only filler material in the closing section. In all, the trumpets supply relatively little independent material, and the movement otherwise closely resembles Bach's other motet-like settings of biblical texts.)

Bach breaks long biblical texts into smaller units. For example, the text of BWV 108/4 consists of three units, each grammatically capable of standing on its own, and each is presented in its own fugue. Bach also divides the text of BWV 68/5 into three sections; the first is set to a fugue, the second to another fugue based on the counter-subject of the first. The two text units, which form an antithesis, are then combined in

Example 8–1 BWV 108/4, mm. 1–14

Table 8–3 *Motet-like chorale movements from the church cantatas*

BWV	Text	Date (Place or Jahrgang)
4/5	"Es war ein wunderlicher Krieg"	(Weimar or earlier)
182/7	"Jesu, deine Passion"	1714 (Weimar)
2/1	"Ach Gott, vom Himmel sieh darein"	6/18/1724 (II)
38/1	"Aus tiefer Not schrei ich zu dir"	10/29/1724 (II)
121/1	"Christum wir sollen loben schon"	12/26 1724 (II)
28/2	"Nun lob, mein Seel, den Herren"	12/30/1725[a] (III)
14/1	"Wär Gott nicht mit uns diese Zeit"	1/30/1735
80/1	"Ein feste Burg ist unser Gott"	*c.* 1744/47

[a] Probably an older composition.
 Dates from Dürr, *Studien;* Dürr, *Chronologie.*

a double fugue, during which the third text phrase is introduced. The perfunctory treatment of the last text phrase is a result of Bach's emphasis of the antithesis presented in the first two. (Note that in BG 16 the editor Rust emended the text underlay in the bass, mm. 37ff. The original reading, which makes the division of text clearer, is restored in NBA I/14.) The third section of the motet "Der Geist hilft unser Schwachheit auf" BWV 226 is also of this type, with a text in three units. The first two text phrases are presented in separate fugues that are then combined in a double fugue, and the third unit is delayed until the last phrase of the section. Mattheson specifically cited texts containing antitheses as suitable for treatment in double fugues, a practice that shows up in Bach's music.[5] In BWV 21/9, Bach combined a biblical text with a chorale cantus firmus. Here, as in BWV 228 and Anh. 159, Bach introduces counterpoint in the voices supporting the chorale. The first stanza uses only the first half of the biblical text; the second stanza adds the second half, creating an effect similar to that produced by a double fugue.

For Bach, a motet-like setting of a chorale in a cantata meant almost exclusively a cantus firmus supported by points of imitation derived from the phrases of the chorale melody. The one exception is BWV 21/9, in which the imitative supporting voices carry a biblical text and have thematically independent material. Bach's contrapuntal technique in motet-like chorale movements is discussed by Platen,[6] and analytical details will not be repeated here, but some chronological observations are appropriate. Table 8–3 lists Bach's motet-like cantata movements using chorales in chronological order.

The earliest pieces (BWV 4/5 and 182/7) are distinguished by their florid and rhythmically active non-cantus-firmus parts, which move substantially faster than the cantus firmus they support. (BWV 182/7 [example 8–2] presents its chorale in half notes, with supporting parts including sixteenth-note motion; BWV 4/5 presents its chorale in quarter-notes, and its supporting parts include motion up to sixteenths.) This is in contrast to some of Bach's later settings (e.g., BWV 38/1, 2/1 [example 8–3]), in which the cantus firmus and other parts move at similar speeds.

[5] See chapter 1.
[6] "Struktur der chorischen Choralbearbeitung."

117

Example 8–2 BWV 182/7, mm. 1–14

In the earlier movements, the thematic relationship between the cantus firmus and its supporting parts is less tightly controlled than in later pieces, partly as a result of the more florid writing in the earlier compositions. The complete saturation of the texture with chorale motives is a characteristic of Bach's later settings. With this strictness in thematic material also comes a generally starker *allabreve* style, evidenced by the abandoning of florid accompanimental writing. One apparent exception is BWV 121/1 (example 8–4). In this movement, though, in contrast to the earlier compositions, the decorative eighth-note figure used throughout is ornamental and not melodically essential, consisting of a neighbor-note subdivision of lines whose essential motion

Example 8–3 BWV 2/1, mm. 1–26

occurs at the quarter- and half-note levels. In essence, the handling of the vocal parts in BWV 121/1 resembles that of its contemporary motet-like chorale movements.

BWV 14/1 is unusual among the motet-like chorale settings for its 3/8 meter. In its use of an instrumental cantus firmus, it is related to BWV 80/1.[7] Bach wrote both of these works well after he composed his yearly cycles of cantatas, apparently marking the use of an instrumental cantus firmus in a motet as a feature of his later compositions. (On the possible significance of this trait for the dating of the Mass in F major BWV 233, see chapter 9.) BWV 80/1 has the added complication of a canonic cantus firmus. This

[7] Cf. Dürr, *Die Kantaten von Johann Sebastian Bach*, 578.

Example 8–4 BWV 121/1, mm. 1–28

movement, with its combination of elaborated motet style and canon, vividly represents Bach's interests during the 1740s both in sophisticated counterpoint and old musical styles.

Movements with sections in motet style

In several cantata movements, Bach used motet style for only one portion of the movement. These movements and the division of their texts are listed in table 8–4. (In addition, the B sections of two *da capo* choruses from Bach's Weimar years, BWV 12/2 and 172/1 [earliest version] use no independent instruments. Unlike true motet-like movements, they use poetic texts. Bach's removal of the instrumental accompaniment probably does not represent motet style, but is rather a fairly typical procedure in the B section of *da capo* arias: the reduction of the accompaniment to continuo only. In another Weimar-era work, BWV 63/7, again on a poetic text, Bach introduces imitative passages using mostly *colla parte* instruments, apparently representing a unique experiment in the combination of motet and concerto techniques for a free poetic text. The choral fugue BWV 198/7 from the so-called *Trauer-Ode*, also on a free text, probably represents Bach's effort to bring some stylistic variety to his setting of Gottsched's long strophic text.)

In two movements with biblical texts, BWV 6/1 and 24/3, the entire short text is treated first in concerted fashion, and then in motet style.[8] In BWV 6/1 (example 8–5), the motet-like section is followed by an abbreviated return of the opening material. Also in this movement, Bach separates the first words of the text ("Bleib bei uns") and constructs a fugal setting on the second part of the text ("denn es wird Abend werden"), reintroducing occasional statements of the first phrase both in the voices and in the occasionally independent instruments.

In the other three biblical movements Bach divided the text, turning to motet style only for the final portion. These three examples and the division of their texts tell us something important about the suitability of particular biblical texts for motet style.

---

[8] Bach's setting of BWV 24/3 in fugal style is interesting in the light of Johann Mattheson's detailed explanation of why such a setting of this text would not be advisable. *Critica Musica*, 2:323.

Table 8–4 *Church cantata movements with sections in motet style*

BWV	Musical type	Text
6/1	concerto	*"Bleib bei uns, denn es will Abend werden und der Tag hat sich geneiget."*
	motet	"Bleib bei uns, denn es will Abend werden und der Tag hat sich geneiget." (Luke 24:29)
22/1	concerto	*"Jesus nahm zu sich die Zwölfe und sprach: Sehet, wir gehn hinauf gen Jerusalem, und es wird alles vollendet werden, das geschrieben ist von des Menschen Sohn."*
	motet	"Sie aber vernahmen der keines und wußten nicht, was das gesaget war." (Luke 18:31, 34)
24/3	concerto	*"Alles nun, das ihr wollet, daß euch die Leute tun sollen, das tut ihr ihnen."*
	motet	"Alles nun, das ihr wollet, daß euch die Leute tun sollen, das tut ihr ihnen." (Matt. 7:12)
76/1	concerto	*"Die Himmel erzählen die Ehre Gottes, und die Feste verkündiget seiner Hände Werk."*
	motet	"Es ist keine Sprache noch Rede, da man nicht ihre Stimme höre." (Ps. 19:2, 4)
105/1	concerto	*"Herr, gehe nicht ins Gericht mit deinem Knecht."*
	motet	"Denn vor dir wird kein Lebendiger gerecht." (Ps. 143:2)
41/1	concerto	*"Jesu nun sei gepreiset,"* lines *1–10* (J. Heermann, 1593)
	motet	"Jesu, nun sei gepreiset," lines 11–14

BWV 22/1 begins with the words of the Evangelist and of Jesus, presented by solo tenor and bass in an orchestrally-accompanied aria. The setting turns to motet style for the final lines concerning the understanding of Jesus' words, the central theological message of the cantata text. In BWV 76/1, Bach sets the first part of the text, a statement of praise, in concerted style; the second, a comment on its universality, in motet style. In BWV 105/1, he divides the text into a supplication for clemency (set in concerted style) and a reason for the request expressing the theme of sinfulness found throughout the cantata text (set in motet style). In all three movements, Bach used motet style only for the portion of the text that addresses a central theological idea in the cantata text in universal terms.

In these pieces, the use of motet style is less strict than in most other motet-like movements, in that the instruments depart to some extent from their normal *colla parte* roles. For example, BWV 22/1 is rounded off with an eight-measure instrumental sinfonia; in BWV 76/1, one contrapuntal trumpet entrance briefly creates a five-part texture at the end; both BWV 6/1 and 24/3 show some divergence between the vocal lines and the instruments that double them, and the latter also has a partly independent trumpet line. These departures from strict motet style sometimes help unify the movements (by rounding off in BWV 22/1) or by accommodating an instrument used in the opening section that would not ordinarily have a place in motet-like

Example 8–5a BWV 6/1, mm. 1–30

compositions (trumpet in BWV 24/3 and 76/1). These features are departures from the motet style that underlies these movements.

In the concerted cantus firmus movement BWV 41/1, Bach uses motet style for the last few lines of the chorale "Jesu, nun sei gepreiset." The switch to imitative

Example 8–5b BWV 6/1, mm. 80–91

Table 8–5 *Selected church cantata movements combining the motet with other principles*

BWV	Text
25/1	"Es ist nichts Gesundes an meinem Leibe für deinem Dräuen und ist kein Friede in meinen Gebeinen vor meiner Sünde." (Ps. 38:4)
101/1	"Nimm von uns, Herr, du treuer Gott" (M. Moller, 1584)
171/1	"Gott, wie dein Name, so ist auch dein Ruhm bis an der Welt Ende." (Ps. 48:11)

chorale-derived polyphony was probably not text-inspired, but was presumably intended to set off the final lines of this long hymn text. The reference to motet style in this New Year's cantata probably also recalls the central-German tradition of Christmas and New Year's motets. As in his other Leipzig settings of this melody (BWV 362, BWV 41/6 = 171/6), Bach here repeats the last lines of text, set to the first phrases of the hymn. In BWV 41/1, the setting returns at this point to the concerted style of the opening. The motet style used in the first statement of the last lines makes a particularly effective contrast with this concerted material that surrounds it.

Movements combining motet style with other principles

The works discussed so far represent Bach's more or less pure use of motet style in cantatas – movements that adhere relatively strictly to eighteenth-century norms of motet writing. Several other cantata movements draw on or refer to motet style, but combine it with other principles. These movements can be placed on a spectrum with pure motet-like movements at one end and movements that are merely informed by motet style at the other. Three cantata movements, listed in table 8–5, stand out as especially closely related to motet style.

BWV 171/1's use of a Psalm text, counterpoint, *allabreve* notation, and *colla parte* instruments marks it as motet-like. To the basic motet framework, Bach adds one thematic trumpet entrance (mm. 23ff.), briefly creating a five-voice contrapuntal texture; and several non-thematic entrances of trumpets and drums in the concluding section of the movement. (Cf. the second half of BWV 46/1, a *colla parte* fugue with independent recorders, and BWV 29/2.) These instrumental parts are additions to the essential motet texture of the movement. BWV 171 was apparently written for New Year 1729, and was assembled largely from extant material. The revision copy character of the first movement suggested to Robert Marshall that BWV 171/1 is a parody;[9] Werner Neumann suggested an origin in an instrumental work.[10] In light of the clear use of motet style, one must wonder whether this music might have been conceived for another text, and that rather than adapting an instrumental work, Bach retexted an older motet-like movement.

BWV 101/1 treats a chorale text using points of imitation in support of a soprano cantus firmus. (See example 8–6.) This construction, the allabreve time signature, and the use of doubling trombones all point to motet style. The movement is also a

9 *Compositional Process*, 1:19, 30.
10 *NBA* 1/4 KB, 105f.

Example 8–6 BWV 101/1, mm. 1–49

Example 8–7 BWV 25/1, mm. 1–21

concerto: it uses independent instruments, but their material is less important than in many similarly constructed cantata movements. The instruments provide interludes between chorale phrases; during the vocal sections, their material is limited mostly to repetitions of a single motive. The concerto element governs the overall structure of the movement, but motet style dominates the presentation of vocal material.

In BWV 25/1, the two phrases of a Psalm text are each presented in separate fugues, and then combined in a double fugue in a motet-like movement to which several

131

complicating elements are added. (See example 8–7.) The first is the use of partly independent strings and woodwinds, which provide a brief introduction and accompaniment to each of the two statements of the first fugue. Their material in these passages is limited to a rhythmically regular, harmonically conceived repeating figure without melodic independence, similar to that in "O Jesu Christ, meins Lebens Licht" BWV 118. In its limited use of instruments – outside this opening section they are either silent or play *colla parte* with the voices – this movement fits Bach's expanded view of the motet discussed in chapter 2.

The second complication in BWV 25/1 is the addition of a chorale played by cornetto and trombones in a style closely resembling that of Bach's four-part vocal harmonizations. The use of these instruments, strongly associated with motet style, and their presentation of a chorale in conjunction with a biblical text recall motet style. Alfred Dürr has suggested that Bach alludes in the instrumental chorale to the second verse of "Ach Herr, mich armen Sünder," which refers to the theme of sin and bodily illness treated in the biblical text.[11] This is exactly the kind of textual relationship between a biblical *Spruch* and a chorale typical of motets, and reinforces the motet character of the movement.

These three cantata movements are the nearest derivatives of the motet, but there are also others that show the influence of motet style to a lesser degree. There are many cantata movements, for example, that treat chorales in imitative settings – a reference to motet style – but that also involve other musical principles, most often the concerto (e.g., BWV 3/1, 4/2, 78/1, 137/1, 177/1). Fugal settings of biblical texts with additional independent instruments are also closely related to motets (e.g., BWV 17/1, 40/1 [middle section], 45/1 [second section], 47/1, 148/1, 176/1). These movements are not strict motet-like pieces, but show the influence of motet style.

The familiar practice of combining a chorale with another text in a concerted work may also be ultimately derived from the motet, which strove for theologically revealing combinations of *Sprüche* and chorales (for example BWV 71/2, an aria that combines the biblical text "Ich bin nun achtzig Jahr" with a chorale verse about aging.) This practice was not restricted to motet-like pieces, nor to combinations of chorales with biblical texts, but the inspiration for this practice may have been the motet. Friedhelm Krummacher's suggestion that the mixing of *Sprüche* and chorales in motets was a feature adopted from the cantata risks ignoring the view expressed by early eighteenth-century writers (see chapter 1) that such combinations were an important element of motet style.[12] The practice of using combinations like these in the cantata may be a legacy of the motet.

---

[11] *Die Kantaten von Johann Sebastian Bach*, 431.
[12] "Mehrchörigkeit und thematischer Satz," 41.

CHAPTER 9

Motet style in Bach's Latin works and oratorios

Motet style in Latin works

The early eighteenth-century concept of "motet" encompassed both *stile antico* works and more modern pieces. In practice, this distinction corresponded in large measure to that between Latin settings and pieces in the vernacular. This is never stated explicitly by contemporary writers, but is implicit in their definitions and borne out by the known repertory; composers of Latin-texted works tended to reach further back to the *stile antico*, whereas German-texted works seemed to call for a more modern style. The cantata movements discussed in chapter 8 represent Bach's use of the aspect of motet style associated with the vernacular, and his Latin-texted vocal pieces in the *stile antico* (like the "Credo" of the Mass in B minor BWV 232) represent his cultivation of "motet" as it related to music of the sixteenth century and its legacy.

Table 9–1 *Motet-like movements from J. S. Bach's Latin works*

BWV	Movement	Text source	Parody model
232/6	"Gratias agimus tibi"	Mass Ordinary	BWV 29/2
232/13	"Credo/Patrem omnipotentem"	Mass Ordinary	BWV 171/1
232/15	"Et incarnatus est"	Mass Ordinary	
232/25	"Dona nobis pacem"	Mass Ordinary	BWV 29/2
233a	"Kyrie eleison"	Mass Ordinary	
233/1	"Kyrie eleison"	Mass Ordinary	BWV 233a
233/6	"Cum sancto spiritu"	Mass Ordinary	BWV 40/1
236/1	"Kyrie eleison"	Mass Ordinary	BWV 179/1
243(a)/10	"Suscepit Israel"	Luke 1:54	
243(a)/11	"Sicut locutus est"	Luke 1:55	
243a/A	"Vom Himmel hoch"	M. Luther	
243a/B	"Freut euch und jubilirt"	(traditional)	

It is important to realize, though, that in his Latin works Bach drew not only on the *stile antico* but also on the kind of motet style associated with German-language *Sprüche* and chorale texts. The two musical styles are distinguishable, but they are closely related,[1] and their relationship is well illustrated by parodies among Bach's compositions. Several

---

[1] See Wolff, *Der Stile antico*, 12, 122ff.

Example 9–1 BWV 233a, mm. 1–27

of Bach's Latin works contain motet-like pieces that originally had German texts, showing that German motet style was considered appropriate for both Latin and German texts. The motet-like movements from Bach's Latin church music are listed in table 9–1, and the large number of parodies – typical, of course, of Bach's Latin music – is particularly striking.

The two Kyrie settings BWV 233a and 233/1 show the use of motet style in settings of the Mass Ordinary especially clearly. BWV 233a, transmitted as a single-

Example 9–2 BWV 233/1, mm. 1–27

movement composition, combines an imitative motet-like setting of the "Kyrie eleison" text with cantus-firmus treatments of "Christe, du Lamm Gottes" (German "Agnus dei," soprano) and "Kyrie eleison" (bass). (See example 9–1.) These two melodies are treated exactly like chorales in motets, except that the material in the voices that support the cantus firmi is not derived from the pre-existent melody (as it is in many of Bach's motet-like chorale movements), but is independent. The contrapuntal structure of BWV 233a also points to motet style. The first "Kyrie eleison" is presented in a fugue, the "Christe eleison" in a fugue on the inversion of the "Kyrie" theme, and the second "Kyrie" in a double fugue combining the two. This treatment recalls the double fugues sometimes encountered in motet-like settings of *Spruch* texts that fall into several textual phrases. BWV 233a is not datable from source evidence, but a Weimar date has been proposed on the basis of the version of the "Kyrie eleison" used.[2] This composition and its likely early date provide further evidence of Bach's cultivation of motet style before his move to Leipzig in 1723.

Bach reused the music of BWV 233a in the "Kyrie eleison" of his Leipzig Mass BWV 233 (see example 9–2). In adapting BWV 233a, Bach reduced the scoring to four voices, and assigned the former soprano cantus firmus to horns and oboes; the continuo part, part-writing, and text underlay were also revised. This movement and the "Cum sancto spiritu," a reworking of BWV 40/1, whose second part is in a free motet-like style, frame the work with motet-style movements.[3] In adapting the cantata movement for the Mass, Bach emphasized its motet-like qualities by removing most of the introductory sinfonia (largely eliminating most of the concerto element) and changing the rhythmic notation from common time to *allabreve*.[4] BWV 233 cannot be dated exactly, but may well be roughly contemporary with Bach's two datable Masses, BWV 234 and 236, which are probably from the late 1730s.[5] The use of a motet with an instrumental cantus firmus, as in BWV 233/1, is a technique also found in BWV 14/1 (1735) and BWV 80/1 (*c.* 1730–*c.* 1745), and is apparently a feature of Bach's later compositions. Its use in BWV 233 may well support a date in the 1730s for that work.

The Kyrie of BWV 236 is also derived from a motet-like cantata movement, BWV 179/1. (See examples 9–3 and 9–4.) The ease with which Bach was able to convert the setting of a biblical prose text into a Mass movement owes a great deal to the nature of the new text. The "Kyrie eleison" text is short, consists of grammatically independent phrases, and is susceptible to melismatic setting. It is thus ideally suited to being fitted to a parody model that originally carried a longer text set syllabically.[6] The musical organization of the model did lead to one unusual feature of this Mass movement. The original cantata movement sets the two parts of its text as fugue subject and countersubject; Bach also builds several imitative sections on a variant of the countersubject, and introduces the inversion of the subject. In making the parody, Bach assigned the text "Kyrie eleison" to the subject and countersubject (treated as one unit), and reserved the text "Christe eleison" for the variant of the countersubject beginning at m. 37. The movement alternates freely between treatments of the two text/music units, eschewing the traditional three-part "Kyrie-Christe-Kyrie" division, and ending with "Christe eleison." This is Bach's only Kyrie setting that does not present a clear tripartite division of this text, relying instead on a musical distinction between "Kyrie" and "Christe" material presented in contrapuntal combination. This feature is an artifact of the parody of a motet-like movement.

[2] Wolff, *Der Stile antico*, 178.
[3] Wolff, *Der Stile antico*, 134.
[4] Cf. Wolff, *Der Stile antico*, 133f.
[5] For the most recent dating of the sources see Kobayashi, "Chronologie der Spätwerke."
[6] On the susceptibility of such movements to parody cf. Wolff, *Der Stile antico*, 124f.

For two movements of the Mass in B minor BWV 232, Bach turned to parodies of the same motet-like cantata movement. The "Gratias agimus tibi" and "Dona nobis pacem" are derived from BWV 29/2, a motet-like piece augmented by partly independent trumpet parts. The particular reason for Bach's choice of a motet model is unclear; presumably the relatively neutral affect of the movement (neutral, at least, for a piece using trumpets and drums) was a factor, as was the melodic material designed for a metrically irregular biblical prose text. Bach reused another motet-like cantata movement for the "Credo/Patrem omnipotentem" of the Mass, drawn from BWV 171/1 or perhaps from its lost model. He made several revisions to the model in creating the Mass version; the most significant from the point of view of motet style is his addition of rhythmically regular non-thematic material in the oboes in the opening section. This figure, which is soon dropped in favor of *colla parte* doubling of the voices, resembles that employed in the motet "O Jesu Christ, mein Lebens Licht" BWV 118 and similar motet-like works.

The "Et incarnatus est" of BWV 232 also shows strong motet-like features. (See example 9–5.) Almost all of its essential material is in the vocal parts, with only an independent bass line and rhythmically regular non-thematic figuration in the violins. The figuration continues throughout the piece, providing an accompaniment to the vocal parts and short instrumental passages articulating the vocal phrases. The vocal parts are primarily homophonic, with close imitative entrances at the beginning of each of the two main sections. This disposition of material in the "Et incarnatus est" is similar to that found in several extended motet-style compositions. The movement shares with "O Jesu Christ, meins Lebens Licht" BWV 118 a pulsating bass part and a tendency toward extended pedal points. The relationship to "Der Gerechte kommt um," a movement from a Passion pastiche (see below) is even more striking, especially in the expressive harmonic language and in the similar vocal entrances. Even in the context of the Credo, the "Et incarnatus est" text is particularly abstract; perhaps for this reason, Bach referred to motet style for its setting.

The two versions of the Magnificat BWV 243 and 243a contain several movements indebted to the motet. The "Suscepit Israel" for three high voices and continuo shows its connection to motet style in its use of imitative vocal parts. In addition, the Magnificat intonation is presented in an instrumental cantus firmus (trumpet in BWV 243a, oboes in BWV 243), in an arguably motet-like combination of a biblical text and a chorale melody. The "Sicut locutus est," also common to both versions of the Magnificat, presents its text in a five-voice fugue recalling a *Spruch* motet. The E♭ major version of the Magnificat includes four interpolated Christmas movements, two of which make no use of independent instruments. "Vom Himmel hoch" BWV 243a/A (example 9–6) is a setting of a chorale melody, presented as a soprano cantus firmus supported by points of imitation based on chorale phrases – classic motet texture. Motet style is here particularly appropriate because of the central-German tradition of Christmas motets on this tune. "Freut euch und jubilirt" BWV 243a/B presents the four phrases of its traditional poetic text[7] in three distinct sections, the

---

[7] See Robert Cammarota, "The Repertoire of Magnificats in Leipzig at the Time of J. S. Bach: A Study of the Manuscript Sources" (Ph.D. diss., New York University, 1986), 297ff.

Example 9–3 BWV 179/1, mm. 1–25

outer two in imitative counterpoint. The connection to motet style is relatively loose, and is further obscured in the opening section by the filler material that precedes each of the contrapuntal entrances, lessening the effect of a strict point of imitation, but motet style certainly influenced this movement.

Motet style in oratorios

Many of the vocal ensemble movements in Bach's oratorios meet the criteria for motet-like compositions: they are settings of biblical texts, and are often accompanied

Example 9–4 BWV 236/1, mm. 1–25

only by *colla parte* doubling instruments, perhaps with the addition of continuous, fast-moving figuration in a few other instruments. What is more, oratorios (especially settings of the Passion) were long dependent on motet style; the tradition includes, for example, settings of the Passion narrative in the form of motets (Lechner), and settings in which the *turbae* are presented as motets (Lassus, Schütz). We should also note here the *turbae* in the spurious St. Luke Passion BWV 246, several of which are *stile antico* motets. Yet it would be wrong to consider all of these choruses motets. For example, it would be difficult to argue that "Wir haben keinen König denn den Kaiser" BWV 245/23f, with its short homophonic phrases and independent instruments, is a motet.

Other choruses, especially some of the more extensive movements, do seem to invite the label (e.g., "Andern hat er geholfen" BWV 244/58d).

Two kinds of pieces from the Passions are particularly interesting from the point of view of motet style. The first group comprises fugal movements with strict *colla parte* doublings, such as "Lasset uns den nicht zerteilen" BWV 245/27b and the pair of choruses "Wir haben ein Gesetz" and "Lässest du diesen los" BWV 245/21f and 23b. These movements are most closely related to motet style. Also closely related are fugal works whose successive imitative entrances are masked by filler, for example the chorus "Sein Blut komme über uns und unsre Kinder" BWV 244/50d. It is also possible to view "Wäre dieser nicht ein Übeltäter" and "Wir dürfen niemand töten" BWV

Example 9–5 BWV 232/15, mm. 1–20

245/16b and 16d in this way.[8] A step further removed from motet style are pieces like "Laß ihn kreuzigen" BWV 244/45b and 50b, which add independent instrumental parts (here, flute) to contrapuntal vocal settings with otherwise strict *colla parte* doubling. The second category of pieces drawing on motet technique consists of ensemble settings of long texts, in which the various phrases are treated one by one, often in short points of imitation. Examples include "Andern hat er geholfen" BWV 244/58d and "Herr, wir haben gedacht" BWV 244/66b. These pieces have the musical and textual structure of a sixteenth-century motet.

Motet style also plays a role in the alto aria "Ach, nun ist mein Jesus hin" BWV 244/30 that opens the second half of the St. Matthew Passion. The aria in Choir I is repeatedly interrupted by a text from the Song of Songs, presented chorally in a series of points of imitation in Choir II. The imitative treatment of a biblical text, doubled *colla parte* by strings, is clearly motet-like. Further, the combination of a biblical text with the aria text recalls the combination of *Sprüche* and chorales so important to motet writing.

The chorus "Ehre sei Gott in der Höhe" BWV 248/21 from the Christmas Oratorio illustrates particularly well the integration of instruments into a motet-like movement. The movement treats a traditional Christmas biblical text as a motet, a setting it often received in the late seventeenth and early eighteenth centuries. Bach divides the text into three short units ("Ehre sei Gott in der Höhe / und Friede auf Erden / und dem Menschen ein Wohlgefallen"), and treats each separately. The two outer sections are imitative; they are set not as extensive fugues, but rather use close imitation in relatively short thematic units. (The imitation in the first section is masked by filler in the other voices, yielding a continuous four-voice texture.)

Bach uses instruments in a different way in each of the three sections of the piece, but the instruments are always subordinate to the vocal parts, maintaining the essential

---

8 Cf. Neumann, *Chorfuge*, 90.

Example 9–6 BWV 243a/A, mm. 1–12

motet-like character of the work. (See example 9–7.) In the first section, all instruments play a transparent chordal accompaniment that provides harmonic support for the voices but no melodic competition with them. In the second section, the strings and flutes are given a rhythmically regular, harmonically conceived three-note accompanimental figure like that found in BWV 118 and other extended motets. The four oboes

142

are given a written-out continuo realization in large note values in conjunction with a *tasto solo* indication in the continuo. The oboes maintain this texture in the third section, in which strings and flutes play *colla parte* with the imitative voices. In all, Bach uses a large orchestra deployed with great variety, but never in violation of the motet style that underlies the movement. The appearance of the text "Ehre sei Gott in der Höhe" in the libretto must immediately have suggested a motet-like setting, and Bach found a way to integrate a large instrumental ensemble into an essentially motet-like treatment of the text.

"Der Gerechte kommt um"

The extended type of motet represented by BWV 118, making limited use of independent instruments, is also found in a piece from another oratorio from the Bach circle. The work is "Der Gerechte kommt um," a five-voice movement that was one of several added to Carl Heinrich Graun's passion cantata "Ein Lämmlein geht und trägt die Schuld." The movement appears in a pastiche, "Wer ist der, so von Edom kömmt," that has several connections to J. S. Bach: the score of the work was once owned by Carl Philipp Emanuel Bach, the principal copyist of that score was Bach's student and son-in-law Johann Christoph Altnickol, and two of the movements added to Graun's cantata are compositions by J. S. Bach.[9]

It has been suggested that "Der Gerechte kommt um" may have been used in Leipzig as an independent motet, and that it may be a work of J. S. Bach.[10] Each of these assertions is difficult to support. A set of parts for the work does survive, but was almost certainly made for use at the Berlin Sing-Akademie in the early nineteenth century, and thus has no connection to Leipzig practice.[11] No performance of the pastiche by Bach can be documented, and it is not possible to establish whether he had any role in the revisions made to BWV 127/1, one of the added movements.[12] Kirsten Beißwenger has argued that J. S. Bach may have been responsible for a pastiche passion on which the pastiche in question was, in turn, based, but that he was probably not responsible for the addition of "Der Gerechte kommt um," which was probably added later.[13] The movement is nonetheless worthy of attention for its use of motet style.

The text of "Der Gerechte kommt um" is a translation of a Matins Responsory for Holy Saturday, "Ecce, quomodo moritur justus" (Isaiah 57:1–2), also used at funerals. A setting by Gallus of the Latin version is found in the motet collection *Florilegium Portense*, and Gallus' composition appears in German versions in the Dresden and

[9] SBB Mus. ms. 8155. "Chorus" ["Der Gerechte kommt um"]. Hands of Johann Christoph Altnickol and an unknown copyist, whose work includes "Der Gerechte kommt um." Full description in John W. Grubbs, "Ein Passions-Pasticcio des 18. Jahrhunderts," *BJ* 51 (1965): 10–42.

[10] Diethard Hellmann, "Eine Kuhnau-Bearbeitung Joh. Seb. Bachs?" *BJ* 53 (1967): 93–99.

[11] SBB Mus. ms. 8185, in the hands of Georg Poelchau and an unidentified copyist, made from the score cited above from Poelchau's collection.

[12] See Andreas Glöckner, "Johann Sebastian Bachs Aufführungen zeitgenössicher Passionsmusiken," *BJ* 63 (1977): 75–119, and Alfred Dürr, "Zum Choralchorsatz 'Herr Jesu Christ, wahr' Mensch und Gott' BWV 127 (Satz 1) und seiner Umarbeitung," *BJ* 74 (1988): 205–9.

[13] Kirsten Beißwenger, *Johann Sebastian Bachs Notenbibliothek* (Cassel, 1992), 89–100.

Example 9–7a BWV 248/21, mm. 1–4

Leipzig hymnals.[14] The text (both in Latin and in German) was also used on Good Friday, where a performance of a setting of the text immediately followed the singing of the Passion.[15] In the pastiche, the text was apparently absorbed into the Passion in the form of "Der Gerechte kommt um," where it forms part of the complex of chorales and choruses that concludes the work.

[14] Leipzig, 1618, and reprints. See Otto Riemer, "Erhard Bodenschatz und sein Florilegium Portense"; Schering, *Johann Sebastian Bachs Leipziger Kirchenmusik*, 121–29; *Neu Leipziger Gesangbuch* (1682) and *Privilegirte Ordentliche und Vermehrte Dreßdnische Gesangbuch* (1725).

[15] See Charles Sanford Terry, *Joh. Seb. Bach Cantata Texts*, 201 and 209; Werner Braun, *Die mitteldeutsche Choralpassion im achtzehnten Jahrhundert* (Berlin, 1960), 188ff.; Bernhard Friedrich Richter, "Zur Geschichte der Passionsaufführungen in Leipzig," *BJ* 8 (1911): 54; Leipzig "Kirchenandachten" (1694), cited by Arnold Schering, *Johann Sebastian Bachs Leipziger Kirchenmusik*, 124f. n. 1.

Example 9–7b BWV 248/21, mm. 25–29

Various musical features of "Der Gerechte kommt um" point to motet style. (See example 9–8.) The composition sets a biblical text in a vocally-dominated style. The vocal parts are supported by partly independent instruments, which provide opening and intermediate ritornellos (based on limited material) and *colla parte* support of the voices (SI=Fl1/2; SII=V1; A=V2; T=Va). The instruments are sometimes rhythmically independent of the vocal parts, and occasionally elaborate a vocal melodic figure, but they are doublings in essence. Their doubling function is made particularly clear in imitative vocal entrances, where the instrumental parts rest and then reenter with the voices. The only independent instrumental writing outside of the ritornellos is in the oboes, whose material is restricted almost entirely to repetitions of a harmonically

Example 9–7c BWV 248/21, mm. 31–35

conceived three-note figure. (In the last few measures, the oboes abandon the harmonic figure and play slow-moving independent material.) Otherwise, all the thematic material resides in the vocal parts and their instrumental doublings.

In these features, "Der Gerechte kommt um" shows close musical similarities to "O Jesu Christ, meins Lebens Licht" BWV 118, which Bach explicitly called a motet. As in "Der Gerechte kommt um," the thematic material of BWV 118 is almost entirely in its vocal parts. The independent material in the oboes in "Der Gerechte kommt um" parallels that in the lituus parts in BWV 118. "Der Gerechte kommt um" represents a kind of piece that Bach considered a motet, one that could include limited instrumental participation: *colla parte* doubling, rhythmically independent harmonic

Example 9–8 Anon., "Der Gerechte kommt um," mm. 1–16

Example 9–9 Johann Kuhnau (attrib.), "Tristis est anima mea," mm. 1–15

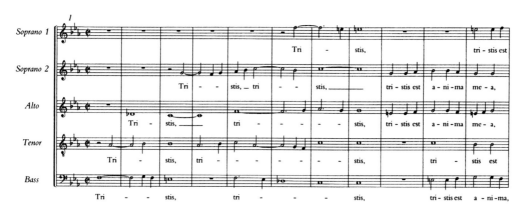

support, and punctuating ritornellos. The movement is also closely related to the motet-like "Et incarnatus est" from the Mass in B minor BWV 232, especially in its harmonic expressivity, and to the cantata movement BWV 25/1.

The motet character of "Der Gerechte kommt um" is reinforced by its apparent origin as an arrangement of a motet attributed to Bach's Leipzig predecessor Johann Kuhnau, "Tristis est anima mea," a work essentially identical to "Der Gerechte kommt um" but lacking the instrumental parts found in the German version.[16] (See example 9–9.) Any number of problems makes the attribution to Kuhnau difficult to evaluate. The oldest source, a score, is of a relatively late date.[17] A set of parts reported by Philipp Spitta in the Leipzig Sing-Akademie is probably related to this score, but is lost in any event.[18] Lora Matthews has pointed out a set of parts in Darmstadt, apparently from the collection of Franz Hauser, and related the Leipzig Sing-Akademie's material.[19] The source used for the preparation of a heavily revised edition by Gustav Schreck is unknown,[20] and nothing is known of a lost copy reported in Dessau by

[16]   See Hellmann, "Eine Kuhnau-Bearbeitung Joh. Seb. Bachs?"
[17]   SBB Mus. ms. autogr. J. Kuhnau 1, from the estate of J. G. Schicht; hand unknown, but not Kuhnau.
[18]   *J. S. Bach*, 2:163 n. 3.
[19]   Personal communication. Hessische Landes- und Hochschulbibliothek, Mus. ms. 528/1–4.
[20]   *Ausgewählte Gesänge des Thomanerchores zu Leipzig*, no. 6 (Leipzig, 1899).

Example 9–10 Orlando di Lasso, "Tristis est anima mea," mm. 1–14

Arnold Schering.[21] In sum, the attribution to Kuhnau is difficult to evaluate on source-critical grounds.

The Latin text of "Tristis est anima mea" (from Matt. 26:38 and some unknown source) is a Responsory for Matins on Maundy Thursday, but it is not specified in the surviving documentation of the Leipzig liturgy of Bach's time. The *Florilegium Portense* lists its two settings of the text "Tristis est anima mea" under the heading "De Passione Domini." One of them, a setting by Lassus (example 9–10) shares with the work attributed to Kuhnau the use of five voices and the tonal center F.[22] The opening phrases are handled similarly, with closely overlapping vocal entries, and both shift to homophonic declamation at the words "Nunc/jam videbitis turbam." Assuming that the text "Tristis est anima mea" was used liturgically in Leipzig, it is possible that the setting attributed to Kuhnau was composed as an up-to-date substitute for the composition by Lassus found in the *Florilegium Portense*. But even this hypothesis puts us no closer to identifying the composer of the work. It is even conceivable that "Tristis est anima mea" is an arrangement of the vocal parts of "Der Gerechte kommt um" and not the other way around. In any event, the labeling of "Tristis est anima mea" as a motet strengthens the assertion that "Der Gerechte kommt um" would have been regarded as a motet as well.

[21] Dessau Herzogl. Singechor D IV, Nr. 35, cited in the Kuhnau worklist in DDT 58/59, xlv.
[22] *O. de Lassus. Sämtliche Werke,* 5:48–50.

The Leipzig origin of the presumed model, the provenance of the score of the Passion pastiche that contains "Der Gerechte kommt um," and the stylistic similarity of that piece to BWV 118 and the "Et incarnatus est" of the Mass in B minor BWV 232 point clearly to the circle of J. S. Bach. It is unlikely that Bach was responsible for the work's composition. Nonetheless, it is clear that "Der Gerechte kommt um" is a kind of motet, one recognized in the Bach circle, and deemed appropriate for the setting of an oratorio text closely associated with motet style.

CHAPTER 10

Bach's use of motet style in concerted works

Bach's use of motet style

The compositions discussed in the previous chapters show that the motet was one element in a repertory of musical styles that Bach brought to the composition of his concerted church music, and was one of the choices available to him in approaching a libretto. Motet style retained its traditional associations with biblical and chorale texts, and in concerted works Bach applied it only to texts to which it was generically suited. The style brought with it certain musical characteristics that continued to be reflected in its use in concerted works: notation in large rhythmic values, counterpoint, and *colla parte* doubling instruments, especially trombones. The close relationship between motets and motet-like cantata movements is supported by the indications that at least one piece (BWV Anh. 160–BWV 231– BWV 28/2) may have served in both capacities. Several other cantata movements are transmitted separately, perhaps intended for independent use as motets, but none of them has yet been associated with such a practice under Bach.

Bach also used elements of motet style in combination with other techniques. In some cantata movements, vocal counterpoint on biblical and chorale texts is combined with the concerto to produce hybrid movements. To recognize motet style as one of the roots of these pieces is to gain insight into their musical workings and the logic of their creation.

For a given text, motet style may have been appropriate, but was Bach's choice of it meaningful? Klaus Hofmann has argued that Bach used a somewhat updated "alter Stil" in the motet-like BWV 28/2 to invoke the general concept of the past in the New Year's season cantata "Gottlob! nun geht das Jahr zu Ende" BWV 28 and to represent a liturgical act (a "frohes Danklied" mentioned in the first movement).[1] In some respects, these insights into Bach's choice of motet style in BWV 28/2 apply to his other motet-like cantata movements as well, particularly his motet-like settings of chorales. In them, the historical associations of motet style go hand-in-hand with the oldest and most venerable aspect of the Lutheran musical tradition, and Bach's use of motet style probably acknowledges that tradition. For Bach, the historical

---

[1] Klaus Hofmann, "Alter Stil in Bachs Kirchenmusik."

significance may well have been musical as well as theological, representing his homage to older settings of these tunes.

It is less certain whether Bach's use of motet style in BWV 28 was also symbolically appropriate to the New Year, because motet-like movements are found in cantatas intended for every part of the church year. There is indeed a concentration of motet-like chorale settings around Christmas and the New Year in Bach's music, but this is probably more a reflection of central-German tradition associating motets with these feasts than an explicit reference to the retrospective theme of the New Year celebration. The motet as a representative of a "liturgical act" could well have been employed at any time during the year, but Bach's use of the style at other times in the church calendar shows that his understanding of motet style went beyond mere reference to "the past."

Another problem with identifying motet style with a general reference to the past is that it is difficult to reconcile this interpretation with the motet-like settings of *Spruch* texts, which make up a large proportion of movements of this type. There are, of course, differences in Bach's musical approach to motet-like settings of chorales and *Sprüche*, but evidence suggests that eighteenth-century musicians regarded them as different manifestations of essentially the same thing. The retrospective and liturgical significance attributed to the motet-like chorale settings does not apply as satisfactorily to motet-like *Spruch* movements. We cannot explain Bach's use of motet style in them as a reference to the past.

We need to look for other motivations for Bach's use of motet style, and they are to be found in the historical tradition of the motet. Bach could choose to set a chorale or biblical *Spruch* in several different ways, but the stylistic attraction between these text types and motet style was as strong as that between madrigalian texts and the recitative and aria, even stronger for the long history of the association between them. The motet may have been old-fashioned, but its style and its textual associations were clearly still part of the musical language of Bach's time.

The argument is occasionally put forward that fugal technique was associated with the law by a metaphorical parallel between the laws of society and the "laws" of strict counterpoint, and that this connection explains why there are so many fugal settings of biblical texts. This is an attractive explanation, one that appeals especially to those in search of strong symbolic connections between texts and the specific musical techniques used in setting them. The association may not have been direct but rather by way of motet style. The most important kind of texts for motets were biblical *dicta*, which were regarded as the Law. Because counterpoint was so strongly associated with motet style, this kind of text apparently became associated in time with counterpoint. Thus, composers may not have set biblical texts (especially those that refer explicitly to the law) contrapuntally because of purported parallels between counterpoint and biblical authority, but rather because they associated such texts with motet style.

Instrumental doubling of motet-like cantata movements

Motet-like cantata movements by definition do not have independent instrumental parts. Nonetheless, in such movements, Bach made extensive use of instruments to provide *colla parte* doublings of the vocal lines.[2] In fact, the overwhelming majority of Bach's motet-like cantata movements have exact instrumental doublings of the vocal parts (see table 10–1). This practice is stylistically significant, because the instrumental doublings consistently employed in motet-like movements represent an important aspect of the early eighteenth-century conception of motet style.

In most of Bach's motet-like movements, there are occasional departures from strict *colla parte* writing: repeated pitches are sometimes combined into longer notes, melodic lines are sometimes slightly ornamented, and there are adjustments made in some lines to accommodate the range of the doubling instruments. Despite these small divergences, it is clear that the instrumental parts in these movements are entirely subordinate to the vocal lines they double, in keeping with the movements' motet style.

Among the motet-like movements, there are only two for which Bach did not specify *colla parte* doublings, both from early cantatas. One is the chorale setting BWV 4/5, one of two movements in the cantata unusual in its use of doubling instruments. (The other is the duet BWV 4/3.) It is difficult to say why BWV 4/5 is not doubled, but it should be noted that we know this work only from Leipzig-era sources; the circumstances of Bach's reperformance of this older work may have something to do with its peculiar use of doubling instruments. The other early undoubled motet-like movement is the *Spruch* setting BWV 71/3, the original score and parts for which make clear that Bach intended performance by solo voices without instrumental doublings. The omission of doubling instruments is again hard to explain, but is exceptional among the motet-like movements.

Bach almost always doubled the vocal parts of motet-like cantata movements with strings; the single exception is BWV 101/1, a movement that combines motet and concerto elements, and there is a clear reason for the lack of string doubling. In this piece, the strings play independent material and are thus unavailable; trombones and a flute double the voices. Oboes, too, almost always double the vocal parts. As table 10–1 shows, there are few exceptions, and they are almost all explainable; in these movements, there are no oboes in the cantata's *Instrumentarium*, or only a single oboe d'amore, or the oboes are occupied with the concerto element in a hybrid movement. The single exception is BWV 179/1, which is the only movement in which Bach apparently did not add doubling oboe parts when the instruments were available. The incomplete survival of sources for this cantata should be noted; only oboe parts survive, and they are conceivably duplicate parts that do not fully represent Bach's practice in the work. (Note that in the Latin parody of this movement, BWV 236/1, Bach apparently did specify doubling oboes.)

The use of cornetti and trombones, especially in full choir, is a particularly important aspect of these instrumental doublings. Trombones had a special association with

---

[2] See Wolff, *Der Stile antico*, 108ff. and Prinz, "Studien zum Instrumentarium."

Table 10–1 Colla parte *doublings in motet-like church cantata movements*

BWV	Strings S/A/T/B	Woodwinds S/A/T/B	Cornetti/Trombones S/A/T/B
		Strict motet-like movements	
Biblical texts			
29/2[a]	V1/V2/Va/[Bc]	Ob1/Ob2/–/–	
64/1	V1/V2/Va/[Bc]	[ob. d'am. in 64/7]	Cto/Tbn1/Tbn2/Tbn3
68/5	V1/V2/Va/[Bc]	Ob1/Ob2/Ta/–	Cto/Tbn1/Tbn2/Tbn3
71/3			
108/4	V1/V2/Va/[Bc]	Ob. d'am.1/Ob. d'am.2/–/–	
144/1	V1/V2/Va/[Bc]	Ob1/Ob2/–/–	
179/1	V1/V2/Va/[Bc]	[oboes in 179/3,5,6]	
Chorales			
2/1	V1/V2/Va/[Bc]	–/Ob1+2/–/–	Tbn1/Tbn2/Tbn3/Tbn4
4/5		[no oboes in cantata]	
14/1	V1/V2/Va/[Bc]	[oboes on cantus firmus]	
28/2	V1/V2/Va/[Bc]	Ob1/Ob2/Ta/–	Cto/Tbn1/Tbn2/Tbn3
38/1	V1/V2/Va/[Bc]	Ob1+2/–/–/–	Tbn1/Tbn2/Tbn3/Tbn4
80/1	V1/V2/Va/[Bc]	[oboes on cantus firmus]	
121/1	V1/V2/Va/[Bc]	Ob.d'am/–/–/–	Cto/Tbn1/Tbn2/Tbn3
182/7	V/Va1/Va2/Vc	Rec/–/–/–	
Combined texts			
21/9	V1/V2/Va/[Bc]	Ob/–/–/Bn	Tbn1/Tbn2/Tbn3/Tbn4
		Movements partly in motet style	
		(doublings shown are for motet-like portion)	
Biblical texts			
6/1[b]	V1/V2/Va/[Bc]	Ob1[c]/Ob2/Ob. da cacc./–	
22/1[b]	V1/V2/Va/[Bc]	Ob/–/–/–	
24/3[b]	V1/V2/Va/[Bc]	Ob1/Ob2/–/–	
76/1[b]	V1/V2/Va/[Bc]	Ob1/Ob2/–/–	
105/1[b]	V1/V2/Va/[Bc]	Ob1[d]/Ob2/–/–	
Chorale			
41/1	V1/V2/Va/[Bc]	Ob1/Ob2/Ob3[e]/–	
		Selected movements combining motet style with other principles	
Biblical texts			
25/1[b]	V1/V2/Va/[Bc]	Ob1/Ob2/–/–	
171/1	V1/V2/Va/[Bc]	Ob1/Ob2[f]/–/–	
Chorale			
101/1		Fl/–/–/– [oboes part of concerto element]	Cto/Tbn1/Tbn2/Tbn3

[a] Tpt1+2 partly independent, partly double S+A
[b] No doubling of first section or first fugal exposition
[c] Ob1 and V1 have a few independent entrances
[d] S also doubled by Hn; occasionally independent
[e] S also doubled by Tpt1; Ob3 occasionally independent
[f] Ob2 initially doubles Ob1

motet style,[3] and this association is reflected in Bach's use of the instrument in his own works (both motets and motet-like cantata movements) and in his performances of motets by other composers. Table 10–2 lists Bach's use of cornetti and trombones.

Bach used obbligato trombone parts in two works: the first version of "O Jesu Christ, meins Lebens Licht" BWV 118, which he explicitly called a motet; and the motet-like cantata movement BWV 25/1, which – like traditional motets – combines a biblical text and a chorale, the latter entrusted to the trombone choir. Bach used trombones mostly in cantatas, and almost exclusively in choruses. Aside from four-part chorale harmonizations, most of the movements that use trombones are motet-like, and six of the seven non-motet movements that use trombones employ a chorale, linking them musically and textually to the motet. Four of the non-motet-like movements use a single instrument to double a chorale cantus firmus; a fifth, BWV 4/2 uses a motet-derived technique of a chorale cantus firmus with imitative supporting voices. The sixth, the presumably solo chorale duet BWV 4/3, is doubled by cornetto and trombone, a departure from Bach's usual practice that is as puzzling as the non-doubling of BWV 4/5. In the Sanctus BWV 238, a single cornetto doubles the soprano. The most difficult to explain among the movements in which Bach used trombones is BWV 23/4, a movement apparently not of a musical type that called stylistically for trombone doubling. Perhaps its trombone parts were added for security when Bach performed BWV 23 at his test for the Leipzig cantorate in 1723.[4]

Bach used trombones for a number of four-part chorales, but only in cantatas in which he also used a full choir of trombones for a larger choral movement. This makes it clear that the motivation for the inclusion of trombones in a cantata's instrumentation was the presence of a movement that called for trombones stylistically, usually a motet-like piece. The use of trombones in the four-part chorales in these cantatas was incidental to their use in other movements.

Bach used *colla parte* trombones in his performances of two works by other composers: Palestrina, *Missa sine nomine* and Knüpfer, "Erforsche mich, Gott." Here again, the connection to motet style is evident – extended in the case of the Palestrina Mass to the *stile antico* in its strictest manifestation. In the Knüpfer motet, the trombones replace *colla parte* woodwinds; this substitution, presumably made for practical reasons, should remind us that Bach may have made similar substitutions in other works. In addition, Durante's Mass BWV Anh. 26, known from a score in Bach's hand that includes the "Christe eleison" BWV 242, calls for trombones doubling A, T and B in tutti sections. (A later addition to the title page reads "NB. In Stimmen fehlen die Trombonen"; it is not known whether this refers to parts by Bach, of which none survive.[5]) The musical style of this work does not clearly call for trombone doubling, though it obviously was not considered out of place.

---

[3] On the use of trombones see Prinz, "Studien zum Instrumentarium," and MacCracken, "Die Verwendung der Blechblasinstrumente." On the close relationship between motet style and the use of trombones see Wolff, *Der Stile antico*, 111f.

[4] Christoph Wolff, "Bachs Leipziger Kantoratsprobe und die Aufführungsgeschichte der Kantate 'Du wahrer Gott und Davids Sohn' BWV 23," *BJ* 64 (1978): 78–94; but cf. Kobayashi, "Chronologie der Spätwerke," 7 n. 4.

[5] See *NBA* II/2 *KB*, 162.

Table 10–2 *J. S. Bach's use of cornetti and trombones*

Composition				Notes

Motet

"O Jesu Christ, meins Lebens Licht" BWV 118 (first version)				Tbns obbligato

Cantata movements

Motet-like biblical	Motet-like chorale	4-part chorale	Other chorale	
	2/1	2/6		
		3/6	3/1	1: Tbn=B; 6: Cto=S
		4/8	4/2–3	
21/9				
			23/4	
25/1		25/6		1: Tbns obbligato
	28/2	28/6		
	38/1	38/6		
64/1		64/2–4–8		
68/5				
			96/1	Tbn=A (replaces Hn)
	101/1	101/7		
	121/1	121/6		
		133/6	133/1	1, 6: Cto=S
		135/6	135/1	1: Tbn=B; 6: Cto=S

Other

	Notes
Sanctus BWV 238	Cto=S

Works by other composers

Palestrina, *Missa sine nomine*	Tbns double all voices
Knüpfer, "Erforsche mich, Gott"	Tbns double Choir II
Durante, Mass BWV Anh. 26	Tbns double ATB

Most of the time, Bach neither notated separate trombone parts in a cantata score nor specified trombones among the instruments in the heading on the score. In most cases, Bach's use of doubling trombones is known from the survival of original performing parts, or from notations on wrappers for scores or parts. Several cantatas for which trombone participation under Bach cannot be documented may nonetheless have been performed with them because of the motet-like movements they contain. Among the Leipzig-era cantatas, no parts survive for BWV 144 or BWV 80, and only oboe parts for BWV 179. The opening motet-like movements in each of these works makes *colla parte* doubling by trombones stylistically appropriate. The surviving parts for BWV 108 include no trombones, and neither Bach's wrapper for the score nor C. P. E. Bach's later wrapper for the parts suggest that there ever were original trombone parts for this cantata. J. S. Bach's autograph parts for BWV 14 include none for trombones, nor does his wrapper for the score specify them. Nonetheless, it is clear that trombone doubling would have been stylistically appropriate in each of these cantatas as well, though perhaps less likely in BWV 14/1 given the use of a horn. Modern performances – and editions – should probably include trombones as an option for these works.

Whether with brass instruments or with the usual woodwinds and strings, Bach nearly always chose to double the vocal lines in motet-like cantata movements. He did so presumably not out of necessity but rather because he considered *colla parte* instrumental participation an essential aspect of motet style. Eighteenth-century writers made it clear that instrumental doubling of a motet was a perfectly ordinary and stylistically acceptable practice; for Bach, in cantata movements in motet style, it was nearly indispensable.

PART FOUR

Bach's contact with seventeenth-century German motets

CHAPTER 11

The history of the Altbachisches Archiv

J. S. Bach and the music of his family

The most important influences on J. S. Bach's mature vocal music are not hard to find; with little doubt, they were Antonio Vivaldi's concertos and Erdmann Neumeister's cantata librettos. These two elements eventually dominated Bach's vocal music, and to recognize and understand the legacy of Vivaldi and Neumeister is to go a long way in appreciating Bach's concerted vocal music. But these modern influences fall short of a complete illumination of Bach's vocal music for several reasons. First, there is a small but important body of vocal works that Bach composed before he encountered Vivaldi's music, and before he turned to Neumeister-type librettos, and these pieces are clearly in the mold of late seventeenth-century compositions. Next, certain vocal genres – the motet foremost among them – were largely unaffected by either the ritornello concerto or the operatic mixed-text libretto, meaning that Bach's compositions in these genres, too, owe more to the late seventeenth century than to the early eighteenth.

Finally, despite the importance of the musical and textual ideas Bach learned in the second decade of the eighteenth century (when he apparently first encountered Vivaldi's music in Weimar, and began composing cantatas on mixed text-type librettos), he was, after all, fully twenty-five years old by then, a musician and composer of no little experience. It is nearly impossible to imagine that any influences – even those as powerful as Vivaldi and Neumeister – could completely overwhelm the musical traditions and the conceptions of genre and style with which Bach had been brought up: those of the late seventeenth century. An understanding of the roots of Bach's music in the late seventeenth century is thus particularly essential in addressing the types of vocal music that were largely immune to changing styles, and in studying certain features of Bach's mature concerted vocal music that draw on long-standing traditions. However important the modern influences, Bach's cultivation of them rested on the foundation of the received traditions of earlier musical styles.

We need a better grasp of the vocal music Bach encountered during his formative years. Unfortunately, the sources that might tell us the most about the musical influences on the young Bach are lost, and it is difficult to identify much of the music with which he would have been familiar. For example, we possess only an inventory of the music collection of the St. Michael's School in Lüneburg, which Bach attended from 1700 to 1702. Much of the repertory is lost, and in any event the extent of Bach's access to it and the extent to which the older music in the collection was actually used are unknown.[1] Another possibility lies in Bach's report that he had assembled a collection of "choice church music" in Mühlhausen during the time he was organist at St. Blasius' church there, but that collection, too, has disappeared altogether.[2] Bach's well-known stay in Lübeck during the tenure of Dieterich Buxtehude almost certainly gave him the opportunity of hearing important and influential music, but the exact repertory to which he was exposed there remains a matter of speculation, except for a few pieces whose texts are known but whose music is lost.[3]

We also know that Bach was extensively exposed to the music of his family; that repertory, to the extent that it survives and can be identified, is another potential clue to his musical upbringing. He spent the first ten years of his life in Eisenach, where both his father Johann Ambrosius and his father's cousin Johann Christoph were active musicians, the latter both as a composer and a performer. After his parents' deaths, the young J. S. Bach lived in Ohrdruf in the home of his older brother Johann Christoph, from whom he received instruction and exposure to repertory. Curiously enough, there is no older family music among the pieces J. S. Bach is known to have received from his brother, and in any event, we know only about keyboard music that passed between them.[4] The frequent Bach family gatherings of the kind described by Johann Nikolaus Forkel must also have given J. S. Bach the opportunity to hear vocal works by members of his family, though the only possible surviving examples of such works are Georg Christoph Bach's vocal concerto [14] "Siehe wie fein und lieblich" and J. S. Bach's own Quodlibet BWV 524.[5] Finally, the members of the family apparently exchanged music among themselves; this is documented in J. S. Bach's acquisition of cantatas by his cousin Johann Ludwig, vocal works by Johann Nicolaus, and suites by Johann Bernhard. Relatively little is known about Bach's acquisition of these works, and there is no evidence that he encountered any of them early in his life. Although we do not know much about the specific family pieces Bach was exposed to in his early years, compositions by members of his family must have been important influences. At the least, from a historical point of view they probably represent a good sample of the kinds of music he was exposed to – one could not ask for a closer match in time, place, and stylistic outlook.

[1] The Lüneburg works in manuscript are listed in Max Seiffert, "Die Chorbibliothek der St. Michaelisschule in Lüneburg zu Seb. Bach's Zeit," *Sammelbände der Internationalen Musik-Gesellschaft* 9, no. 4 (1908): 593–621; printed music in W. Junghans, "Johann Sebastian Bach als Schüler der Partikularschule zu St. Michaelis in Lüneburg oder Lüneburg eine Pflegstätte kirchlicher Musik," in *Programm des Johanneums zu Lüneburg: Ostern 1870*. On the collection in general see Friedhelm Krummacher, *Die Überlieferung der Choralbearbeitungen in der frühen evangelischen Kantate* (Berlin, 1965); on Bach's access see Gustav Fock, *Der junge Bach in Lüneburg 1700 bis 1702* (Hamburg, 1950), 80f.

[2] Bach's "guthe apparat der auserleßensten kirchen Stücken" is mentioned in a letter to the Mühlhausen town council (*Dok* I/1).

[3] Snyder, *Dieterich Buxtehude*, 104ff.

[4] See Robert Hill, "'Der Himmel weiss, wo diese Sachen hingekommen sind': reconstructing the lost keyboard notebooks of the young Bach and Handel," in Peter Williams, ed., *Bach, Handel, Scarlatti: Tercentenary Essays* (Cambridge, 1985), 161–72.

[5] Johann Nikolaus Forkel, *Ueber Johann Sebastian Bachs Leben, Kunst und Kunstwerke* (Leipzig, 1802), 3.

It turns out that J. S. Bach's exposure in his early years to music by members of his family represents only one of his two encounters with it. The second came late in his life, when his interests turned to music of the past. The best-known example of this historical interest is Bach's study of Palestrina-style counterpoint (the *stile antico*) both in its original form and in modern manifestations. His cultivation of this repertory is documented both in study and performance, and this music has been shown to have been an important influence on his own compositions in the last years of his life.[6] But in these late years, Bach also explored the music of his ancestors. His interest in the musical past and in his own family intersect in a remarkable body of material known as the Altbachisches Archiv (ABA), a collection of compositions by older members of the Bach family, owned and probably assembled by J. S. Bach himself. Bach's ownership of the ABA shows that he was familiar with its repertory, but his contact went beyond collection and preservation of the material for historical and sentimental reasons. It is clear from documentary evidence that Bach performed pieces from the collection, mostly motets. The repertory of the ABA thus represents simultaneously the kind of music with which Bach grew up and a reflection of Bach's interests in his family and in their music in his later years.

There has never been a systematic evaluation of the ABA and of J. S. Bach's contact with it. Philipp Spitta began his biography of J. S. Bach with a discussion of older family members and their compositions, but little of the ABA material was available to him. Max Schneider published most of the compositions in the ABA and a number of related pieces in an important edition in 1935, and Karl Geiringer presented brief analytical discussions of many of the pieces in his book on the Bach family.[7] Only Schneider had access to the source materials themselves, because the ABA has periodically disappeared and resurfaced over the years, and his work obviously predates the substantial progress that has been made in recent decades in source-critical studies of Bach repertory.

The time is ripe for a closer look at the ABA and at J. S. Bach's relation to it. Unfortunately, there is a major obstacle, because the ABA sources are once again unavailable. Nonetheless, newly discovered photographs of many of them, combined with other reproductions, descriptions, and a few surviving items make possible a reconstruction of the ABA and a closer examination of Bach's contact with it. What emerges is a fascinating pattern of Bach's involvement late in his life with an old-fashioned repertory, and a glimpse into his exploration of his musical roots. It also emerges that Bach took a particular interest during his later years in the genre of the German motet. This is clearly documented in the evidence of his copying and performing of a significant number of older motets by his family, and by his study and performance of at least one other seventeenth-century motet in these years.

---

[6] See Wolff, *Der Stile antico*.
[7] Spitta, *J. S. Bach*; Max Schneider, ed., *Altbachisches Archiv*, 2 vols., EDM 1/2 (Leipzig, 1935); Karl Geiringer and Irene Geiringer, *The Bach Family: Seven Generations of Creative Genius* (New York, 1954).

C. P. E. Bach's ownership of the Altbachisches Archiv

The first reference to music by older members of the Bach family owned by the younger generations appears in the obituary of J. S. Bach by C. P. E. Bach and Johann Friedrich Agricola.[8] The authors begin their discussion – as did Forkel, Spitta, and others after them – with an outline of J. S. Bach's distinguished musical ancestry, listing five composers as "particularly worthy of mention on account of their composing." Hans-Joachim Schulze has demonstrated that C. P. E. Bach used the genealogy compiled in 1735 by J. S. Bach in preparing the obituary of J. S. Bach,[9] and it is clear from a comparison of wording and facts that the descriptions of these five men were also based on their entries in the family genealogy. What C. P. E. Bach knew about his ancestors, he apparently learned from his father.

The obituary continues: "There are still extant works by all of these, which sufficiently demonstrate the skill of their composers both in vocal and instrumental composition." C. P. E. Bach lists five composers and apparently knew of extant works by all of them. It can be deduced that he owned pieces by at least four of the five: motets, concertos, and arias by Johann Michael and Johann Christoph (listed in his estate catalogue),[10] instrumental works by Johann Bernhard (also listed in the estate catalogue), and cantatas by Johann Ludwig (sold before C. P. E. Bach's death and thus not listed in the estate catalogue).[11] In the obituary, then, C. P. E. Bach mostly singled out those composers whose music he owned. He presumably also already owned Georg Christoph Bach's [14] "Siehe, wie fein und lieblich" (listed in the estate catalogue); why he did not mention him is not clear.

Heinrich Bach's inclusion as a composer is puzzling, because C. P. E. Bach is not known to have owned any music attributed to him in his sources. He may have been listed out of family pride; Heinrich, as Johann Michael's father, was C. P. E. Bach's great-grandfather. It is also possible that C. P. E. Bach did own – or thought he owned – music by Heinrich Bach. [6] "Ach, daß ich Wassers gnug hätte" is attributed to Johann Christoph Bach in C. P. E. Bach's estate catalogue, but may be a composition of Heinrich Bach. [16] "Nun ist alles überwunden," anonymous in the ABA listing, is signed "Arnstadt 1686," and could be a work of Heinrich, but there is no evidence that C. P. E. Bach thought so. Only two other vocal works attributed to Heinrich are known, and C. P. E. Bach had no known contact with them.[12] The three organ chorales

---

[8] *Dok* III/666.

[9] "Marginalien zu einigen Bach-Dokumenten," *BJ* 48 (1961): 82f.

[10] *Verzeichniß des musikalischen Nachlasses des verstorbenen Capellmeisters Carl Philipp Emanuel Bach* (Hamburg, 1790) "estate catalogue." Facsimile edition, *The Catalog of Carl Philipp Emanuel Bach's Estate*, ed. Rachel W. Wade, Garland Reference Library of the Humanities, no. 240 (New York, 1981). Transcription by Heinrich Miesner, "Philipp Emanuel Bachs musikalischer Nachlass," *BJ* 35 (1938): 103–36; 36 (1939): 81–112; 37 (1940/48): 161–81.

[11] The cantata scores and parts were sold to an unknown purchaser during C. P. E. Bach's lifetime. See William Scheide, "Johann Sebastian Bachs Sammlung von Kantaten seines Vetters Johann Ludwig Bach," part 1, *BJ* 46 (1959): 55f.

[12] "Ich danke dir, Gott" from the Michaeliskirche in Erfurt (SBB St 342); see Elizabeth Noack, "Die Bibliothek der Michaeliskirche zu Erfurt," *Archiv für Musikwissenschaft* 7 (1925): 68. "Alß der Tag der Pfingsten erfüllet war," listed in the inventory from the Michaelisschule in Lüneburg; see Seiffert, "Die Chorbibliothek der St. Michaelisschule in Lüneburg," 599.

generally attributed to Heinrich are probably spurious; in any event, C. P. E. Bach is not known to have had any role in their transmission.[13] If C. P. E. Bach owned any music attributed to Heinrich Bach, it cannot be identified today.

Much of what is known about C. P. E. Bach's ownership of family material (aside from the listing in his estate catalogue; see below) comes from his correspondence with Johann Nikolaus Forkel and from Forkel's writings based on it. The material is first mentioned in a letter from Bach of 13 January 1775 answering Forkel's questions, many of which apparently concerned the influence of other composers on J. S. Bach. In earlier letters, now lost, Forkel must have expressed interest in the family, for at the end of this letter Carl Philipp Emanuel mentions a Bach family tree that he had sent earlier, and offers to supply Forkel with works by Johann Christoph Bach.[14]

The first reference to a systematic collection of compositions by older Bachs appears in a letter from late in the same year; Forkel had apparently taken C. P. E. Bach up on his offer.

> Herewith I have the pleasure of sending you something from my *alten Bachischen Archive*, namely two works by the worthy Joh. Christoph and one by his worthy brother Johann Michael Bach, my late grandfather on my mother's side. I would ask that you return them to me at some point – n.b. well preserved, as they are somewhat brittle. The twenty-two-voice work is a masterpiece. My late father performed it once in church in Leipzig; everyone was astounded at the effect. I do not have enough singers here; otherwise I would gladly perform it.

> (Hierbey, habe ich das Vergnügen, Ihnen etwas aus meinem alten Bachischen Archive zu überschicken, nehmlich 2 Stücke von dem braven Joh. Christopf, und 1 von deßen braven Bruder Joh. Michel Bach, meinem seeligen Großvater mütterlicher Seite. Ich bitte, sie gelegentlich mir, NB gut conservirt, weil sie etwas mürbe sind, wieder zu schicken. Das 22stimmige Stück ist ein Meisterstück. Mein seeliger Vater hat es einmahl in Leipzig in der Kirche aufgeführt, alles ist über den Effekt erstaunt. Hier habe ich nicht Sänger genug, außerdem würde ich es gerne einmahl aufführen.[15])

One of the two works by Johann Christoph Bach that C. P. E. Bach sent was the vocal concerto [1] "Es erhub sich ein Streit"; the other is unknown. Both [4] "Lieber Herr Gott, wecke uns auf" and [3] "Der Gerechte, ob er gleich zu zeitlich stirbt" are good candidates. The surviving score of the former (SBB P 4/2) is extremely fragile (cf. C. P. E. Bach's description), is in a wrapper citing the date 1775 in C. P. E. Bach's hand, and the accompanying parts show that he had performed the motet. He had recently used the latter in a cantata, so it may have been on his mind. The work by Johann Michael Bach cannot be identified.

This letter marks the earliest known use of the name "Altbachisches Archiv" for the collection. We do not know whether it was Carl Philipp Emanuel's name or was

---

13   "Erbarm dich mein, O Herre Gott" and "Da Jesus an dem Kreuze stand," printed in Diethard Hellmann, ed., *Orgelwerke der Familie Bach*, 2nd edn. (Frankfurt, 1985); "Christ lag in Todesbanden," a work of Buttstedt or Pachelbel, printed in Christoph Wolff, ed., *Johann Michael Bach: Sämtliche Orgelchoräle* (Neuhausen-Stuttgart, 1988).

14   "Mit einigen Sachen von J. Xstopf kann ich aufwarten, wenn ich soll." *Dok* III/803. The family tree is mentioned in earlier letters (*Dok* III/801 and 802).

15   *Dok* III/807 (20 September 1775).

applied earlier. The original sense of the word "Archiv" was a depository for official documents; this meaning can be traced at least as far back as the sixteenth century. The secondary meaning of the term is a collection of documents, and is found in the late seventeenth century. This sense of the word is thus old enough to have been applied to the family music collection before C. P. E. Bach's time, perhaps by J. S. Bach.[16]

Forkel was able to examine the three pieces that C. P. E. Bach sent him in 1775; he reported that he had also had the opportunity of visiting C. P. E. Bach in his later years and of hearing several ABA works in his presence.[17] Nonetheless, for his discussion of older Bachs in his biography of J. S. Bach he seems to have relied little on this first-hand experience, paraphrasing instead several second-hand accounts of the ABA. Forkel drew on the ABA listing in C. P. E. Bach's estate catalogue, taking from it, for example, his description of Johann Michael Bach's compositions.

Forkel's discussion of Johann Christoph Bach relies especially heavily on the obituary of J. S. Bach, from which he took his discussion of Johann Christoph's purported use of the augmented sixth.[18] He first mentions it in his *Allgemeine Geschichte der Musik*, where he explicitly acknowledges his indebtedness to the obituary.[19] (Johann Christoph's use of the interval is also cited by Ernst Ludwig Gerber in his *Neues historisch-biographisches Lexikon der Tonkünstler* in an entry almost certainly paraphrased from the obituary.[20]) No surviving work by Johann Christoph Bach makes use of the augmented sixth; either C. P. E. Bach knew a work that does not survive, or he was reporting a piece of Bach family lore that cannot be confirmed today. At the least, the anecdote exemplifies the high regard in which Johann Christoph Bach was held in the family.

C. P. E. Bach was clearly interested in family history, as witnessed by his revision of his father's genealogy and by the prominence of Bachs in his large portrait collection (Johann Ambrosius, Johann Sebastian, Anna Magdalena, Wilhelm Friedemann, Johann Christoph Friedrich, Johann Christian, Hans, and Johann Ludwig).[21] His interest is also documented in his performances of several ABA works, for which he prepared parts and added performance markings to old materials. He also used one ABA motet in an otherwise original cantata and had several old scores recopied.

C. P. E. Bach wrote to Forkel that he did not have enough singers to perform [1] "Es erhub sich ein Streit," but he was apparently referring to his situation in Hamburg, because the ABA contains a score and set of parts in the hand of his principal Berlin copyist, doubtless for a performance there, though the occasion is unknown.[22] All the other documentary evidence of C. P. E. Bach's contact dates from his years in Hamburg.

The "Alt-Bachisches Archiv" is a major subdivision in C. P. E. Bach's estate catalogue, and is the only music referred to as an integral collection. An explanatory paragraph introduces the ABA:

[16] See Hans Schulz, *Deutsches Fremdwörterbuch*, 3 vols. (Strasbourg, 1913), and Friedrich Kluge, *Etymologisches Wörterbuch der deutschen Sprache*, ed. Walther Mitzka, 20th edn. (Berlin, 1967).

[17] Forkel, *Ueber Johann Sebastian Bachs Leben, Kunst und Kunstwerke*, 2.

[18] Forkel, *Ueber Johann Sebastian Bachs Leben, Kunst und Kunstwerke*, 2.

[19] 2 vols. (Leipzig, 1788–1801), 2:466n.

[20] S.v. "Bach, Johann Christoph."

[21] Estate catalogue, 95f.

[22] An300. See Paul Kast, *Die Bach-Handschriften der Berliner Staatsbibliothek*, Tübinger Bach-Studien, nos. 2/3 (Trossingen, 1958).

Alt-Bachisches Archiv, consisting of the following vocal works, choruses and motets by Johann Christoph Bach, organist in Eisenach until 1703, Johann Michael Bach, Johann Christoph's brother and Joh. Sebastian's father-in-law, organist in Gehren, Georg Christoph Bach, Cantor in Schweinfurt, 1689, and others; excellently crafted for sundry voices.

(Alt=Bachisches Archiv, bestehend In folgenden Singstücken, Chören und Motetten von Johann Christoph Bach, Organisten in Eisenach bis 1703, Johann Michael Bach, Joh. Christophs Bruder und Joh. Sebastians Schwiegervater, Organist im Amte Gehren, Georg Christoph Bach, Cantor in Schweinfurt, 1689, und andern; in verschiedenen Stimmen vortrefflich gearbeitet:)[23]

As in the family section in J. S. Bach's obituary, the descriptions of Johann Christoph and Johann Michael Bach are drawn from J. S. Bach's genealogy; Johann Michael is further identified as J. S. Bach's father-in-law, showing C. P. E. Bach's bias toward his mother's side of the family. The information on Georg Christoph Bach is probably from the informative title page of his vocal concerto [14] "Siehe, wie fein und lieblich," which gives his position as Cantor and the date 1689.

The description of the ABA compositions as "excellently crafted" ("vortrefflich gearbeitet") was presumably meant to bring these greatly outdated pieces to the attention of potential purchasers. Most of the music in the catalogue was still useful, such as C. P. E. Bach's compositions and the cycles of church cantatas "von verschiedenen Meistern," most of which are described in practical detail, including the extent of performing parts and lacunae in yearly cycles. Among the music "von verschiedenen Meistern" listed in the catalogue, most of the occasional pieces and material of historical interest can be traced, having been bought by collectors, especially Georg Poelchau. But there is no trace of the cycles of cantatas by Benda, Telemann, and Stölzel. One suspects that they were purchased relatively early by musicians who could make use of them. The ABA material, together with a few items by other composers, was substantially older and of much less practical value, and most of this more esoteric material was apparently sold only in 1805 with the leftovers.[24] The laudatory description of the ABA was a recommendation of the musical merit of its compositions, despite their great age compared to much of the material in the catalogue.

The ABA listing is carefully ordered. First come the attributed works: seven by Johann Christoph Bach, six by his brother Johann Michael, and one by Georg Christoph Bach. Then come anonymous compositions: one identified with initials and a date ("J. B. 1696"), one with a place and date ("Arnstadt 1686"), and finally four others, one with the date "1696". Within the sections, vocal concertos, choral arias, and motets (corresponding to the "Singstücken, Chören und Motetten" mentioned in the introductory paragraph) are freely mixed.

A comparison of the catalogue entries with the title pages, wrappers, and annotations on the ABA material shows that the catalogue listing was made from those sources. It is not known with certainty who drew up the entries in the estate catalogue,

[23] Estate catalogue, 83f.
[24] I owe this insight to Dr. Kirsten Beißwenger.

although it has been suggested that they are based on C. P. E. Bach's draft.[25] The issue is important with respect to the ABA because of the several anonymous pieces in the collection, and because of the apparently speculative nature of the attributions assigned to some of them.

The anonymous works in the ABA listing are unattributed presumably because C. P. E. Bach was uncertain about their authorship. If C. P. E. Bach was indeed the compiler of the ABA listing, though, it is strange that he did not venture a guess about the authorship of the composition attributed to "J. B." or the one signed "Arnstadt 1686," given his knowledge of family history.

Perhaps the most difficult problem concerns Johann Christoph Bach, to whom seven works are attributed. In the sources, three works are labeled only "J. C. B.," and the attribution on one work is unknown. Three of the seven can be reasonably securely attributed to the Eisenach bearer of the name, who was highly respected as a composer in the Bach family, but there were several Johann Christoph Bachs who might conceivably have composed the other works: Johann Christoph (13) (1642–1703) of Eisenach; Johann Christoph (12) (1645–93), who worked in Erfurt and Arnstadt; and Johann Christoph (22) (1671–1721, J. S. Bach's brother), to name just the most important. J. S. Bach commented about Johann Christoph Bach (13) in his genealogy "war ein profonder componist"; C. P. E. Bach added "Dies ist der große und ausdrückende Componist." C. P. E. Bach's remark is generally taken simply to support J. S. Bach's comment, but his emphasis has most likely been misunderstood. C. P. E. Bach probably meant this comment to be read "*This* is the great and impressive composer," in an attempt to distinguish the Eisenach Johann Christoph from the others. This strongly suggests that there was uncertainty within the family about the various Johann Christoph Bachs, and perhaps about the identity of the "J. C. B." listed in the ABA.

It is possible that works attributed only to "Johann Christoph Bach" or simply "J. C. B." gravitated to the Eisenach composer under the pull of his strong reputation in the family. Unfortunately, two of the three questionable pieces in the ABA are simple four-part arias that do not permit an attribution based on style. The tendency to attribute good pieces to the Eisenach Johann Christoph was also a problem in regard to [17] "Ich lasse dich nicht" BWV Anh. 159. It is also possible (if unlikely) that [1] "Es erhub sich ein Streit," attributed in two sources to Johann Michael Bach, was not Johann Christoph's either.

The listing in the estate catalogue is often cited as an authority for the attributions of ABA works, but the ascriptions there are only as good as C. P. E. Bach's information. Fully one quarter of the works are anonymous in the catalogue, and others are transmitted with attributions that are ambiguous, some perhaps speculative. It also cannot be ruled out that some of the compositions are not by Bachs at all, but are old pieces that found their way into the collection by accident at any point in its transmission.

---

[25] See Wade's preface to the estate catalogue, vii.

Later owners of the Altbachisches Archiv

C. P. E. Bach's estate catalogue was printed partly to offer copies of pieces for sale, but no early copies made from the ABA material are known. The collection is next mentioned in the catalogue of the 1805 auction at which the remaining portion of C. P. E. Bach's musical estate was offered.[26] The purchaser of the ABA, Georg Poelchau, was perhaps the most important music collector of his time, and an early champion of the music of J. S. Bach.[27] It thus comes as no surprise that he purchased the ABA, along with a great deal of other material from C. P. E. Bach's estate. The ABA and Poelchau's purchase of it attracted the attention of the lexicographer Gerber, who mentioned Poelchau's ownership in the entry for C. P. E. Bach.[28]

Poelchau eventually gave most of the ABA materials to Carl Friedrich Zelter, the director of Sing-Akademie zu Berlin, who also had a strong interest in the Bach family. Poelchau retained certain items for himself, and had copies made of several others. Like Johann Sebastian and Carl Philipp Emanuel Bach, Poelchau was particularly interested in Johann Christoph Bach, who is the composer of the three attributed works of which Poelchau kept copies. He made a copy of the twenty-two-voice [1] "Es erhub sich ein Streit," and kept the signed and dated autograph of [4] "Lieber Herr Gott, wecke uns auf." [3] "Der Gerechte, ob er gleich" may have attracted his attention because C. P. E. Bach had used it in a cantata whose original materials Poelchau had also acquired. [17] "Ich lasse dich nicht" was considered by some at the time to be J. S. Bach's composition, perhaps explaining why Poelchau kept a copy of it. These materials were eventually sold to the Royal Library in 1841 with Poelchau's collection.

Poelchau was a member and the librarian of the Sing-Akademie zu Berlin, and his collection was a source of repertory for that organization. As a result, it must have been difficult to draw a clear line between the collector's personal material and that belonging to the Sing-Akademie. (A similar problem was to arise with respect to Zelter's collection at his death.) The blurring of the distinction between the two collections may explain why performing parts from the Sing-Akademie ended up in Poelchau's collection.

At the Sing-Akademie, Zelter prepared wrappers and title pages for several works, and supplied attributions and other information, sometimes based on the listing in the estate catalogue. The ABA is listed sketchily in the catalogue of Zelter's estate, a document drawn up in the course of a legal dispute over the ownership of musical materials at the Sing-Akademie.[29] The catalogue lists nineteen works, attributed generally to Johann Michael and Johann Christoph Bach. It is likely that the twentieth (making the

---

26 *Verzeichniß von auserlesenen . . . meistens Neuen Büchern und Kostbaren Werken . . welche nebst den Musikalien aus dem Nachlaß des seel. Kapellmeisters C. P. E. Bach . . . öffentlich verkauft werden sollen.* Hamburg, [1805] (SBB Mus. Db 313). See Dok III/957.

27 See Klaus Engler, "Georg Poelchau und seine Musikaliensammlung."

28 *Neues Lexikon,* s.v. "Bach, Carl Philipp Emanuel."

29 *Catalog musikalisch – literarischer und practischer Werke aus dem Nachlasse der Königl: Professors Dr. Zelter* (SBB N. Mus.ms. theor. 30). See Friedrich Welter, "Die Musikbibliothek der Sing-Akademie zu Berlin," in *Sing-Akademie zu Berlin: Festschrift zum 175jährigen Bestehen,* ed. Werner Bollert (Berlin, 1966), 33–47. On the dispute see Georg Schünemann, *Die Singakademie zu Berlin 1791–1941* (Regensburg, 1941), 67ff.

total listed in C. P. E. Bach's estate catalogue) was [17] "Ich lasse dich nicht," which Zelter considered a work of J. S. Bach.[30] It was apparently during Zelter's ownership of the ABA that Johann Friedrich Naue used it as the basis for an edition of its nine motets. Presumably also during this time, the Sing-Akademie rehearsed and performed ABA works under Zelter's direction, documented by parts for [3] "Der Gerechte, ob er gleich" (SBB St 344) and [4] "Lieber Herr Gott" (SBB St 168).

The Sing-Akademie came into legal possession of the ABA in 1835 with the purchase of Zelter's musical estate. The collection is next mentioned in connection with the Sing-Akademie's sale of a large part of its Bach material to the Royal Library in 1854.[31] At the time, the Sing-Akademie was in serious financial trouble, and the sale produced much-needed cash. Most of the works sold were by J. S. Bach, but two ABA compositions were sold as well: a score (SBB P 4/1) of [17] "Ich lasse dich nicht," which was regarded at the Sing-Akademie as a composition of J. S. Bach; and C. P. E. Bach's score and set of parts for [1] "Es erhub sich ein Streit" (SBB P 1 and St 166), sold apparently by accident.[32] This work by Johann Christoph Bach is listed under the cantatas of Johann Ludwig Bach; William Scheide has made a convincing case that [1] "Es erhub sich ein Streit" was included to make the expected total of eighteen Johann Ludwig Bach cantatas, the original eighteenth ("Denn du wirst meine Seele" BWV 15) having been separated from the rest and attributed to J. S. Bach.[33]

Some time after this sale, the ABA material remaining in the Sing-Akademie disappeared. The sources were unknown to Philipp Spitta. When Max Schneider published his thematic catalogue of Bach family works in 1907, he apparently did not know that the Sing-Akademie owned the ABA materials. It fell to Schneider himself to rediscover them when he undertook a catalogue of the Sing-Akademie's collection.[34] The material Schneider recovered probably included original ABA materials, C. P. E. Bach's scores and parts, and more recent Sing-Akademie material. Some time during World War II, most of the Sing-Akademie's library vanished. Of the ABA, only the material sold to the Berlin Library by the Sing-Akademie and by Poelchau's estate is known to survive.

Reconstructing the Altbachisches Archiv

Despite the losses in original source material, a substantial portion of the ABA can be reconstructed. A few sources survive; the Berlin libraries hold several original manuscripts from the ABA, items that Georg Poelchau retained when he gave the collection to Zelter and several that the Sing-Akademie sold to the Library. It also turns out that

[30] The listing is summarized in Welter, "Die Musikbibliothek der Sing-Akademie," 37.
[31] Martin Tielke, "Die Erwerbung der Bach-Autographen durch die Königliche Bibliothek / Preussische Staatsbibliothek in Berlin" (thesis, Bibliothekar-Lehrinstitut des Landes Nordrhein-Westfalen, Cologne, 1980), 30; and Werner Neumann, "Welche Handschriften J. S. Bachscher Werke besaß die Berliner Singakademie?" in *Hans Albrecht in Memoriam*, ed. Wilfried Brennecke and Hans Haase (Cassel, 1962), 136–42.
[32] SBB Mus. ms. theor. Kat 427, the transmission list, includes descriptions of the material purchased by the Royal Library. Kat. 429, possibly prepared as an inventory of candidates for the sale, preserves a similar list.
[33] "Bachs Sammlung von Kantaten seines Vetters Johann Ludwig Bach."
[34] EDM 1:112.

there are photographs of many of the lost ABA sources. Max Schneider published a few reproductions of ABA sources in the two volumes of his edition, but two more sets of photographs exist as well, previously little known or entirely unknown. The first was made by the Staatliches Institut für deutsche Musikforschung, and comprises essentially complete photographs of eight items from the ABA, preserved in the SBB.[35] The other set of photographs was in the possession of Friedrich Welter, who took over Schneider's cataloging at the Sing-Akademie in 1928. Welter retained partial photographs of many ABA sources, photographs that are now also in the SBB.[36]

There are descriptions, as well, of some of the ABA sources. Schneider's edition includes critical notes and descriptions of the oldest layer of ABA sources. Unfortunately, these appear to have been heavily edited for publication, and contain irresolvable ambiguities concerning copyists. In his edition, Schneider reported only on the oldest layer of the ABA, and for the most part he did not mention later copies, including those made for C. P. E. Bach. He also omitted from the edition and did not report on four works that were already in print; as a result, less is known about them than about the others. (They are [1] "Es erhub sich ein Streit," [4] "Lieber Herr Gott, wecke uns auf," [6] "Ach, daß ich Wassers gnug hätte," and [17] "Ich lasse dich nicht.") In addition, Schneider could not locate the ABA source of one work at the Sing-Akademie ([12] "Nun hab ich überwunden"), and little is known about its source. Friedrich Welter's estate also preserves what appear to be cataloging notes for almost all of the ABA sources, which contribute occasional details. These notes are typed on the back of flyers announcing Sing-Akademie performances in the 1920s, suggesting that they were taken at the Sing-Akademie from the original sources. Welter's notes occasionally remark on the absence of watermarks. The only other hint about the watermarks on the ABA sources is a suggestion that some or all of the sources may have borne the common Arnstadt "A" with a trefoil.[37]

Table 11–1 summarizes the ABA sources for the compositions listed in C. P. E. Bach's estate catalogue. There are four layers of sources listed: original ABA sources, sources from J. S. Bach's circle, sources from C. P. E. Bach's circle, and sources from Georg Poelchau and the Sing-Akademie, layers that correspond to the successive owners of the ABA.

A survey of Bach family vocal works and their sources raises an important question. Were there once more works in the ABA than the twenty vocal compositions listed in C. P. E. Bach's estate catalogue? That is, are there additional Bach family works that were transmitted within the family, especially through J. S. Bach? There are at least two such pieces: the motets "Unsers Herzens Freude" and "Herr, nun läßest du deinen Diener," both transmitted in a convolute manuscript from the collection of

---

[35] SBB Fot Bü 41 and 42. Photographs of one composition are cited by Hans-Joachim Schulze in *Studien zur Bach-Überlieferung*, 178ff.

[36] Cited in Welter, "Die Musikbibliothek der Sing-Akademie," n. 22. These photographs were graciously made available to me by his widow, Elisabeth Welter, and have since been donated to the SBB (N. Mus. Nachl. 106).

[37] Conrad Freyse, ed., Johann Christoph Bach, *Aria Eberliniana*, Veröffentlichung der Neuen Bachgesellschaft, no. 39/2 (Leipzig, 1940).

Table 11–1 *Sources of the Altbachisches Archiv*

Composition and listing in C. P. E. Bach's estate catalogue, p. 83ff.	Original ABA sources	JSB-circle sources	CPEB-circle sources	Poelchau/Sing-Akademie circle sources
[1] Es erhub sich ein Streit etc. Ein Singstück mit 22 Stimmen, von Joh. Christoph Bach.	[Score SA] Photo Welter (p.1) Copyist: ABA–6	[Parts–perf. reported by CPEB]	Score SBB P 1 Copyist: An300 Parts SBB St 166 Copyists: An300, 4 anon	Score SBB P 2
[2] Meine Freundinn, du bist schön etc. Ein Hochzeitstück mit 12 Stimmen, von demselben.	[Parts SA] Photo EDM (B, text) Copyists: JAB, anon	Title page Copyist: JSB		
[3] Der Gerechte, ob er gleich etc. Motetto. Mit 5 Singstimmen und Fundament, von demselben.	[Score SA] Photo Welter (p.1) Copyist: prob. JCB	[Parts SA] Photo EDM (Org) Copyist: JSB	Score SBB P3 (Cantata vers. H. 818) Copyist: CPEB Parts SBB St 167 (Cantata vers. H. 818) Copyist: An304	Score SBB P 4/2 SBB P 5 Score SBB St 344
[4] Lieber Herr Gott, wecke uns etc. Motetto mit 8 Singstimmen in 2 Chören und Instrumenten, von demselben. 1672.	SBB P 4/2 Copyist: JCB [Vocal Parts SA] Photo SBB Fot Bü Copyist: JCB	[Instr. Parts SA] (Photo SBB Fot Bü) Copyists: JSB, Anon. H	[revisions to JCB/JSB parts] Copyist: CPEB	Score SBB P 5 Parts SBB St 168
[5] Mit Weinen hebt sichs etc. Für 4 Singstimmen und Fundament, von demselben. 1691.	[Score SA] Photo Welter (p.1) Copyist: ABA–1 [Parts SA] Copyist: ABA–1?			
[6] Ach, daß ich Wassers gnug etc. Für den Alt, 1 Violine, 3 Viol di Gamben und Baß, von demselben.	[SA] Copyist: ?			
[7] Es ist nun aus etc. Sterb–Arie für 4 Singstimmen, von demselben.	[Score SA] Photo Welter (p.1) Copyist: ABA–1 [Parts SA] Copyist: ABA–1?			
[8] Ich weiß, daß mein Erlöser etc. Motetto mit 5 Singstimmen und Fundament, von Joh. Michael Bach.	[Score SA] Photo Welter (p.1) Copyist: ABA–6 [Parts SA] Copyist: ?			
[9] Ach, wie sehnlich wart ich etc. Für den Discant, 5 Instrumente und Fundament, von demselben.	[Parts SA] Photo SBB Fot Bü (all); EDM (V) Copyist: ABA–2			
[10] Das Blut Jesu Christi etc. Mit 5 Stimmen, von demselben, 1699.	[Score SA] Photo Welter (p.1) Copyist: ABA–1 [Parts SA] Photo EDM (Cornetto) Copyist: ABA–1			

[11] Auf! laßt uns den Herren loben etc. Für den Alt und 4 Instrumente, von demselben.	[Parts SA] Photo SBB Fot Bü Copyist: ABA-2	[Score SA] Photo Welter Copyist: Michel
[12] Nun hab ich überwunden etc. Für 8 Singstimmen in 2 Chören, von demselben. 1679.	?	
[13] Herr, wenn ich nur dich habe etc. mit dem Choral: Jesu, du edler etc. Für 5 Singstimmen, von demselben.	[Score SA] Photo Welter (p.1) Copyist: ABA-1 [Parts SA] Copyist: ABA-1?	
[14] Siehe, wie fein und lieblich etc. Mit 2 Tenoren, 1 Baß, 1 Violine, 3 Viol di Gamben und Fundament, von Georg Christoph Bach. 1689.	[Parts SA] Photo SBB Fot Bü Copyist: ABA-3	
[15] Unser Leben ist ein Schatten etc. mit dem Choral: Ich weiß wol, daß unser Leben etc. Mit 9 Singstimmen in 2 Chören, von J. B. 1696.	[Score SA] Photo EDM (title page) Copyist: ABA-1 [Parts SA] Copyists: ?	
[16] Nun ist alles überwunden etc. Arie für 4 Singstimmen. Arnstadt 1686.	[Score SA] Copyist: ABA-4 [Parts SA] Copyist: ABA-1 [Text, SA] Copyist: ABA-7 Photo SBB Fot Bü (all)	
[17] Ich lasse dich nicht etc. Motetto von 4 Singstimmen und Fundament. [BWV Anh.159]	Score SBB P 4/1 Copyists: JSB, P. D. Kräuter	
[18] Sey nun wieder zufrieden etc. Ein Chor mit 8 Singstimmen und 4 Instrumenten.	[Parts SA] Photo SBB Fot Bü (all); EDM (Sopr. 1) Copyist: ABA-5, rev. ABA-1	
[19] Weint nicht um meinen Tod etc. Arie für 4 Singstimmen. 1699.	[Score SA] Copyist ABA-1 [Parts SA] Photo SBB Fot Bü (all) Copyist: ABA-1	
[20] Die Furcht des Herrn etc. Für 9 Singstimmen und 5 Instrumente.	[Score frag. SA] Photo SBB Fot Bü Copyist: JCB	Score SBB P 4/2 Copyist: Michel

JSB = Johann Sebastian Bach
JCB = Johann Christoph Bach (13)
JAB = Johann Ambrosius Bach
CPEB = Carl Philipp Emanuel Bach
ABA-1/7 = anonymous copyists of the ABA

Photo Welter = SBB N. Mus. Nachl. 106
Photo SBB Fot Bü = SBB Fot Bü 41 and 42
Photo WDM = Max Schneider, ed., *Altbachisches Archiv*, EDM 1/2

Georg Poelchau (SBB P 4/2). Their existence strongly suggests that Carl Philipp Emanuel's family material represents only a portion of the ABA. To the extent that the provenance of these additional ABA materials may be traced to other Bach family members, they suggest that the collection may well have been divided at J. S. Bach's death, just as his own music was.

Johann Christoph Bach's motet "Unsers Herzens Freude" is transmitted in a score in the hand of J. S. Bach and an anonymous copyist. The score was apparently made from a set of parts, and is on a paper well known from other Bach sources.[38] A second copy (SBB P 5) in the hand of Georg Poelchau was made from Bach's score, and supplies the date 1669 not found on the model. Where Poelchau got this date is unknown; perhaps there was once a wrapper. Even more important, Poelchau's copy is dated "Bückeburg 24.ix.17." If he acquired the score in Bückeburg, it is possible that it once belonged to Johann Christoph Friedrich Bach. Poelchau is known, in fact, to have acquired several manuscripts of works by J. S. Bach from Johann Christoph Friedrich's estate. Because C. P. E. and Johann Christoph Friedrich exchanged some material, it is also possible that the older son once owned "Unsers Herzens Freude" at some point.[39] In any event, the work clearly once belonged to J. S. Bach.

The second family work with a connection to J. S. Bach is the motet "Herr, nun läßest du deinen Diener in Friede fahren." This work is transmitted in a score in the early hand of J. S. Bach's youngest son Johann Christian, with the exception of the last two pages, which are in a different, anonymous hand. The watermark in the paper, a crowned monogram under a tree, is not found in other Bach sources.[40] The copy probably dates from the last years of J. S. Bach's life, and it seems likely that this motet was also from J. S. Bach's collection.[41] There are serious part-alignment errors in the last section of the work, suggesting that it was scored up from a set of parts, perhaps also once in Bach's possession.

The provenance of the score before Poelchau's ownership is unknown, so the attribution to Johann Christoph Bach in Poelchau's hand is not verifiable. There was once another attribution at the head of the score, but it was crossed out and is now illegible, except for the name "Bach." Erhard Franke has implicitly argued for the authenticity of the attribution of the motet to Johann Christoph Bach by proposing that it was written for an Eisenach funeral sermon preached on the text of this motet, the song of Simeon (German Nunc Dimittis) on 12 February 1691. But this text was one of the most common for funerals, and the date must be considered doubtful at best.

The identification of these two Bach family motets as almost certainly from J. S. Bach's library has several implications. First, it clearly suggests that the ABA was once more extensive than the twenty works listed in C. P. E. Bach's estate catalogue.

---

[38] *c.* 1746/47; Kobayashi, "Chronologie der Spätwerke," 57.

[39] See Yoshitake Kobayashi, "Zur Teilung des Bachschen Erbes," typescript (1988).

[40] Similar watermarks (*NBA* ix/1, Nachtrag 2) are found in a duplicate continuo part for BWV 129 (Leipzig Stadtarchiv) and in Bach's testimonial for Johann Christoph Altnickol of 25 May 1747 (*Dok* I/81).

[41] It is apparently later than the earliest known musical document in his hand, dated 23 October 1748 (reproduced in Hans-Joachim Schulze, "Frühe Schriftzeugnisse der beiden jüngsten Bach-Söhne," *BJ* 50 [1963/64]: 61–69), but probably dates from before his move to Berlin in the opinion of Joshua Rifkin (personal communication).

Second, these two compositions also suggest that other Bach sons may have inherited portions of the ABA (or material closely related to it), because "Unsers Herzens Freude" probably came through Johann Christoph Friedrich Bach, and "Herr, nun läßest du" possibly through Johann Christian Bach (though this is far from certain).

These two motets are relatively easy to identify as candidates for having once been part of the ABA, because they almost certainly came from J. S. Bach's library. Several other family vocal works transmitted in sources close to the Bach circle may be related to the ABA, but are more difficult to connect to J. S. Bach. Peter Wollny has recently discussed the sources for an eight-voice motet, "Merk auf, mein Herz" BWV Anh. 163, that resurfaced unexpectedly.[42] The motet, an unusual setting of seven verses of the chorale "Vom Himmel hoch," is attributed in its three sources to J. S. Bach, to "Bach in Eisenach," and to "Sigl. Bach Cugino del Sigl. Giov. Seb. Bach." Wollny has argued from stylistic evidence that the most likely composer of the composition was Johann Christoph Bach (13). The principal source is a set of parts in the hand of an anonymous copyist active at the Leipzig Thomasschule around 1750, on a paper known to have been used by J. S. Bach.[43] The Leipzig provenance of the sources for this composition and the possibility that its composer was Johann Christoph Bach have led Wollny to suggest that "Merk auf, mein Herz" was part of the ABA.

There are any number of difficulties with this hypothesis. The identity of the motet's composer is uncertain, and we should be cautious in attributing works to Johann Christoph on the basis of his reputation. The motet's connection to J. S. Bach is also uncertain, because the copyist of the parts is not known to have worked for Bach, or even in Leipzig at all during his lifetime. "Merk auf, mein Herz" would also be the only older Bach family motet to have entered the repertory of the Thomasschule; none of the other ABA compositions can be documented there. Nonetheless, the Leipzig provenance of the work in a period so close to Bach's tenure certainly makes BWV Anh. 163 a candidate for inclusion in the ABA.

Another repertory with a possible connection to the ABA is transmitted in a group of motet manuscripts from the Amalienbibliothek in which members of the Bach family figure prominently. Although no direct connection to J. S. Bach is known, the concentration of works by Bachs suggests that the manuscripts may be related to the ABA, a hypothesis first proposed by Erhard Franke.[44] The compositions in these manuscripts might have been transmitted through Wilhelm Friedemann, Johann Christian, or Berlin-based students of J. S. Bach. The three convolute manuscripts (SBB AmB 90, SBB AmB 116, and SBB AmB 326) are in the same unknown hand on apparently the same paper, and the neat regular handwriting and extremely free use of paper suggest a professional copyist.[45] Each composition is on its own fascicle in the three manuscripts,

---

[42] See the edition by Peter Wollny (Carus-Verlag, in press), to whom I am grateful for information on this work and its sources.

[43] Eda Kuhn Loeb Music Library, Harvard University, Mus. 627.273.579 Merritt Room; the paper is *NBA* ix/1, no. 73.

[44] *Johann Christoph Bach: Sämtliche Motetten* (Leipzig, 1982), 133.

[45] Designated "J. S. Bach XXV" by Eva Renate Blechschmidt, *Die Amalien-Bibliothek: Musikbibliothek der Prinzessin Anna Amalia von Preußen (1723–1787): Historische Einordnung und Katalog mit Hinweisen auf die Schreiber der Handschriften* (Berlin, 1965).

Table 11–2 *Bach family motets in three Amalienbibliothek manuscripts (SBB AmB 90, AmB 116, and AmB 326)*

Composer/text	Voices	Source
Johann Christoph Bach		
"Fürchte dich nicht"	8	AmB 116, f. 1
Johann Michael Bach		
"Fürchtet euch nicht"	8	AmB 90, f. 1
"Herr, du lässest mich erfahren"	8	AmB 116, f. 92
"Herr, ich warte auf dein Heil"	8, Bc	AmB 116, f. 98
"Dem Menschen ist gesetzt"	8, Bc	AmB 116, f. 111
"Halt, was du hast"	8	AmB 326, f. 212
Johann Ludwig Bach		
"Gott sey uns gnädig"	8, Bc	AmB 90, f. 7
"Das ist meine Freude"	8	AmB 90, f. 25
"Uns ist ein Kind gebohren"	8	AmB 90, f. 33
"Die richtig für sich gewandelt haben"	10	AmB 326, f. 94
"Ich will auf den Herren schauen"	8, Bc	AmB 326, f. 101
"Wir wißen so unser irrdisches Haus"	8	AmB 326, f. 115
"Unsere Trübsal die zeitlich und leicht ist	6	AmB 326, f. 153
"Das Blut Jesu Christi"	8	AmB 326, f. 160
"Sey nun wieder zufrieden"	8	AmB 326, f. 168
"Gedenke meiner, mein Gott"	8	AmB 326, f. 194
Johann Sebastian Bach		
"Sey Lob und Preis mit Ehren" BWV 231	4	AmB 116, f. 40
"Der Geist hilft unsrer Schwachheit auf" BWV 226	8	AmB 116, f. 64

and their gathering into three volumes is apparently largely arbitrary. The volumes contain attributed works of several composers as well as anonymous pieces, but the attributed works are dominated by compositions by Bach family members. The Bach family works in the manuscripts are listed in table 11–2.

There is no overlap between the Bach family motets in these volumes and the motets in C. P. E. Bach's portion of the ABA. In fact, all but one of the pieces in these manuscripts by Johann Michael Bach and Johann Christoph Bach are unica, as are all their motets in C. P. E. Bach's collection. The complementary relationship of the Amalienbibliothek manuscripts and C. P. E. Bach's collection suggests that the copyist of the former may have had access to a different part of the ABA than the one C. P. E. Bach inherited. The presence in the manuscripts of works by [Johann Matthäus] Schmiedeknecht (who was born and worked in and around Gotha) and by [Johann Conrad] Geisthirt (cantor in Eisenach in 1708) may point to the origin of the repertory in Thuringia; nothing is known of J. C. Gundelach, whose name also appears.[46] There may also be a more direct link to J. S. Bach suggested by the presence of two of his motets.

These manuscripts are also the only known sources of most of Johann Ludwig Bach's motets. A large proportion of his other surviving vocal music (Masses and cantatas) is transmitted in sources originating with J. S. Bach, and it worth considering

---

[46] On these composers, see their entries in New Grove, *MGG*, and Robert Eitner, *Biographisch-Bibliographisches Quellen-Lexikon*, 10 vols. (Leipzig, 1900).

whether Johann Sebastian might have had a role in the transmission of Johann Ludwig's motets as well. If so, one wonders whether J. S. Bach may have considered music by his contemporaries to be part of the ABA, including compositions he owned by Johann Ludwig and perhaps also Johann Nicolaus and Johann Bernhard.

We should not rule out the possibility that there was an instrumental component of the ABA in addition to the vocal works we know about. Perhaps, too, J. S. Bach's family genealogy and some of the Bach family portraits in C. P. E. Bach's large collection were considered part of the Altbachisches Archiv as well. Beyond the two motets by Johann Christoph Bach discussed above, it is difficult to say for certain what other compositions may once have been part of the ABA, but the Bach family's collection of its own music was most probably larger than the listing in C. P. E. Bach's estate catalogue would suggest.

CHAPTER 12

J. S. Bach and the Altbachisches Archiv

The reconstruction of the Altbachisches Archiv in the hands of J. S. Bach gives us the opportunity of reevaluating Bach's role in its assembly and the extent of his contact with it. This reconsideration shows that late in his life, Bach took a strong interest in the late seventeenth-century motet. We can also begin to explore the extent to which the repertory of the ABA may have been an influence on his own music, a matter that depends a great deal on the chronology of Bach's contact with the collection.

Who assembled the Altbachisches Archiv?

The generally accepted view, first proposed by Max Schneider, is that the ABA was assembled by Johann Ambrosius Bach, from whom it passed to his son Johann Sebastian, who expanded it and passed it in turn to his son Carl Philipp Emanuel.[1] Indeed, most of the ABA can be traced with certainty to C. P. E. Bach, and several of the sources show clearly that they were once in the possession of J. S. Bach. But even though it is appealing to imagine a Bach family collection handed down over several generations – Johann Ambrosius to Johann Sebastian to Carl Philipp Emanuel – there are several problems with this hypothesis.

First, there is very little evidence of Johann Ambrosius Bach's contact with the collection. He is the copyist of only one piece by Johann Christoph Bach, and it is even possible that the material he copied never belonged to him. Further, the concentration of copies apparently made in the late 1690s makes it unlikely that a large part of the ABA ever passed through the hands of Johann Ambrosius, who died in 1695.

Second, as Schneider himself points out, we would have to account for the collection between the death of Johann Ambrosius Bach in 1695 and its ownership by J. S. Bach, because it is hardly conceivable that the collection would have been turned over to a ten-year-old. If Johann Ambrosius Bach did assemble the Altbachisches Archiv, the collection may have followed J. S. Bach to Ohrdruf into the care of his older brother Johann Christoph (22). Unfortunately for this hypothesis, there is no evidence that the Ohrdruf Bach ever owned the collection. It is possible that the two keyboard variation sets in his hand attributed to Johann Christoph Bach document

---

[1] EDM 1:v, 111.

his contact with family music, but it is not clear which Johann Christoph Bach was the composer of these pieces, or whether these works have any connection to the Altbachisches Archiv.[2] At the least, there is no evidence that the Ohrdruf Bach owned any older family vocal material, the only kind of music we can trace to the ABA with any certainty.

A third problem with the theory that J. S. Bach inherited the Altbachisches Archiv is that there is no evidence that he had any contact with the collection before the late 1740s. It was formerly believed that the copy of "Ich lasse dich nicht" BWV Anh. 159 in Bach's early hand documented his ownership of the ABA in the early years of the century, but it is now clear that this work is not properly part of the collection. All of the surviving evidence of J. S. Bach's contact comes at the end of his life, and it is possible that he did not come into possession of it until quite late. (It is also possible, of course, that he acquired the material earlier, but made no traceable use of it until his later years.) In sum, if Johann Ambrosius Bach did assemble the collection or a substantial part of it, then it must have come to J. S. Bach along a path that cannot now be traced.

The final difficulty with the traditional view of the ABA's transmission is the assumption that the collection was continuously passed along as a unit. We know that C. P. E. Bach owned all the material listed in his estate catalogue, but there is no way to be sure that he acquired all of it from his father. Even if he did, J. S. Bach may not have received the collection all at once. It is equally possible that he acquired the material over time from various sources – that he compiled it himself.

In fact, for several reasons, it is likely that J. S. Bach was indeed the compiler of the ABA. First, he was in a position to receive material from two branches of the family – his father's, and that of Johann Michael, his father-in-law by his first marriage. We do not know what became of Johann Michael Bach's estate, but it is possible that some musical materials passed into the hands of J. S. Bach. This possibility seems all the more likely given that two of Johann Michael's daughters lived with him: his first wife Maria Barbara, and her eldest sister Friedelena Margaretha, who lived with the family until her death in Leipzig in 1729.[3] J. S. Bach is also a likely candidate for the compiler of the Altbachisches Archiv because of his strong interest in family history, documented by his preparation of a family genealogy in 1735.[4] It is easy to imagine that the assembly and organization of the ABA was related to this genealogy Bach made in his fiftieth year.

J. S. Bach is also known to have acquired and performed music by several other Bach family members (Johann Ludwig, Johann Nicolaus (27), and Johann Bernhard (18)) besides those represented in the ABA. Bach's role as teacher of several members of the younger generation may have given him access to various family materials. His students included two sons of his older brother Johann Christoph Bach (22): Johann Bernhard (41) and Johann Heinrich (43); two grandsons of Georg Christoph (10):

---

[2] "Aria Eberliniana" (Eisenach, Bachhaus, 6.2.1.05); "Aria" (Zürich, Zentralbibliothek, Ms. Q 914). See Robert Hill, "The Möller Manuscript and the Andreas Bach Book: Two Keyboard Anthologies from the Circle of the Young Johann Sebastian Bach" (Ph.D. diss., Harvard University, 1987), 114ff.

[3] See *Dok* II/45, II/162.

[4] *Dok* I/184.

Johann Elias (39) and Johann Lorenz (38); Johann Ernst (34), son of Johann Bernhard (18); and Johann Ludwig's son Samuel Anton (75). Samuel Anton came to J. S. Bach shortly after his father's death in 1731, and may have brought inherited family material with him. Johann Valentin (21) died in 1743; his son Johann Elias (39) was with J. S. Bach from 1738 to 1742, and Johann Ernst (34) was with J. S. Bach from 1737 to 1742, dates that accord with the time of J. S. Bach's documentable contact with the Altbachisches Archiv. Perhaps these relatives had some role in J. S. Bach's acquisition of the material.[5]

Even the next stage of the transmission of the ABA (from J. S. Bach to C. P. E. Bach) is not fully illuminated. We know from documentary evidence that some of the pieces listed in C. P. E. Bach's estate catalogue came from his father, and it is probably a fair assumption that the rest of the collection came from Johann Sebastian as well. But we cannot be sure, because among the surviving and reconstructed materials are sources that bear no trace of J. S. Bach's contact. This makes it impossible to say with certainty whether he once owned these materials, as likely as this may be. Perhaps only by chance, none of the ABA material in the hand of the best-represented copyist (ABA–1) shows any evidence that J. S. Bach ever owned it, nor is J. S. Bach known to have performed any music by Johann Michael Bach. We should note, though, that the wrapper for Sebastian Knüpfer's motet "Erforsche mich, Gott" known to be from Bach's library is in the hand of the apparently aged ABA–1, probably showing a point of contact between this scribe and Bach. In sum, it is conceivable that J. S. Bach never owned parts of the ABA listed in C. P. E. Bach's estate catalogue; this is improbable, though, and we would be hard pressed to say where C. P. E. Bach got the material if not from his father.

J. S. Bach's contact with the Altbachisches Archiv

It is most likely that Carl Philipp Emanuel Bach acquired all of his ABA material from his father. For some works we can only infer from circumstantial evidence that J. S. Bach was their owner but for others Bach's contact is documentable, and it is clear that it went beyond mere ownership. Table 12–1 lists the works of the ABA for which J. S. Bach's direct contact is known.

Max Schneider claimed in his edition of compositions from the ABA that the sources of two additional works contained revisions and performance markings in Bach's hand.[6] In [16] "Nun ist alles überwunden," Schneider ascribed to J. S. Bach one text correction in the score and the entire text sheet that accompanied the score and parts. The correction in the score is reflected in the set of parts, which were probably copied before J. S. Bach owned the materials, making it unlikely that he was responsible for the corrections. A photograph of the text sheet survives, and it shows clearly that Schneider's identification of Bach as the copyist was in error. There is thus no evidence of Bach's contact with this work.

[5] On all these Bachs, see Christoph Wolff et al., "Bach," *New Grove.*
[6] EDM 1:114.

Table 12–1 *Compositions from the Altbachisches Archiv showing J. S. Bach's contact*

Composition	Source (copyist)	Date
Joh. Christoph Bach, [1] "Es erhub sich ein Streit"	[Leipzig performance reported by C. P. E. Bach]	1723 or later
Joh. Christoph Bach, [2] "Meine Freundin, du bist schön"	[SA] Title page (JSB)	?
Joh. Christoph Bach, [3] "Der Gerechte, ob er gleich"	[SA] Parts (JSB)	*c.* 1743/44
Joh. Christoph Bach, [4] "Lieber Herr Gott, wecke uns auf"	[SA] Parts (JSB, Anon. H)	1748 or later
Joh. Christoph Bach, "Unsers Herzens Freude"	SBB P 4/2 Score (JSB + anon., from parts)	*c.* 1746/47
?Joh. Christoph Bach, "Herr, nun läßest du deinen Diener"	SBB P 4/2 Score (J. Christian Bach + anon.)	*c.* 1748–50

Dates of sources from Kobayashi, "Zur Chronologie der Spätwerke."

In [7] "Es ist nun aus mit meinem Leben," Schneider reported that J. S. Bach had written out the strophes of text in the parts, altered several notes in the bass voice in both the score and parts, and added three trills to the soprano. The only purported Bach entries in the one partial photograph of the score are two trills in the soprano. These do not resemble Bach's trills, and in any event are too small a sample from which to identify Bach's hand. Schneider's identification of Bach's entries in the parts cannot be verified, and in light of his incorrect identification of Bach's hand in [16] "Nun ist alles überwunden," his claim that Bach edited the parts of [7] "Es ist nun aus" must be considered dubious. (There is one possible point of contact between J. S. Bach and one of these arias that has gone unnoticed: the text of [7] "Es ist nun aus," first published in 1673,[7] was also set or arranged by J. S. Bach in the so-called Schemelli Gesangbuch [Leipzig, 1735; no. 847, BWV 457]. Bach apparently did not draw on the older aria for his version.)

For other works in the ABA, our knowledge of Bach's contact is on firmer ground. In 1775, Carl Philipp Emanuel Bach wrote to Johann Nikolaus Forkel, sending him several items from the ABA including a "twenty-two-voice work" that is clearly identifiable as Johann Christoph Bach's [1] "Es erhub sich ein Streit," the first item in the ABA listing in the estate catalogue. C. P. E. Bach wrote that his father had performed the work in church in Leipzig, but this performance cannot be dated.[8] It must have taken place after 1723, when Bach moved to Leipzig, but it is not clear whether it was before or after C. P. E. Bach's departure from that city in 1734. Carl Philipp

---

[7] Magnus Daniel Omeis, *Der Geistlichen Erquickstunden . . . H. Doct. Heinrich Müllers . . . Poetischer Andacht-Klang* (Nuremberg, 1673); see Albert Fischer and W. Tümpel, *Das deutsche evangelische Kirchenlied des 17. Jahrhunderts*, 6 vols. (Gütersloh, 1904–16), 5:149.

[8] See *Dok* III/807 and chapter 11.

Emanuel wrote expressly that the performance took place in a church, and given the work's text – a description of the battle between St. Michael and the dragon – it seems most likely that Bach used it on St. Michael's Day. The old-fashioned, purely biblical libretto of "Es erhub sich ein Streit" might not have been appropriate on its own in the modern Leipzig liturgy; perhaps Bach used it as part of a pastiche.

Bach's performing materials have not survived, and there is no suggestion from the listing in C. P. E. Bach's estate catalogue or anywhere else that a set of parts accompanied the ABA score. J. S. Bach's parts (either original parts or new ones of his own making) may well have become separated from the score at the division of his estate. That C. P. E. Bach went to the trouble of having new parts written out suggests that he did not own the old set, but it is possible that he wished to make a new set because of the archaic notation of the old (he did have a new score copied in reduced note values) and possibly its decrepit condition.

J. S. Bach also made a new wrapper for another vocal concerto from the ABA, Johann Christoph Bach's [2] "Meine Freundin, du bist schön." It is not possible to say whether he performed the work, but the existence of a nearly complete set of parts would have made this possible without there being a documentary trace.

It is striking that besides his performance of "Es erhub sich ein Streit" and his making a wrapper for "Meine Freundin, du bist schön," all of J. S. Bach's other documented contact with the ABA involves motets. This contact took place in the last years of his life, and the composer of all of the works we know he dealt with – concertos as well as motets – is Johann Christoph Bach (13). J. S. Bach's concentration on this composer is a reflection, or perhaps a source, of the high regard in which he was held in the family.[9] His focus on motets probably reflects both practical considerations and his musical interest in the genre.

The existence of newly-made parts for [3] "Der Gerechte, ob er gleich" and [4] "Lieber Herr Gott, wecke uns auf" shows clearly that Bach performed these motets. J. S. Bach's performing material for "Der Gerechte, ob er gleich" (figure 12–1) comprises five vocal parts and an organ part with his own figures, dating from *c.* 1743–46.[10] Bach's organ part is in the same key as the vocal parts (F), showing that the performance took place at *Chorton* pitch, with voices and organ notated in the same key. This was not his usual Leipzig practice, which was to perform at the lower *Cammerton* pitch with a transposed organ part. (Bach also performed Palestrina's *Missa sine nomine* this way; his vocal parts, cornetto/trombone parts, and organ part are notated in D minor *Chorton*, violone and cembalo in E minor *Cammerton*.)[11] Bach retained the large note values of the original in his parts for "Der Gerechte, ob er gleich," as he did in other old motets and in many of his own motet-like compositions.

Bach's instrumental parts for [4] "Lieber Herr Gott, wecke uns auf" (1748 or after, figure 12–2)[12] document one or more performances under his direction. Once again,

[9] See *Dok* I/184 and III/666.
[10] Kobayashi, "Chronologie der Spätwerke," 53.
[11] SBB Mus. ms. 16714. See Karl Gustav Fellerer, "J. S. Bachs Bearbeitung der Missa sine nomine von Palestrina," *BJ* 24 (1927): 123–32, and Wolff, *Der Stile antico*, 20, 161.
[12] Kobayashi, "Chronologie der Spätwerke," 62.

Figure 12–1 Continuo part in the hand of J. S. Bach for Johann Christoph Bach, "Der Gerechte, ob er gleich" (Sing-Akademie zu Berlin, lost; photograph EDM 1)

the parts show a pitch disposition atypical of Bach's Leipzig practice. The vocal parts and organ part for this motet (Johann Christoph's originals) are notated in E minor *Chorton*, the *colla parte* woodwinds and strings (J. S. Bach's) in G minor *tief Cammerton*. The use of mixed pitches in Bach's performing material for this work was probably prompted by considerations of vocal and instrumental range. The low tessitura of the vocal parts (SI descends to c'; AI and AII to f; TI to B; TII to C; BI and BII to E') required a relatively high performing pitch. Bach thus performed the work in E minor *Chorton* using the original vocal parts and new *Cammerton* instrumental parts. This had the additional advantage of moving the vocal lines, which often descend below the range of the normal doubling instruments, closer to the range of those instruments. Bach presumably chose *tief Cammerton* (a minor third below *Chorton*) to avoid having winds and strings play in the relatively awkward key of F minor, as they would have had to in "normal" *Cammerton* (a major second below *Chorton*). It is not clear why Bach had a new organ part copied out; the old one, which served as the copyist's model for the new part, was presumably usable.

Figure 12–2 Oboe 1 part in the hands of J. S. Bach and Anon. H for Johann Christoph Bach, "Lieber Herr Gott, wecke uns auf" (Sing-Akademie zu Berlin, lost; photograph SBB Fot Bü)

In *c.* 1746/47, J. S. Bach participated in the copying of "Unsers Herzens Freude" from a set of parts (see figure 12–3). (The lost model is betrayed by an alignment error made by the unidentified copyist and corrected by Bach.) The model was old, as demonstrated by the archaic use of accidentals. Bach modernized them, but the other scribe retained old forms; some of these were later corrected, perhaps by Bach. He used a small stroke in place of a barline in one passage, as he did in other works in large note values, declining to break up notes and phrases with barlines. The score also contains an unfigured continuo line that was probably part of the model. Bach's access to both parts and a newly-made score suggests that he performed this work as well. Just as he used an old set of parts for his performance of [4] "Lieber Herr Gott, wecke uns auf," he may have done the same with "Unsers Herzens Freude."

Johann Christian Bach's copy of "Herr nun läßest du deinen Diener" (figure 12–4) was copied late in J. S. Bach's life, and was almost certainly made for his father; it is difficult to imagine that the young Johann Christian would have had any other reason to copy an antiquated motet. The exact material from which the score was made is

184

Figure 12–3 Score in the hands of J. S. Bach and an anonymous copyist of Johann Christoph Bach, "Unsers Herzens Freude hat ein Ende" (SBB P 4/2), f. 1

unknown, and whether J. S. Bach performed the work is an open question, but he apparently owned the parts necessary for a performance of it, just as he did for "Unsers Herzens Freude." At the least, this was a work of interest to him, and one consistent with his apparent stylistic preference among the older works.

An assessment of J. S. Bach's contact with the repertory of the ABA must start with a reevaluation of the date at which he is thought to have come into possession of the collection. We cannot be sure when he acquired the material – possibly over a period of time – but the available evidence points to his involvement with the ABA later than has generally been believed. Some of Bach's performances of works from the ABA (e.g., of [1] "Es erhub sich ein Streit") cannot be dated exactly, but the evidence for other contact and presumed performances points to the last decade of Bach's life, perhaps even just the last five years.

There is no evidence, in fact, that the ABA was in J. S. Bach's possession before the late 1740s. The one suggestion to the contrary might be in the genealogy Bach compiled in 1735, which gives the birthdate of Georg Christoph Bach. This date is specified on the title page of [14] "Siehe, wie fein und lieblich," so one might argue that J. S. Bach owned at least that work, if not more of the ABA, by 1735. But it should be noted that the birth dates in the genealogy, (including Georg Christoph Bach's) are concentrated in J. S. Bach's immediate family and may have come from some older family document and not from the ABA sources. It is also possible that J. S. Bach acquired [14] "Siehe, wie fein und lieblich" before 1735, but other compositions only later. Bach did not necessarily rely on the ABA materials for his genealogy, and so need not have acquired them early.

In the light of the date and nature of Bach's documented contact with the ABA, some widely-held assumptions need to be reconsidered. For example, the specific repertory of the ABA is often cited as an influence on the development of Bach's own vocal style. This view needs to be approached with caution given the strong suggestions that he may not have come in contact with the ABA until well after he had composed the bulk of his vocal music. The ABA is probably best regarded as representative of the kind of repertory with which Bach grew up, but not necessarily as a direct source of inspiration in his younger years.

This point is illustrated by the example of [1] "Es erhub sich ein Streit," which has been cited as an influence on J. S. Bach's own cantatas for St. Michael's Day, "Herr Gott, dich loben alle wir" BWV 130, "Es erhub sich ein Streit" BWV 19, and "Man singet mit Freuden vom Sieg" BWV 149.[13] The available evidence does not permit us to say with any authority that the older composition influenced Bach's cantatas for the day. The martial style used both in Johann Christoph Bach's cantata and in J. S. Bach's compositions for St. Michael's Day was, if not a convention, then an almost inevitable consequence of the biblical texts for the feast, and so does not necessarily show direct influence. Further, William Scheide has demonstrated that the fragment "Nun ist das Heil und die Kraft" BWV 50, whose eight-voice disposition has been interpreted as a

---

[13] See Geiringer, *The Bach Family*, 57f.

Figure 12–4 Score in the hands of Johann Christian Bach and an anonymous copyist of ?Johann Christoph Bach, "Herr, nun läßest du deinen Diener" (SBB P 4/2), f. 1

response to "Es erhub sich ein Streit," does not reflect Bach's original scoring[14] – if the work is Bach's at all. It is thus extremely difficult to argue that the polychoral ABA work served as a model for it or for any other St. Michael's Day cantata by J. S. Bach. Other proposed influences of ABA works are at least as dubious; the suggestion that [2] "Meine Freundin, du bist schön" influenced a similarly-texted movement from the St. Matthew Passion BWV 244/30 is difficult to fathom.[15] The numerous writers who cite "Ich lasse dich nicht" BWV Anh. 159 as an influence on J. S. Bach's later motets were, of course, more right than they knew.

The preponderance of motets, both single- and double-choir compositions, among the works from the ABA that J. S. Bach performed is particularly significant. The material amply documents Bach's interest in motet style, especially in the last years of his life, an interest clearly coordinated with his cultivation of the related *stile antico*. (See chapter 13 on Bach's performances of a motet by Sebastian Knüpfer during the same period.) This interest in German motet style in Bach's late years is less markedly observable in his compositions than is his cultivation of the *stile antico*. This is partly because motet style had been a continuous part of Bach's compositional palette all through his career, and so the use of motet style was nothing new in his music. Nonetheless, motets and motet-like movements figure prominently in Bach's works dating from 1735 and after (including the motet-like "Et incarnatus est" from the Mass in B minor BWV 232 from 1749), perhaps reflecting his heightened interest in the style.

In J. S. Bach's hands, the ABA sources were both archival and practical. The collecting and organizing of family music represents the kind of project that clearly interested him most in his older age, but Bach was not content simply to study and preserve these pieces. He put them to practical use, honoring their historical significance to his family in living performances, performances concentrated in the venerable but still vital genre of the motet.

---

[14] "'Nun ist das Heil und die Kraft' BWV 50."

[15] Hans Grüß, "Johann Christoph Bachs Hochzeitsstück 'Meine Freundin, du bist schön' aus dem Altbachischen Archiv," in *Johann Sebastian Bachs Traditionsraum*, ed. Reinhard Szeskus, Bach-Studien, no. 9 (Leipzig, 1986), 78–83.

CHAPTER 13

Sebastian Knüpfer, "Erforsche mich, Gott"

The catalogue of Carl Philipp Emanuel Bach's estate contains the following entry in the section headed "Von verschiedenen Meistern": "Motetto: Erforsche mich, Gott &c von Sebastian Knüpfer. Partitur und Stimmen."[1] The material referred to, previously unidentified, is from J. S. Bach's music library. It is preserved in the SBB, and consists of a score with annotations in Bach's hand and a set of autograph vocal and instrumental parts. The parts, contemporary with the documents showing Bach's contact with the Altbachisches Archiv, further establish his interest in and performance of seventeenth-century motets late in his life, and add to our knowledge of his motet performance practice.

Sources

"Erforsche mich, Gott" is transmitted in a score, SBB Mus. ms. autogr. Knüpfer, S. 1. (See figure 13–1.) Its title page, perhaps once part of a wrapper, reads "Motetta. / Erforsche mich Gott. / à/8 / C.A.T.B. 1. Chori. / C.A.T.B. 2. Chori. / [in a different ink and hand:] di Seb: Knüpfer." On the first page of music is the following heading: "Sebastiani Knüpfers, in Obitum Johannæ Laurentiæ Lipsiensis Consulis Uxoris. Est Text[us] Con[solationis?]." The manuscript consists of twelve pages, approximately 19.5 x 16.5 cm. There is only a fragment of a watermark visible.[2]

The motet is also transmitted in a set of parts, SBB Mus. ms. 11788. (See figure 13–2.) The parts comprise nineteen single leaves, each *c.* 17 x 21 cm., in the hand of J. S. Bach. All are headed Motetto.

Canto 1 Chori	[=]	*Violino 1*
Alto 1 Chori	[=]	*Violino 2*
Tenore 1 Chori	[=]	*Viola*
Basso 1 Chori	[=]	*Violoncello*

---

[1] p. 88.

[2] The title page and first page of music are reproduced in facsimile, and a transcription of the motet printed in *Threnodiae Sacrae: Beerdigungskompositionen aus gedruckten Leichenpredigten des 16. und 17. Jahrhunderts*, ed. Wolfgang Reich (Wiesbaden, 1975), EDM 79. Reich's edition is a conflation of this score and the early printed version (see below); the set of parts was not taken into consideration.

Canto 2 Chori	[=]	*Hautbois 1*
Alto 2 Chori	[=]	*Hautbois 2*/verso: *Trombona 1* [*Chorton*]
Tenore 2 Chori	[=]	*Taille*/verso: *Trombona 2* [*Chorton*]
Basso 2 Chori	[=]	*Bassono*/verso: *Trombona 3* [*Chorton*]

Violone

Cembalo [figured; probably not completely autograph; second, unidentified hand on the verso]

Organo [figured; *Chorton*]

The Cembalo part bears a watermark with the upper half of the letters "HR," identical to NBA ix/1 no. 59. The others contain a watermark not found in any other Bach source: a swan with the monogram JCH as a countermark. The versi of

Figure 13–1 Score in an unknown hand, with annotations by J. S. Bach, of Sebastian Knüpfer, "Erforsche mich, Gott" (SBB Mus. ms. autogr. Knüpfer, S. 1), f. 1

Figure 13–2 Alto I part in the hand of J. S. Bach for Sebastian Knüpfer, "Erforsche mich, Gott" (SBB Mus. ms. 11788)

the vocal parts are ruled but unused. Additionally, the set includes two duplicate violin parts in the hand of C. P. E. Bach's copyist Michel.

The score was originally part of SBB P 4/2, a convolute manuscript from Georg Poelchau's collection; a penciled note on the title page, in fact, reads "war in P 4." The score was removed and recatalogued early in the twentieth century, and has proved elusive; Ortrun Landmann listed it as "augenblicklich vermißt" in 1960 and George Buelow as "?lost" in 1980.[3]

All of the descriptions of the score as an autograph appear to be based on Poelchau's assertions in P 4/2 and in the catalogue of his manuscript collection.[4] The score apparently dates from the seventeenth century and is catalogued as an autograph, but is almost certainly not in Knüpfer's hand. It does not match what is known of the composer's handwriting, although that is little enough. The manuscripts described by Ortrun Landmann as autographs are in several different hands, none identical with that in "Erforsche mich Gott,"[5] and yet a different hand appears in SBB Mus. ms. 11780 (no. 13, "Der Herr ist König"), described by the Berlin RISM catalogue (in progress) as an autograph solely on the basis of the dates of composition at the end of the score.

3   Ortrun Landmann, "Das Werk Sebastian Knüpfers im Überblick" (Diplomarbeit, Leipzig, 1960); George Buelow, *New Grove*, s.v. "Knüpfer, Sebastian." But cf. Kast, *Die Bach-Handschriften der Berliner Staatsbibliothek*, 3.
4   SBB Mus. ms. theor. Kat 41.
5   "Das Werk Sebastian Knüpfers im Überblick," 4f.

None of these manuscripts is in the same hand as two letters of Knüpfer's, one in Latin, and one in German.[6]

The supposed autograph score of "Erforsche mich, Gott" also contains gross copying errors that could hardly have been made by the composer; they are certainly not evidence of compositional activity, as has been claimed.[7] The origin of the errors is easy to find. The score was apparently made from a copy of the original print of the work (see below), which was laid out in choirbook format. The unknown copyist eliminated a repeat of the final section while copying, but in the process miscopied the bass I and bass II parts. The errors were corrected in the score, partly by a hand that may be that of the original copyist, and partly by J. S. Bach, who also completed the text, and prepared for the copying of parts by counting long rests and writing their lengths in the score. Because most of the corrections are written on irregular, hand-drawn staff lines, identification is difficult, but the corrections in the bass II part on the last page are most probably Bach's. It is also possible that a few other revisions in the score, principally the strengthening of cadences by raising leading tones, are in Bach's hand. (Curiously, an entry on the SBB catalogue card, dating from before World War II, correctly identifies the corrections in Bach's hand.)

Arnold Schering speculated that the words "di Seb: Knüpfer" on the title page of this score were in J. S. Bach's hand, but this appears not to be correct.[8] The title page for the motet is, in fact, in the hand of the principal scribe of the Altbachisches Archiv,[9] suggesting that the score was transmitted in close connection with that collection, and perhaps that the score of "Erforsche mich, Gott" came from outside of Leipzig. On the other hand, the inscription on the first page is in a hand appearing in several documents related to Johann Kuhnau, Bach's Leipzig predecessor: a manuscript copy of Kuhnau's *Fundamenta compositionis* (SBB Mus. ms. autogr. theor. Kuhnau, J.), and the inscription at the top of a score of Kuhnau's Magnificat,[10] possibly implying that the score was from the Thomasschule. The score of "Erforsche mich, Gott" does not appear in any known inventory of the school's library, though.[11]

Landmann has discussed the set of parts for the motet in connection with Knüpfer, but they were apparently unknown to Schering, and are not mentioned by Reich. Bach's handwriting in them is clearly late, and by Yoshitake Kobayashi's criteria dates from *c.* 1746/47.[12] The watermark on the Cembalo part is found in Bach sources that have been dated between *c.* 1743 and 1747, including Bach's copy of Johann Christoph Bach's "Unsers Herzens Freude" from the ABA. The other paper in the parts, unique in Bach sources, is from the Zwickau mill of Johann Christian Hermann, who was

[6] The Latin letter is reproduced in Arnold Schering, *Musikgeschichte Leipzigs*, vol. ii (Leipzig, 1926), following p. 48; the German letter is Leipzig, Stadtarchiv, Act. Schul zu St. Thomas, Stift VIII B 2 C.

[7] EDM 79: 136.

[8] DDT 58/59, xviii and xx.

[9] ABA–1; see chapter 11.

[10] SBB Mus. ms. autogr. Kuhnau, J. 2; first page reproduced in *Johann Kuhnau: Magnificat*, ed. Evangeline Rimbach, Recent Researches in the Music of the Baroque Era, no. 34 (Madison, 1980), xi.

[11] On the Thomasschule library see Arnold Schering, "Die alte Chorbibliothek der Thomasschule in Leipzig," *Archiv für Musikwissenschaft* 1 (1918–19): 275–88; Knüpfer's own works are only summarized there, but are listed in detail in DDT 58/59, xixff.

[12] Kobayashi, "Chronologie der Spätwerke," 57.

active starting in 1742.[13] J. S. Bach used another Zwickau paper made by Johann Gottlieb Hermann; the relationship between the two Hermanns is not known.[14]

The score and set of parts passed from Johann Sebastian to C. P. E. Bach, whose performance of the motet is documented by the existence of duplicate violin parts in the hand of Michel, one of his principal Hamburg copyists. The material was acquired from C. P. E. Bach's estate by Georg Poelchau, and is listed in the catalogue of his collection (SBB Mus. ms. theor. Kat. 41, f. 90). Poelchau's catalogue also lists a second copy of the motet score, "in neuer Abschrift" (now part of SBB Mus. ms. autogr. Romberg, A. 2). This score is in the hand of one of Poelchau's copyists, and bears a note in Poelchau's hand to the effect that it was made from the "original" score in his possession. From Poelchau, the material for the motet passed to the Berlin Library.

The motet and J. S. Bach's contact

"Erforsche mich, Gott" is a motet in archaic style for two four-voice choirs by Sebastian Knüpfer (1633–76), who was Thomascantor from 1657 until his death; the text is Psalm 139:23–24: "Erforsche mich, Gott, und erfahre mein Herz; prüfe mich, und erfahre, wie ichs meine. Und siehe, ob ich auf bösem Wege bin. Leite mich auf ewigem Wege." ("Search me, O God, and know my heart: try me, and know my thoughts: And see if there be any wicked way in me, and lead me in the way everlasting.") (See example 13–1.) The motet was performed at the funeral of Johanna Lorentz von Adlershelm, wife of the mayor of Leipzig, who died on 28 April 1673, and was printed in 1674 in conjunction with her funeral sermon.[15]

Bach's performing material comprises parts for eight voices, three continuo instruments, and *colla parte* strings, woodwinds, and brass. Bach retained two archaic notational features of the motet in his parts: he kept the Dorian signature of G minor notated with only one flat, introducing E♭ by accidental; he also retained the *allabreve* notation of the score, with half-notes as the principal syllable carriers, often using a small stroke in place of a barline. (Cf. Bach's use of this notation in his performing materials for Johann Christoph Bach's [4] "Lieber Herr Gott" and [3] "Der Gerechte, ob er gleich," and other works.[16]) Bach made only one substantive change in the motet, rewriting one imitative subject to eliminate an exposed cambiata figure. This correction is not found in the score from which he copied; he must have made the change as he wrote out the parts.

Bach doubled Choir I with *colla parte* strings and Choir II with woodwinds, the same disposition as in the original parts for "Der Geist hilft unser Schwachheit auf"

---

[13] See Kobayashi, "Chronologie der Spätwerke." A similar but not identical paper is found in the autograph score of a Sanctus by J. L. Krebs, SBB Mus. ms. 30196. I am grateful to Dr. Kobayashi for identifying the watermark.

[14] *NBA* ix/1, no. 22.

[15] *Der . . . Frauen Johannen / Gebohrnen Beckerin von Rosenfeld / Des . . . Herrn Christian Lorentz von Adlershelm . . . Hertzgetreuen Ehe-Liebsten / Selbst beliebt und erwehlter Leichen-Text . . . in die Music gebracht / und bey derer . . . Leichen-Begängnüß / am 14. May. des 1673 Jahres . . . abgesungen von SEBASTIANO Knüpffern / Asch. Varisc. der Music zu Leipzig Directore, und der Schuel ad D. Thomae Cantore* [Leipzig: Christian Michael, 1674].

[16] See also Wolff, *Der stile antico*, 41f.

Example 13–1 Sebastian Knüpfer, "Erforsche mich, Gott," mm. 1–23

BWV 226 and in his parts for Johann Christoph Bach's motet [4] "Lieber Herr Gott, wecke uns auf." Bach also allowed for the woodwinds doubling the second choir to be replaced with trombones, whose *Chorton* parts (notated a whole step lower) are written on the versi of three of the woodwind parts. The *Chorton* brass parts could not date from very much later than those for the woodwinds, because Bach's hand is essentially the same in both. There is no brass part doubling the soprano voice; perhaps a cornettist supported it, reading from the oboe I part. That this would have presented no problem to Bach's cornetto players is suggested by the existence of *Cammerton* cornetto parts in G clef for the cantatas BWV 25, 101, and 133.[17] It is possible but unlikely that there was a lost cornetto part to replace oboe I; Bach would presumably have written out a replacement part on the verso of oboe I, just as he did with the others. He may alternatively have used a mixed ensemble to support the second choir (oboe and three trombones), although such a practice by Bach is not otherwise documented.

There are complex additions and erasures to the labels on the woodwind and brass parts that make it difficult to reconstruct the multiple versions exactly. Bach added the words "ô Trombona 1" and "ô Trombona 2," respectively, to the headings on the parts for Hautbois 2 and Taille; these additions were later erased. The *Chorton* side of the Bassono/Trombona 3 part first read "Bassono," then "Bassono ô Trombona 3," and then simply "Trombona 3." (The *Cammerton* side reads simply "Bassono.") These confusing and inconsistent markings could mean several things. Most likely, Bach originally intended the labels on the parts to refer to the entire sheets containing the woodwind and (added) brass parts, but later relabeled each side separately. Bach may also have asked his trombone players to transpose at sight from *Cammerton* parts, but later wrote out new *Chorton* parts because they had had difficulty. It is also possible but unlikely that the erased labels meant what they said: that Bach intended trombones to play at pitch from *Chorton* parts, or bassoon from a *Chorton* part. This would imply a previously undocumented retuning of the strings, or a *Chorton* bassoon, also unknown in Leipzig; from all other evidence, Bach's bassoons in Leipzig were invariably at *Cammerton* pitch.[18] A retuning of the strings up a whole step (which would be necessary if trombones were to play from *Cammerton* parts) has been only speculatively proposed for the second version of "O Jesu Christ, mein Lebens Licht" BWV 118.[19] And although retunings to *tief Cammerton* pitch are known, there is no evidence suggesting any retunings a half-step below that, which would be necessary if a *Chorton* part were played on a *Cammerton* bassoon.

Bach's three continuo parts (violone, harpsichord, and organ) make up a basso seguente part, following the lowest-sounding voice. Knüpfer's early print of the motet also contains a figured bass part, but Bach did not use it, if he knew the print at all. Bach's continuo part is an active participant in the polyphony, whereas Knüpfer often simplified rhythmic activity and eliminated repeated, passing and ornamental notes. Bach also made the continuo part reflect good voice leading and dissonance treatment by occasionally introducing a second voice to allow proper resolution of dissonances. These added voices in the Cembalo and Organo parts may also have served as conducting aids, showing difficult vocal entrances.

The existence of both organ and harpsichord parts could conceivably suggest that the motet was performed with dual accompaniment. Because the harpsichord part is on different paper from the rest of the parts, and because it was prepared from the

---

[17] See MacCracken, "Die Verwendung der Blechblasinstrumente," 80.
[18] See Dreyfus, *Bach's Continuo Group,* chapter 4.
[19] See MacCracken, "Die Verwendung der Blechblasinstrumente," 77f.

Figure 13–3 Plaque bearing the text "Erforsche mich, Gott" in the Nikolaikirche, Leipzig

Chorton organ part (as demonstrated by a few peculiarities of notation), it is more likely to have been a later addition for a performance with harpsichord in place of the organ. This strengthens the suggestion of multiple performances implied by the replacement brass parts.

The late date of Bach's performances of "Erforsche mich, Gott" places the composition alongside the ABA motets in documenting Bach's interest in seventeenth-century motet repertoire. It may be significant that the title page of the score Bach used is in the hand of ABA–1, the principal ABA copyist. If this score did originate outside of Leipzig (which this copyist's presence would seem to suggest), it is possible that Bach did not acquire it until relatively late in his life, perhaps along with the ABA. As with the ABA material, he was not content merely to study the work; he went to the trouble of copying an extensive set of parts to put this bit of Leipzig's musical history to practical use.

Bach's parts strongly suggest that he performed Knüpfer's motet more than once, but it is not clear on what occasions. The funeral of a von Adlershelm family member is a possibility – that is, a connection with the original dedicatee of the motet – but no such occasion is known. Bach did have a distant connection with the family: as Thomascantor, he was one of the beneficiaries of a fund endowed in 1688 by von Adlershelm's husband that paid for meals at the Thomasschule and for the yearly singing of chorales in the Nikolaikirche. (There are receipts for payments to Bach from 1723 to 1750.[20]) Bach had to provide music for numerous funerals, at which he presumably also performed certain of his own motets and those of his ancestors. It is clear from Bach's letter to Georg Erdmann that he depended on income from such events,[21] but there is little documentation of this aspect of his Leipzig duties. These occasions represent a more important part of Bach's job than has been suspected, and they gave him the opportunity of performing a repertoire different from the one he cultivated in his other work.

Bach must have been aware, from the inscription on the score and from Knüpfer's authorship, that "Erforsche mich, Gott" represented a piece of Leipzig's musical history. In addition, in the south chapel of the Leipzig Nikolaikirche there is an enormous epitaph bearing the Psalm text "Erforsche mich, Gott." (See figure 13–3.) In more than twenty-five years of performing in the church, Bach can hardly have missed seeing it; perhaps he also noticed that the plaque had been donated in 1672 by Johanna Lorentz von Adlershelm. It should come as no surprise that the identifiable music Bach performed in the exercise of his duties includes motets of a predecessor in Leipzig and of Bach family members. These composers represent Bach's musical patrimony, and for him this was a heritage to be honored not just in study, but also in performance.

[20] *Dok* II/155; see Schulze, "Marginalien zu einigen Bach-Dokumenten."
[21] *Dok* I/23, 28 October 1730.

Appendix: Original texts of motet definitions cited in this study (chronological order)

Daniel Speer, *Grundrichtiger Unterricht der musikalischen Kunst* (2nd edn. Ulm, 1697), p. 285.

p. 285   Motteti, ein fein Chor-Stuck / ohne certiren der Stimmen.

Sebastien de Brossard, Dictionaire de Musique (2nd edn. Paris, 1703), pp. 55–56.

p. 55   MOTETTO. au plur. Motetti. D'autres écrivent Motteto, d'autres, Moteto, &c. en Latin, Motettus, ou Mottetus, Motectum, Moteta, Canticum, Modulus, &c. en François, MOTET. C'est une composition de Musique, fort figurée, & enrichie de tout ce qu'il y a de plus fin dans l'art de la composition, à 1. 2. 3. 4. 5. 6. 7. 8. & plus encore de Voix ou de Parties, souvent avec des Instrumens, mais ordinairement, & presque toûjours, du moins avec une Basse-Continuë, &c. Et cela sur une Periode fort courte, d'où luy vient selon quelques-uns le nom de Motet, comme si ce n'étoit qu'un Mot. Quand la Compositeur prend la liberté d'y employer tout ce qui luy vient dans l'esprit, sans y apliquer aucune parole, ou s'assujettir à en exprimer le sens & la passion, les Italiens l'apellent pour lors Fantasia, & Ricercata, & les François Fantaisie, Recherche, &c. On étend plus loin apresent la signification de ce

p. 56   terme à | touts les pieces qui sont faites sur des Paroles Latines sur quelques sujet que ce soit, comme sont les loüanges des Saints, les Elévations, &c. On fait même des Pseaumes entiers en forme de Motet, &c.

Martin Heinrich Fuhrmann, *Musicalischer-Trichter* (Berlin, 1706), pp. 82–83.

p. 82   Motetto seu Muteta, ist eine Kirchen-Harmonie von 4. Stimmen starck / (bißweilen sind mehr vorhanden) ohne Instrumenten nach dem Hammer-schmiedischen Fuß gesetzet / darin die Stimmen gar nicht / oder wenig fugiren und concertiren. Ich sage / eine gute Muteta soll nur von 4. Stimmen starck seyn / denn diese fallen am besten ins Gehör und können auch wol verstanden werden / sonderlich / wenn solche aus wolbekandten Texten bestehen. Wenn aber dieselbe von 6. 8. 10. und mehr Stimmen starck (dergleichen der itztgedachte Hammerschmied zwar auch geschmiedet; aber wenig approbatores heute darin findet) so disgoustieren sie wegen der überhäufften Tertien, als welche man nicht gerne gedoppelt sehet / [(]wo nicht

p. 83 in transitu & motu contrario, weil | solche einem zarten Gehör eine gelinde dissonantz) Quinten, Sexten, Octaven und Unisonorum, und können / insonderheit wenn der Text den Zuhörern unbekannt / von denselben nicht wol verstanden werden. Ich halte also viel von einer 4. auffs höchste 5stimmigen Muteta, so aus 2. Discanten / 1. Alt und 1. Tenor und 1. Bass bestehet; Aber wo 2. Tenor-Stimmen darin vorhanden / so wünsch ich schon weit davon zu seyn / ratio, der andere Tenor incommodiret durchgehends den Bass in seinem Horizont; Nemlich der Bass vagiret mehr in den 4fußigen als in den 8fußigen Clavibus, in diesen aber hausiret der zweite Tenor und also muß eine Stimme der andern nothwendig in ihren Sphæra die Circulos turbiren / so aber nicht leicht geschehen solte; daher kan man auch in einer solchen Muteta den Bass und 2ten Tenor von ferne schwerlich von einander unterscheiden / so seltzam gehet alles durch einander / &c.

Johann Mattheson, *Das neu-eröffnete Orchestre* (Hamburg, 1713), pp. 141–42.

[Von der Composition unterschiedenen Arten und Sorten]

p. 141 Den Choralen folgen mit recht die Motetti, welche meines wenigen erachtens / mit mehrer raison à motu, als motto und mutare, deren eines ein Wort / das andere / verändern heist / führen / ich will indessen die jenigen sich über den Nahmen der Etymologie dieses Wortes den Kopf zerbrechen lassen / die mehr Zeit dazu haben / und grösser Plaisir daran finden. Es sind aber diese so genannten Motetti gemeiniglich lateinische Kirchen-Stücke / die vormahls

p. 142 bloß aus Singstimmen | bestunden / und aus lauter Fugen zusammen gesetzet waren; nunmehro aber dehnet man die Bedeutung dieses Wortes weiter aus / und macht Motetti, so wol mit Instrumental- als Vocal-Chören. Weil sie aber nicht gern ein Solo leiden / sondern in **steter Bewegung** eine Fuge nach der andern anfangen / und durch alle Stimmen reine ausführen / auch billig keine / oder doch nur einen gar geringen Absatz oder generalen Einhalt haben solten / so muss bey dieser Gelegenheit ein wenig mehr von den Fugen / was dieselben nemlich / und wie vielerley sie sind / auch wie sie ohngefehr müssen gemacht werden / Meldung geschehen.

Johann Heinrich Buttstedt, *Ut, mi, sol, re, fa, la* (Erfurt, 1716), pp. 62–63, 86.

[Von den unterschiedenen harmonischen Arten und Sorten]

p. 62 Der Stylus Motecticus ist Majestätisch / prächtig / wird also genennet weil
p. 63 sein Modus oder Tonus durch Vermischung ande | rer Sonen also künstlich verdeckt wird / daß man ihn nur am Ende erkennen kan.

[Von der Composition unterschiedenen Arten und Sorten]

p. 86   Die Bedeutung des Worts Motetti dehnet man heut zu tage freylich weiter aus / daß also die Motetten so jetzo componiret werden / mehr Concerten als Motetten zu nennen sind: Was aber Stylus Motecticus sey / und warum er so genennet werde / habe oben fol. 61. & 62. aus dem Kirchero angeführet.

Johann Mattheson, *Das beschützte Orchestre* (Hamburg, 1717), pp. 116, 119–20, 133.

[De Stylis Musicis]

p. 116   Stilo Motectico, ist ein bunter Styl / der alle Veränderungen und allen Zierrath der Kunst annimmt / einfolglich geschickt ist verschiedene Affecten auszudrücken / vor allen aber Verwunderung / Bestürtzung / Schmertzen u.s.w. siehe Mottetto.

    . . .

p. 119   Besagter Extract [Athanasius Kircher, *Musurgia Universalis*, German
p. 120   translation] beschreibet den Stylum Motecticum, daß er sey / Majestä⎟tisch / prächtig / &c. ist wohl alle gut / das beste aber vergessen / nemlich: Summa varietate floridus, nulla subjecto adstrictus, das heist: **Er ist voller bunter Veränderungen und an keinem Themate gebunden.** Mich deucht / diese Eigenschaften müssen nothwendig beschrieben werden / sonst möchte man fragen: Wo bleibt das Essentiel und was zu wissen höchst nöthig ist? Brossard hat solches sehr wohl beobachtet.

[Erklärung. Zum Kirchen-Styl gehören]

    . . .

p. 133   (2.) Motecticus, vel Muteticus Stylus, welcher die Fugen / allabreven, doppelte Contrapuncten, und andere unzehlige künstliche Sachen in Kirchen-Musiken begreifft. In so fern denn auch die Canones als fuge in conseguenza paßiren können / gehörte der Stylus Canonicus mit hieher.

Friedrich Erhard Niedt, *Musicalische Handleitung Dritter Theil* (Hamburg, 1717), pp. 34–37.

p. 34   *III. Capitel.*

                                  von

                    Moteten oder Muteten.

1. Die Explication über die Moteten überlasse ich denen Thüringischen Bauren / als welche solche von dem Hammerschmid Zeit ihres Lebens (gleichwie die Altenburgische Bauren-Mägde ihre Stiefeln / und die Spanier ihre kurtze Mäntel von ihren Vorfahren angeerbet) behalten werden.

2. Es ist sonst eine Art Moteten / so im Kirchen-Styl gebräuchlich / wo ein Vers aus einem Choral oder Kirchen-Lied mit eingeführet wird / welchen

ordinairement der Discant singet; die andere Stimmen / als Alt, Tenor, und Bass, führen dazwischen figuraliter ein Dictum oder Spruch aus der Bibel / als folgender Text zeigen wird: |

p. 35

Choral.

Wenn du die Todten wirst am jenem Tag erwecken /
So thu auch deine Hand zu meinem Grab ausstrecken /
Laß hören deine Stimm / und meinen Lieb weck auf /
Und führ ihn schön verklärt zum auserwehlten Hauf.

Text. 1 Cor. XV. 52. 53.

Es wird die Posaune schallen / und die Todten werden auferstehen unverweßlich / und wir werden verwandelt werden: Denn diß verweßliche muß anzeihen das unverweßliche / und diß Sterbliche muß anzeihen die Unsterblichkeit.

3. Wolte man mich nicht vor einen Musicalischen Pietisten halten, könte ich mehr dergleichen hersetzen / und zeigen / auf welche Art ich sie zu componiren pflege / weil aber der Raum solches mit Noten zu thun / nicht leidet / verspare ich es für dieses mahl / und will indessen die Liebhaber an die von andern klugen Componisten verfertigte Moteten gewiesen haben. Wo Gott will / so werden bald 2. von meinen Musicalischen Geburten das Licht sehen / nehmlich:

1. Das bey des sel. Hn. Gen. Lieutenant Trampens Beerdigung gehaltene Helden-Drama, und
2. Das jüngste Gericht in einem Sing-Gedichte.

In beyden diesen Stücken wird man verschiedene Choral-Gesänge mit Muteten eingeführet finden / woraus man schon die Arten / wie solche zu setzen sind / wird erlernen können.

4. Das meiste / was ich dabey nöthig halte zu observiren / ist / daß der Biblische Text mit dem Choral einerley Sinn führe / und gleichen Innhalt und Verstand exprimere; denn sonsten würde es eben so lächerlich heraus kommen / als jenes Dorff-Cantors in Sachsen Invention, auf die Kirchweyhe / oder / wie es beym gemeinen Mann heisst / Kirmeß / gerichtet; deren Text ward / wie gebührlich / aus Lucæ.XIX.9. von der Cantzel erkläret / und fügte gedachter Cantor solchen mit folgendem Choral zusammen: |

p. 36

Text. Luc. XIX.9.

Heute ist diesem Hause Heil wiederfahren / sintemahl er auch Abrahams Sohn ist.

Choral

Sie lehren eitel falsche List /
Was Menschen-Witz erfindet /
Ihr Hertz nicht eines Sinnes ist /
In Gottes Wort gegründet /
Der wehlet diß / der andre das /

201

Sie trennen uns ohn alle Maß /
Und gleissen schön von aussen.

Das reimte sich nun / wie Speck zur Märte / oder als eine Faust aufs
Auge.

5. Noch lächerlicher war folgendes / welches ein Schulmeister in Thüringen seines
Hn. Pfarrers Jungfer Tochter zu Ehren componiret / diese hatte der liebe Gott
(ihrem Vorgeben nach unwissend) mit Liebes-Frucht gesegnet; weßwegen sie /
wie denn gebräuchlich ist / öffentliche Kirchen-Busse thun solte; da denn der
Gesang: Erbarm dich mein O Herre GOtt &c. wenn die Predigt geschlossen /
und das liebe Töchtergen vor den Altar kniend ihren Text anhören soll / vorhero
gesungen wird. Nun gab der Herr Pfarrer / dem Schulmeister / welcher sich
gantz feste einbildete / der galanteste Componiste zu seyn / den Anschlag / er
solte das Lied: Erbarm dich mein O Herre GOtt &c. als eine Motete musiciren /
so würde seiner lieben Tochter der Schimpff nicht so groß sein. Der Anschlag
war gut! Der Schulmeister wehlete sich / seine Motete ansehnlich zu machen /
zu gedachtem Choral folgenden Text:

Text aus dem 128. Psalm.

p. 37

Wohl dem / der den HErrn fürchtet / und auf seinen Wegen gehet: du
wirst dich nähren deiner Hände Arbeit / wohl dir / du hast es gut. Dein
Weib wird seyn / | wie ein fruchtbarer Weinstock um dein Haus
herum; deine Kinder / wie die Oel-Zweige um deinen Tisch her &c.

Choral

Erbarm dich mein / O HErre GOtt /
Nach deiner grossen Barmhertzigkeit /
Wasch ab / mach rein mein Missethat /
Ich erkenne meine Sünd / und sind mir leid /u.s.f. den gantzen Vers durch.

Wie tröstlich solche Motete wird geklungen haben / kan auch
ein halb-kluger leichte sehen.

**Heinrich Bokemeyer, *Der melodische Vorhof*, with commentary by Johann
Mattheson, *Critica Musica*, 2 vols. (Hamburg, 1722–25), vol. ii, pp. 295–96, 301–2,
322–23.**

[Von dem Texte]

p. 295 [Bokemeyer] Der Text, worunter man die Worte verstehet, so gesungen
werden, ist das edelste und vornehmste Stück einer guten Music, es mögen
nun Biblische Sprüche, b) Psalmen, oder Geist- und Weltliche Gedichte seyn.

p. 296 [Mattheson] b) Biblische Sprüche, zumal in Teutscher Uebersetzung, sind
zur Music am allerunbequemsten, außer den vollen Chören, Fugen und
Recitativ. Die Psalmen aber, man nehme sie in welcher Uebersetzung man
wolle, haben und behalten allemal was poetisches, als ohne welchem keine
gute, bewegliche Melodie bestehen kan. Zur Noth setzet man sich auch

wohl auf einen harten, unförmlichen Stein nieder; aber auf einen bequemen Stuhl sitzet sichs doch besser. Das ist meine unmaßgebliche Meynung. In solchen Verstande mag der Text gern ein Sitz der Vocal-Melodie seyn.

. . .

p. 301 Ein solcher musicalischer Text ist entweder ligatus oder prosaicus, eine Poesie, oder gebundene Rede. Ein poetischer Text schickt sich besser zur Music, als ein prosaischer. Ratio: Es ist ein justes metrum (Sylben-Maß) und folglich ein geschickter rhythmus darin; da hergegen in prosa die verschiedene pedes sich nicht allezeit wohl zusammen fügen lassen. t) Wiewohl unter den prosaichen sich ein Text besser zu Music schickt, als der andre. Im

p. 302 Teutschen | lassen sich die meisten Biblischen Sprüche gut singen: u) denn die pedes sind so vermischet, daß sie einen angenehmen rhythmum geben: wenn nur einige Sylben etwas länger gesungen werden, und sonst ein verständiger darüber kömmt. Doch weil die particulae connectendi offt die repetion hindern, so schicket sich alles viel besser, wenn geistreiche Poeten die dicta in Verse bringen, und die bey einem musicalischen Texte bedungene requisita beobachten.

> t) Das ist wahr, und klüglich geschrieben, daß sich eine gebundene Rede beßer, als eine ungebundene, zum Music schickt. Donius, dessen Worte p. 40 huj. Tomi angeführt sind, sagt, daß eine prosaische Music die beste grace verliehret, in so weit selbige vom Text herrühret. Ich habe an verschiedenen Orten eben dasselbe, und noch ein mehrers, behauptet. Die ratio aber steckt nicht allein im Metro, sondern vornehmlich im Styl.

> u) Im Teutschen lassen sich die Biblische Sprüche lange so gut nicht singen, als in Lateinischen, und doch wolte auch obgedachter Donius diese letzten nicht einmal bey der Music wißen. Die Teutschen dicta schicken sich, meines wenigen Erachtens, zu sonst nichts, als zum vollen Chor, zu Fugen, zur Moteten-Art und zum Recitativ. Auch bey diesem findet einer manchesmal seine Noth, wenn er nicht die Sylben, wieder ihren Accent, zu lang oder zu kurtz setzen will. Ich habe es offt versucht, und allemal sehr verwirrte rhythmos, fast nie aber einen angenehmen gefunden. Z. E. Und die Kriegs-Knechte flochten eine krone &c. Von dem an trachtet Pilatus, wie er ihn loßliesse. &c. die Hohenpriester antworteten &c. Es ist hier nicht die Frage, was ein verständiger und versuchter Componist daraus machen kann; sondern obs sich, natürlicher Weise, gut singen lasse, und einen angenehmen rhythmum gebe? Daran sollte ich sehr zweiffeln.

. . .

p. 322 Und hierin stecket auch der Grund zu urtheilen, wo eine Fuge im Text anzubringen, oder nicht denn solche schicken sich nicht überall. Wo die Rede von vielen Personen ist, da schicken sich solche ohne Zweiffel am besten. E. g. Ps. II. 3. Lasset uns zureissen ihre Bande, und von uns werffen ihre Seile. Ps. XXXIV. 4. Preiset mit mir den Herrn, und lasset uns mit einander seinen Namen erhöhen. In General-Sätzen gehen sie auch an. E. g.

Alles was ihr wollet, das euch die Leute thun sollen, das thut ihr ihnen. Ps. CIII. 15. Ein Mensch ist in seinem Leben wie Graß, er blühet, wie eine Blume auff dem Felde. Sonderlich aber in solchen periodis, die ein Lob in sich fassen. E. g. Ps. XIX. 2. Die Himmel erzehlen die Ehre Gottes, und die Veste verkündigen seiner Hände Werk. Ps. XXXIII. 1. Freuet euch des Herrn ihr Gerechten, die Frommen sollen ihn schön preisen. Auch in solchen periodis, die aus zwey contrairen Sätzen bestehen. E. g. Ps. XX. 9. Sie sind niedergestürzt und gefallen; wir aber stehen aufgerichtet. Ps.

p. 323 XXXIV. 11. Die Reichen müssen darben und hungern; | aber die den Herrn suchen, haben keinen Mangel. (Dieser Punct muß noch besser untersucht werden, weil zuweilen wiedrige Affecten zusammen kommen, wie hier im letzten Exempel. i)

[Mattheson's other notes omitted]

i) Um Vergebung! Es kommen keine wiedrige Affecten zusammen in den Worten: Die Reichen müssen darben und hungern; aber die den HErrn suchen, haben keinen Mangel. Es ist eine blosse Betrachtung der Freundlichkeit Gottes, und eine Vergnügung über seiner Gerechtigkeit, daß er die Reichen hungern, und es den Gottesfürchtigen an nichts fehlen, läßt. Diese antitheses geben gute Doppel-Fugen ab, weil sie, ob gleich mit verschiedenen Ausdrückungen, doch zu einerley Ende, concurriren. In der Affecten-lehre muß also vorher eine viel grössere Insicht erhalten werden, wenn man hievon gesund urtheilen will.

Johann Gottfried Walther, *Musicalisches Lexicon* (Leipzig, 1732), pp. 424–25, 584–85.

p. 424 Motetto, plur. Motetti [ital.] Motet, plur. Motets [gall.] Andere schreiben: Motteto; noch andere Moteto; Lateinisch: Motettus oder Mottetus, Motetus, Motectum, Moteta, &c. ist eigentlich eine mit Fugen und Imitationibus starck ausgeschmückte, und über einen Biblischen Spruch bloß zum Singen ohne Instrumente (den General-Bass ausgenommen) verfertigte musicalische Composition; doch können die Sing-Stimmen auch mit allerhand Instrumenten besetzt und verstärckt werden. Ja die Ausländer extendiren nunmehro die Bedeutung dieses termini: Motetto, auch auf eine solche geistliche Composition, deren Text lateinisch, aus Arien und Recitativ bestehet, und worzu noch verschiedene Instrumente, mit à parten Melodien abwechselnd, gesetzt sind; wie, unter andern, aus des Gio. Batt. Allegri erstem Wercke zu ersehen. Anlangend die Etymologie dieses termini; so deriviren ihn einige vom

p. 425 lateinischen Wort: motus, weil dergleichen Composition | in steter Bewegung ist, und immer (wie bereits gesagt worden) eine Fuge und imitation nach der andern anfängen, durch alle Stimmen ausführen, und anbringen soll; andere von mutare, verändern; und noch andere, vom Italiänischen motto, und Frantzösischen Mot, so ein Wort, item etliche Worte, Zeilen, oder einen Spruch bedeuten, und vom alten lateinischen Worte Muttum, welches gleichfalls ein Wort geheissen, herkommen. Denn, bey dem Festo bedeutet mutire so viel, als loqui, reden; und bey dem Lucilio findet man: Non audet dicere multum, er getrauet sich nicht ein Wort zu sagen oder zu muchsen. s Ménage Dictionaire Etymologique, unter dem Articul: Mot. Und hiervon mag wohl die oben gemeldte verschiedene Schreib-Art entstanden seyn. conf. Prætorii Synt. Mus. T. 3. p. 6. woselbst, über berührte derivationes und Schreib-Arten, noch einige andere, und wie insonderheit die Wörter Motetta und Motecta von den Auctoribus bald als Foeminina, bald as Neutra, Motetta in Neutro plurali, und Muteta in foeminino gebraucht worden, zu lesen stehen. Sonsten handelt die Histoire de la Musique, Tome 4. im ersten Articul des 1sten Stücks gewisse Regeln ab, wornach von der Güte eines Motet zu judiciren sey.

. . .

p. 584   stilo Motetctico, lat. stylus Motecticus, oder Muteticus ist ein bunter Styl, der alle Veränderungen und allen Zierrath der Kunst annimmt, einfolglich geschickt ist, verschiedene Affecten, vor allen aber Verwunderung,

p. 585   Bestürtzung, Schmer|tzen, u.s.w. auszudrucken. Er begreifft die Fugen, allabreven, doppelte Contrapuncte, und Canones oder Fugen in Consequenza, und demnach den Stylum canonicum in sich.

**Johann Adolph Scheibe, *Compendium Musices* (manuscript, *c.* 1726–36),
transcribed in Peter Benary, *Die deutsche Kompositionslehre des 18. Jahrhunderts*, p. 79.
Original p. 27.**

[de Stylo]

p. 27   [Motetten] werden aber bald mit bald ohne Instrumente gesetzt; sind Instrumente dabey, so stehen solche meistentheils mit denen Singe Stimmen in Ripieno. In die Motetten aber pflegt man nichts anders als Fugen und Contrapuncte zumachen, und solche gravitaetisch niemahls aber allzu lustig einzurichten, Solo schicken sich par hinein, da zumahl sehr selten Instrumente dabey sind, und die Abwechselung bestehet am meisten darinnen, daß bald 2. 3. oder 4 Stimmen mit einander singen.

Kurtzgefaßtes Musicalisches Lexicon **(Chemnitz, 1737; 2nd edn. 1749), p. 240.**

p. 240   Moteta, ist eine prächtige Kirchen-Harmonie von vier auch wohl mehr Stimmen starck, ohne und auch mit Instrumenten, darinne die Stimmen gar nicht, oder doch wenig fugiren und concertiren. Ein anderer spricht: Moteten-Art gehet meistens gravitätisch, mit vielen Sing-Stimmen, bißweilen auch mit Instrumenten zugleich oder Umwechselungs-weise durch Chöre, oder aber einfach zusammen.

Johann Mattheson, *Der vollkommene Capellmeister* (Hamburg, 1739), pp. 74–75.

[Von der musicalischen Schreib-Art]

p. 74 §39. Wollen wir nun weiter gehen und betrachten, was der Moteten-Styl für Eigenschafften habe, so darff man nur Hammerschmidts, und seines gleichen, Wercke zu Hand nehmen. Ich will dieses aber gar nicht spöttisch gesagt, vielweniger damit zu verstehen gegeben haben, als ob etwa nicht viel schönes, absonderlich in Ansehung der Vollstimmigkeit, in mancher Motete von diesem ehmahls berühmten Mann, vom Orlando Lasso und andern, enthalten, auch kan ich nicht leugnen, daß noch bis itzo vieles daraus zu lernen sey. Man mag billig von ihnen sagen: sie haben Musicam gelernet und geistliche Lieder gedichtet; sie sind alle zu ihren Zeiten löblich gewesen, und bey ihrem Leben gerühmt, und haben ehrliche Nahmen hinder sich gelassen. |

p. 75 §40. "Was die Ehre Gottes betrifft, hat Hammerschmidt darin mehr gethan, als tausend Operisten nicht gethan haben, noch hinfüro thun werden. Er ist auch, welches das höchste Stück seines unsterblichen Ruhms, derjenige, welcher die Music fast in allen Dorff-Kirchen (der Lausitz, des Thüringer, Sachsen-Landes und daherum) bis auf den heutigen Tag erhalten. Dieser Punct soll ihm billig, als ein unverwelckliches Lorber-Blat, in den Krantz seines immergrünenden Nachruhms eingeflochten★ werden."

§41. Allein die itzigen Zeiten lassen dergleichen Schreib-Arten, in ihrem ehmaligen Zusammenhänge, nicht mehr zu. Es litte sowol der Wort-Verstand, d.i. der Sinn des Textes, als auch die rechte, natürliche Führung einer angenehmen Melodie, bey diesem Moteten-Styl gar zu sehr. Sonst läßt er viel buntes, verbrämtes, mit Fugen, Allabreven, Contrapuncten u.s.w. durchwircktes künstliches Wesen zu, dabey iedoch nur wenig Worte zum Grunde geleget werden: so daß er auch daher vermuthlich den Nahmen bekommen hat, nehmlich von dem welchen Motto, so ein Wort★★ bedeutet; nicht aber, wie Kircher mit schlechter Urtheils-Krafft lehret, vom bedecken, motecticus a tegendo, weil er mit lauter Künsten bedeckt ist. Andrer ungereimter Herleitungen zu geschweigen.

§42. Daß dem Moteten-Styl aber canonische deswegen unterworffen seyn sollte, weil auch bisweilen Canones in den Moteten vorkommen, solches folget gar nicht: in dem sowol in Kammer- als Theatralischen Sachen ebenfalls dergleichen Kunst-Stücke, ja mehr als in Kirchen-Stücken angebracht werden, ohne daß sich sonst das geringste Motetenmässige dabey meldet.

§43. Obgedachter [Marco] Scacchi sagt in dem angeführten Manuscript: es müsten die Sätze in diesem Styl mit solcher Geschicklichkeit verfertiget werden, daß sie weder der Schaubühne, noch der Kammer zu nahe kämen, sondern gleichsam die Mittel-Strasse hielten: ingleichen daß man bey den Italiänern seiner Zeiten die Moteten-Art in den Oratorien zu gebrauchen

★   Sind Worte aus Joh. Beerens musical. Discursen, im 22. Capitel.
★★ C'est une composition sur une Periode fort courte, d'ù lui vient selon quelques uns le nom de Motet, comme si ce n'etoit qu'un mot. Brossard.

pflegte. Unsre heutige Oratorien aber haben keine Spur davon. Die Verwunderung, den Schmertz und andre Gemüths-Bewegungen hat der Moteten-Styl ausdrücken sollen; und er ist doch, wegen Abganges einer edlen Einfalt und nothwendigen Deutlichkeit, gewißlich am allerunbequemsten dazu.

§44. Fugen sind gerne zu leiden und wol zu hören; aber ein gantzes Werck von lauter Fugen hat keinen Nachdruck, sondern ist eckelhafft; und aus solchen Fugen, oder Fugenmäßigen Sätzen bestunden die ehmaligen Moteten, ohne Instrumente, ohne General Baß; wiewol man in den jüngern Zeiten nicht nur den General-Baß zugelassen, sondern auch eben dasjenige, was die Stimmen singen, durch allerhand Instrumente verstärcket, und mit zu spielen für gut erachtet hat. Doch machen hiebey die Spielende keine Note mehr, anders, oder weniger, als die Sänger, welches ein wesentlicher Umstand der Moteten ist.

Johann Adolph Scheibe, Critischer Musikus (2nd edn. Leipzig, 1745), pp. 177–85.

p. 177 Ich muß noch etwas bey der andern Abtheilung der Kirchenmusik stehen bleiben; ich muß auch von den Motetten reden; denn diese Stücke finden noch hin und wieder ihre Liebhaber, und ihre Annehmlichkeit und Pracht wird noch nicht den Beyfall der vernünftigen und aufmerksamen Zuhörer verlieren.

Ludewig Viadana, ein Italiener, der Erfinder des Generalbasses, war ein großer Feind der Motetten. Er verwarf sie ganz und gar, und brachte hingegen eine andere Art musikalischer Stücke auf; diese nannte man Concerten. Denn, da vorher in den Motetten alles zu bunt durch einander gieng, und man dabey keine Beschaffenheit der Worte in Acht nahm, die Abtheilungen der Rede versteckte, daß folglich die Deutlichkeit nirgends zu finden war, so führte er eine neue Einrichtung ein, und suchte diese Fehler durch ein regelmäßiges Verfahren zu verbessern. Diese geschah im Anfange des vorigen Jahrhunderts.

Diese Verbesserung der Motetten legte aber den eigentlichen Grund zu der ordentlichen Einrichtung der Missen, die ich im vorigen Stücke beschrieben habe, und man hat sie nach und nach in einen fast unverbesserlichen Stand gesetzt, wenn wir nur einige Fehler, an welchen die Gewohnheit Schuld ist, ausnehmen. |

p. 178 Die Motetten haben hingegen an dieser Aenderung sehr wenig Theil genommen. Die Aufdeckung der Fehler half nur so viel, daß man ein wenig behutsamer ward, und sie auch nicht so häufig, als vorher, gebrauchte, imgleichen auch mit den Instrumenten anders verfuhr, indem man sie fast gänzlich davon absonderte. Zur Ersetzung dieses Mangels aber erschien nunmehro der Generalbaß, wiewohl man diesen endlich auch wieder wegließ, und die Motetten nur allein von Singestimmen verfertigte. Hammerschmied, der größte Meister in der Kunst, Motetten zu machen, war insonderheit in der Mitten des vorigen Jahrhunderts berühmt. Er brachte, nebst noch einigen andern, die zu selbiger Zeit lebten, die Motetten wieder in großes Ansehen. Sie zierten sie mit vielen und mancherley Canonen aus, und machten sie endlich so wichtig, daß sie in Deutschland fast in allen Kirchen und Schulen ausdrücklich eingeführet wurden.

Allein, diese Bemühung gab auch den Motetten fast eine ganz veränderte Gestalt. Man warf sie in der Ausarbeitung und auch in ihren äußerlichen Ansehen um; und man machte sie nunmehro weit ordentlicher, deutlicher und angenehmer, daß also eine Motette, nach dieser Einrichtung, wenn sie mit unsern itzigen Auszierungen, und mit unserer Setzart verbunden wird, nicht wenig gefallen muß, zumal, wenn alle darzu gehörige Regeln wohl beobachtet sind. Diese Regeln wollen wir anitzo etwas ausführlicher betrachten.

Zu einer guten Motette gehöret erstlich eine kluge Wahl der Worte, und dann eine scharfsinnige, deutliche und vollstimmige Ausarbeitung. Wir wollen beydes untersuchen.

Die Worte sind insgemein ein Spruch, oder mehrere aus der heiligen Schrift; hierzu kömmt noch, doch nur bey gewissen Gelegenheiten, ein Vers, oder zweene, aus einem geistreichen Liede, oder Lobgesange. Bey der Wahl der Worte hat man vornehmlich auf den Gebrauch der Motetten zu sehen, ob sie nämlich bey Begräbnissen, bey Hochzeiten, bey Geburtstagen, oder auch den Sonntagen und Festtagen gebrauchet werden sollen. Ferner *p. 179* muß man auch solche Worte | auslesen, die sich von sich selbst zu Chören und vielstimmigen Sätzen schicken. Sie müssen auch so beschaffen seyn, daß man sie ohne Zwang in zweene, drey, oder vier Sätze abtheilen kann; denn so lang soll eigentlich eine Motette seyn. Die Einrückung gewisser Verse aus Liedern, oder Lobgesängen giebt den Worten sehr oft einen sonderlichen Nachdruck. Sie müssen aber mit den Worten überaus wohl übereinstimmen, und keinen widersinnigen und lächerlichen Ausdruck, oder Auslegung erwecken, wie man dergleichen Exempel sehr oft findet. Die Andacht und Erläuterung der Worte müssen allein die Endzwecke seyn, worauf man in der Wahl der Verse sehen soll; weil sie in jene eingerücket, und mit ihnen zugleich abgesungen werden. Diese Einrichtung aber ist nicht allemal nothwendig; denn man machet auch Motetten, in welche man keine Gesänge einmischet; man machet auch so gar welche, worzu man nur allein Verse aus geistreichen Liedern, oder Lobgesängen, nimmt, und also gar keine biblische Sprüche. Diese letztere Art aber ist nicht so gebräuchlich, als die erstere. Man machet auch Motetten in lateinischer Sprache. Hierzu nimmt man allemal einen biblischen Spruch, oder auch eine oder zwo Strophen aus den Lobgesängen der alten Heiligen. Und dergleichen Motetten sind auch annoch in einigen Klöstern der römischen Kirchen gebräuchlich. Im übrigen aber ist ihre musikalische Ausführung mit den übrigen Motetten von einerley Beschaffenheit.

Daß man auch weltliche Motetten verfertiget, mögen ihre Verfasser verantworten. Mich deucht, man sollte diese Art musikalischer Stücke nur zu geistlichen Verrichtungen und zur Aufmunterung zur Andacht und Erbauung anwenden. Andere Absichten werden diese ernsthaften und geistreichen Stücke nur unordentlich, verdächtig und verächtlich machen; ja sie werden auch den ganzen Charakter derselben verändern und verwirren. Eine geistliche Motette, wenn sie in ihrer völligen Stärke genommen wird, verursachet eine außerordentliche Fröhlichkeit des Herzens; sie machet uns *p. 180* munter und | doch beachtsam; sie erhebet das Gemüthe zur Betrachtung; und indem sie uns zugleich mit einer angenehmen Wollust überschüttet, so empfinden wir mit Entzücken, wie süße es sey, die Früchte der wahren Religion zu schmecken[1]. Wer wollte sich nun wohl erkühnen, so herrliche Lobgesänge, die eine so heilige Wirkung haben, unziemlicher Weise zu entheiligen?

Ich habe nunmehr von der Wahl der Worte geredet, zugleich aber den Hauptcharakter und die Absichten der Motette bemerket, die also auch der Componist zum Grunde seiner Arbeit legen muß. Ich muß aber nun auch von der Composition selbst weitläuftiger handeln. Hierbey hat man auf die Einrichtung, auf den Ausdruck der Worte und auf die Ausarbeitung zu sehen.

Was nun erstlich die Einrichtung betrifft, so wird folgendes zu merken sein. Im Anfange der Motette stehet allemal ein deutlicher und prächtiger Satz, in welchem vornehmlich mehr eine vernünftige Nachahmung, als eine vollkommene Fuge, herrschet. Hierauf folgt eine starke Fuge, wobey aber dennoch die Deutlichkeit beobachtet seyn muß. Bey dem Eintritte des Hauptsatzes derselben soll schon in einer andern Stimme der Gegensatz erscheinen; weil sonst | der einstimmige Gesang, zumal wenn keine *p. 181* Instrumente dabey sind, zu leer und zu einfach klingt, und das Ohr keinesweges befriediget. Nach dieser Fuge folget abermal ein völliger und deutlicher Satz, worinnen auch nur die Nachahmung statt findet; wiewohl man diesen letzten Satz noch mit einer zierlichen Fuge verbinden kann. Ist die Motette länger, so kann man in die Mitten derselben auch wohl einen zweystimmigen, oder dreystimmiten Satz einrücken; ein einstimmiger Satz aber thut gar keine Dienste, weil er wegen Mangel gehöriger Begleitung, in dieser Art musikalischer Stücke gar nicht statt findet. Wenn auch der Generalbaß darzu gespielet, und noch eine völlige Instrumentalbegleitung

---

[1] Ich finde im 405 Stücke des englischen Zuschauers eine unvergleichliche Stelle, welche die Hoheit der Kirchenmusik in ihr rechtes Licht setzet. Sie steht im fünften Theile der deutschen Uebersetzung, auf der 47sten S. Ich will sie meinen Lesern ganz hersetzen: "Die Leidenschaften, heißt es, welche durch die ordentlichen Compositionen erregt werden, rühren durchgängig von solchen albernen und eitlen Gelegenheiten her, daß sich ein Mensch schämen muß, wenn er ernstlich darüber nachdenket. Allein die Furcht, die Liebe, der Kummer, der Unwille, welcher in dem Herzen durch Lobgesänge und geistliche Lieder erwecket wird, machen das Herz besser; und rühren von solchen Ursachen her, welche insgesammt vernünftig und preiswürdig sind. Vergnügen und Schuldigkeit gehen neben einander, und je größer unser Vergnügen ist, desto grösser ist unsere Religion."

darzu gesetzet würde: so widerspricht ein einstimmiger Satz dennoch der Motette, wie wir solches hernach aus der Beschaffenheit der Instrumentalbegleitung sehen werden.

Bey der Einrichtung hat man ferner zu merken, daß man die Motetten mit einem Chore von vier, fünf, oder sechs Singestimmen, und auch mit zween Chören, und also von acht und mehr Singestimmen, und endlich wohl gar mit drey Chören zu setzen pflegt. Die zweychörichten Motetten sind die besten, weil sie dem Ohre am meisten Genüge thun. Sind Verse aus Liedern dabey, so läßt man den einen Chor damit, doch zu gewisser Zeit, eintreten, der zweyte Chor aber muß den Hauptspruch der Motette ungehindert fortsingen. Hierbey kann auch ein Wechsel statt finden, daß man also den Choral bald diesem, bald jenem Chore giebt. Ist aber die Motette nur von einem Chore, so muß der Choral mit einer oder zwo Stimmen gesungen werden, die übrigen aber müssen ihre Hauptsätze ordentlich und ungehindert durcharbeiten.

Weil man auch die Motetten bald mit, bald ohne Instrumente setzet: so sind dahero noch folgende Anmerkungen zu machen. Der Generalbaß sollte swar allezeit dabey seyn; allein, man kann ihn selten gebrauchen, weil die meisten Motetten nur von einem Chore Sänger aufgeführet werden, es müßten denn andere Instrumente mehr dabey seyn, oder man | müßte sie bey gewissen Gelegenheiten in der Kirche aufführen. Es muß sich aber der Generalbaß eigentlich nach dem tiefsten Singebaß richten, bloß daß er, wenn in diesem Pausen vorkommen, der untersten Stimme, die inzwischen klinget, und so nach allen Veränderungen, folget. Da auch die Harmonie sehr rein seyn muß, so wird ein vorsichtger Componist die Ziefern gehörig darüber setzen. Die übrigen Instrumente gehen nun ordentlich mit den Singestimmen, und zwar um nicht hervorzuragen, sondern diese nur deutlich zu machen. Wollte man sie besonders darzu einrichten, so würde man schon die Schreibart verändern, und in die ordentlichen Kirchenconcerten, oder Missen verfallen. Hieraus erhellet zugleich, warum man keinen Satz einer Stimme allein kann singen lassen; denn wer wollte eine einzige Stimme, ohne die geringste Begleitung, einen ganzen Satz hindurch, ohne Ekel anhören können?

In Ansehung des Ausdrucks der Worte sieht man in der Motette mehr auf den Hauptverstand derselben, und auf die Zeit und den Ort, wenn und wo die Motette gebrauchet werden soll. Da ferne die Schreibart fast allemal erhaben seyn muß so hat man insonderheit auf ein männliches und durchdringendes Wesen zu sehen, damit alles mit gleichem Nachdrucke in die Ohren fällt. Und man muß dahero auch die Motetten, wo es nur möglich ist, sehr stark von Sängern besetzen, sonst wird der Ausdruck dennoch schwach und matt bleiben, wenn schon der Componist alle Mühe angewendet hat, dieses zu verhindern. Die lebhaften Sätze müssen alles Kräuseln vermeiden, und die langsamen niemals zu lange anhalten, auch nicht allzu traurig und langsam eingerichtet werden. Man hat also bey traurigen Worten

p. 182

mehr einen deutlichen Vortrag, als einen allzueigentlichen Ausdruck der Worte zu beobachten, damit die Zuhörer, weil die Veränderung der Sänger und der Instrumente mangelt, nicht müde gemacht, sondern in besserer Aufmerksamkeit erhalten werden. Die lebhaften Worte muß man im Gegentheil auch etwas mäßigen, damit kein wüßtes, wildes, oder allzu|

p. 183 lustiges Geräusche und Geschrey daraus entstehe, sondern die Hauptcharaktere der Kirchenmusik müssen durchgehends die Oberhand haben. Die Ehrfurcht gegen das göttliche Wesen, die Andacht und die Ehrbarkeit und die Sittsamkeit des Ortes und der Zeit sollen allemal unsern Erfindungen die gehörigen Gränzen setzen, damit alles in seiner Ordnung und in gebührender Uebereinstimmung mit den festgesetzten Absichten geschehe.

Die Ausarbeitung erfordet endlich noch einige Anmerkungen. Daß überhaupt keine ordentliche und durchaus herrschende Hauptmelodie in den Motetten seyn kann, ist bereits aus angeführten Vorerinnerungen zu schließen; es muß also darinnen vornehmlich auf einen wohleingerichteten harmonischen Zusammenhang gesehen werden. Alle harmonische Ausfüllung, die man zur Erhebung einer Melodie, welche die Hauptstimme führet, gebrauchet, kann keine Statt finden, sondern es muß beständig eine überaus flüßige und bündige Arbeit durch alle Stimmen zu hören seyn.

Man brauchet also zu der Ausarbeitung nichts als vollstimmige Nachahmungen, Fugen, und Doppelfugen. Zu desto mehrerm Nachdrucke aber gehören die Contrapuncte, nach ihrem verschiedenen Gattungen, wie auch die Canonen.

Da auch die Pracht und die Deutlichkeit zu beobachten sind, so muß man keine allzugekräuselte, oder auch gebrochene Hauptsätze zum Grunde der Ausführung legen, sondern es muß ein leichter, fließender und kurzer Satz, ohne chromatische, oder gekünstelte Ausschweifungen, die Worte und die Sätze mehr deutlich machen, als verstecken. Die übrige harmonische Durchführung des Hauptsatzes muß sich auch von allen außerordentlichen und enharmonischen Ausweichungen enthalten. Die Gänge in die Quinte, Sexte, Terz, Quart und Secunde, oder in weichen Tonarten in die Septime müssen nur allein beobachtet werden; die Ausweichung in fremde und ungewöhnliche Tonarten soll man insonderheit meiden, zumal in solchen

p. 184 Motetten, so keine In|strumente, oder kein Generalbaß dazu gebrauchet werden; denn es verwirren dergleichen übersteigende und ungewöhnliche Sätze den Zuhörer, und bringen die Sänger sehr leicht aus dem Tone, wo sie zumal nicht allzu tonfeste sind. Von der Unterlegung der Worte unter die Noten ist zu merken, daß ein beständiges Wechseln der Singestimmen die Worte immer mehr erheben soll, daß machmal die nachfolgenden Worte zugleich mit dem vorhergehenden können gesungen werden, wenn jene diese erklären, oder nachdem auch die Stimmen, wegen ihrer fugirenden Sätze angefangen, abgehen, oder wieder eintreten. Die eingerückten Choräle sollen aber allemal gleichsam einen Gegensatz zu dem Hauptsatze der Motette ausmachen; dahero muß man sich bey der Erfindung und Ausarbeitung desselben, wie auch derer dazu gehörigen, oder damit verbundenen Contrapuncte jederzeit richten. Es würde ein großer Uebelstand seyn, wenn mann diese Vorsorge nicht gebrauchet hätte, und man müßte alsdann bey dem Eintritte des Chorals die bisherige Ausarbeitung der vorhandenen Sätze verlassen, und ganz neu erfinden.

Von der Aus[ar]beitung der zweychörichten und dreychörichten Motetten muß ich noch erinnern, daß die Chöre allemal besondere, gegen einander streitende, Sätze führen müssen, also, daß jeder Chor seinen eigenen Hauptsatz und dessen Ausarbeitung für sich selbst bekömmt. Daß aber diese Sätze alle zusammenstimmen müssen, brauchet keiner Erinnerung. Man kann aber auch gar leicht erachten, daß dergleichen starke Motetten, zumal wenn sie dreychöricht sind, mit außerordentlichem Fleiße zu arbeiten sind, wo sie anders prächtig, nachdrücklich und ungezwungen klingen sollen. Sie erfordern ihren Meister, und ein Componist, der nicht besonders in allen Arten von Fugen und Contrapuncten wohl beschlagen ist, wird unmöglich geschickt seyn, eine dergleichen künstliche Motette zu verfertigen. Wem nicht auch die verborgensten Schlupfwinkel der Harmonie bekannt sind, der mag ja unterlassen, sich an diese Stücke zu wagen, wie leicht dörfte er nicht seine Schwäche verrathen, und wie bald

p. 185 würde | man sehen, wie wenig er die Geheimnisse der Harmonie versteht?

Das sind also die vornehmsten Regeln, wie eine Motette zu verfertigen ist. Und man hat nicht zu zweifeln, daß, wenn man alle Motetten nach diesen Vorschlägen einrichten würde, dieselben bald mehr in Obacht genommen, und höher gehalten werden dörften. Es muß aber auch zugleich ein guter und tonfester Chorsänger seyn, der diese Motetten absingen sollte. Sie müssen alle deutliche, vernehmliche und reine Stimmen haben, und es muß auch jedwede Stimme mehr verschiedenemal besetzt seyn.

Der größte Fehler, der noch in der Aufführung der Motetten begangen wird, ist wohl dieser, daß viele geschickte Sänger diese Art musikalischer Stücke für schülerhaft halten, sich folglich ihrer schämen, und sie nur als Kleinigkeiten ansehen, bey denen es nicht darauf ankömmt, ob man sie eben so genau absingt, da doch keine geringe Geschicklichkeit darzu erfordert wird, diese Stücke ihrer Natur gemäß abzusingen. Dieser Umstand nöthiget viele große Städte, diese sonst so prächtige Zierde des Gottesdienstes zu verbannen, weil nicht überall die Schulen in solchem Stande sind, daß man damit den musikalischen Chor in der Kirche besetzen kann. Diejenigen Städte haben in der That einen großen Vorzug in der Musik, da man für die Unterhaltung eines guten Chores von Sängern aus den Schulen bedacht ist, da man gewisse kleine Belohnungen unter diese jungen Leute austheilet, damit man sie desto mehr aufmuntere, die Ordnung des Gottesdienstes zu erhalten, und da man sich mit gleichem Ernste bestrebet, dem Vaterlande geschickte Gelehrte, und erfahrne Musikanten mitzutheilen.

Friedrich Wilhelm Marpurg, *Abhandlung von der Fuge*, 2 vols. (Berlin, 1753–54), vol. ii, pp. 131–32.

[Von der Singfuge]

p. 131 §10. So viele Glieder oder Abschnitte in dem Texte stecken, so viele Sätze muß auch die Fuge haben. Man sieht daraus, daß man sich nicht leicht einen Text über drey oder vier Sätze zu wählen hat. Sind mehrere Glieder darinnen, oder sind solche so beschaffen, daß sie dem Inhalte nach einander entgegen lauffen, und man sie folglich nicht mit einander vereinigen kann:

p. 132 so fugiret man jeden Satz kurz einmahl durch alle Stimmen durch, | und fänget mit jedem neuen Gliede des Textes einen neuen Satz an. Das wird alsdenn eine Motette, d. i. ein aus vielen kleinen Fugen zusammengesetztes musikalisches Kirchenstück. Ich nehme das Wort Motette in dem Verstande, als es vordem genommen worden ist. Die Solocantaten, die man heutiges Tages an vielen Oertern der römischen Kirche, nach Italienischer Art, zum Offertorio singet, sind als eine Erfindung neuerer Zeit auch mit einem neuen Nahmen zu benennen, und können so wenig als alle Gattungen der geistlichen Musik bey den Franzosen ohne Unterscheid, den Nahmen der Motetten führen.

§11. Man verbindet in einer solchen Motette öfters zweyerlei Texte, oder man führet eben denselben Text auf zweyerley Art durch. Dieses geschicht wenn dieselbe über den Vers eines Kirchenliedes verfertiget wird, wo man den vesten Gesang dieses Chorals in einer dazu vestgesetzten Stimme nach Maßgebung der eintretenden Glieder oder Sätze, vermittelst der Vergrösserung, oder doch in einer andern etwas abstechenden Bewegung, dagegen anbringet. Jenes geschicht wenn die Motette über eine biblische Prose ist, mit welcher auf eben diese Art in einer andern Stimme der veste Gesang eines sich dazu schickenden Chorals verbunden wird. Diese leztere aber kann auch in einer ordentlichen Fuge geschehen.

Bibliography

Bach, Carl Philipp Emanuel. *Verzeichniß des musikalischen Nachlasses des verstorbenen Capellmeisters Carl Philipp Emanuel Bach.* Hamburg, 1790. Facsimile edition, *The Catalog of Carl Philipp Emanuel Bach's Estate.* Ed. Rachel W. Wade. Garland Reference Library of the Humanities, no. 240. New York, 1981. Transcribed by Heinrich Miesner. "Philipp Emanuel Bachs musikalischer Nachlass." *BJ* 35 (1938): 103–36; 36 (1939): 81–112; 37 (1940–48): 161–81.

—— *Verzeichniß von auserlesenen . . . meistens Neuen Büchern und Kostbaren Werken. . . welche nebst den Musikalien aus dem Nachlaß des seel. Kapellmeisters C. P. E. Bach . . . öffentlich verkauft werden sollen.* Hamburg, [1805]. (Exemplar SBB Mus. Db 313.)

Bach, Johann Christoph and Johann Michael Bach. *Neun Motetten für Singchöre von Johann Christoph Bach und Johann Michael Bach Ites [IItes/IIItes] Heft. Kirchenmusik verschiedener Zeiten und Völker, gesammelt von F. Naue. No I [II/III] Leipzig bei Fried: Hofmeister [1821/22/23].*

Bach, Johann Sebastian. *Joh. Seb. Bach's Motetten in Partitur Erster Heft [Zweites Heft] . . . Leipzig bey Breitkopf und Härtel.* [1802/3].

Bach-Archiv Leipzig. *Bach-Dokumente.* Vol. i, *Schriftstücke von der Hand Johann Sebastian Bachs (Dok I).* Ed. by Werner Neumann and Hans-Joachim Schulze. Leipzig and Cassel, 1963. Vol. ii, *Fremdschriftliche und gedruckte Dokumente zur Lebensgeschichte Johann Sebastian Bachs 1685–1750 (Dok II).* Ed. Werner Neumann and Hans-Joachim Schulze. Leipzig and Cassel, 1969. Vol. iii, *Dokumente zum Nachwirken Johann Sebastian Bachs 1750–1800 (Dok III).* Ed. Hans-Joachim Schulze. Leipzig and Cassel, 1972.

Bachmair, J. "'Komm, Jesu, komm': Der Textdichter. – Ein unebekanntes Werk von Johann Schelle." *BJ* 29 (1932): 142–45.

Beißwenger, Kirsten. *Johann Sebastian Bachs Notenbibliothek.* Catalogus Musicus, no. 13. Cassel, 1992.

Blechschmidt, Eva Renate. *Die Amalien-Bibliothek: Musikbibliothek der Prinzessin Anna Amalia von Preußen (1723–1787): Historische Einordnung und Katalog mit Hinweisen auf die Schreiber der Handschriften.* Berliner Studien zur Musikwissenschaft, no. 8. Berlin, 1965.

Bokemeyer, Heinrich. *Der melodische Vorhof.* In Johann Mattheson, *Critica Musica.* 2 vols. Hamburg, 1722–25.

Brainard, Paul. "The aria and its ritornello: the question of 'dominance' in Bach." In *Bachiana et alia musicologica: Festschrift Alfred Dürr,* ed. Wolfgang Rehm, 39–51. Cassel, 1983.

Braun, Werner. *Die mitteldeutsche Choralpassion im achtzehnten Jahrhundert.* Berlin, 1960.

Breig, Werner. "Grundzüge einer Geschichte von Bachs vierstimmigem Choralsatz." Part 1. *Archiv für Musikwissenschaft* 45, no. 3 (1988): 165–85.

Brossard, Sebastien de. *Dictionaire de Musique.* 2nd edn. Paris, 1703.

Buttstedt, Johann Heinrich. *Ut, mi, sol, re, fa, la.* Erfurt, 1716.

Cammarota, Robert. "The Repertoire of Magnificats in Leipzig at the Time of J. S. Bach: A Study of the Manuscript Sources." Ph.D. diss., New York University, 1986.

Dadelsen, Georg von. *Beiträge zur Chronologie der Werke Johann Sebastian Bachs.* Tübinger Bach-Studien, nos. 4/5. Trossingen, 1958.

Dammann, Rolf. "Geschichte der Begriffsbestimmung Motette." *Archiv für Musikwissenschaft* 16, no. 4 (1959): 337–77.

Danckwardt, Marianne. "Zur Aria aus J. S. Bachs Motette 'Komm, Jesu, komm!'" *Archiv für Musikwissenschaft* 44, no. 3 (1987): 195–202.

David, Hans T. and Arthur Mendel, eds. *The Bach Reader*. 2nd edn. New York, 1966.

Dreyfus, Laurence. *Bach's Continuo Group: Players and Practices in his Vocal Works*. Cambridge, Mass., 1987.

Dürr, Alfred. *Die Kantaten von Johann Sebastian Bach*. Cassel, 1971.

—— *Zur Chronologie der Leipziger Vokalwerke J. S. Bachs*. 2nd edn. Cassel, 1976.

—— *Studien über die frühen Kantaten Johann Sebastian Bachs*. 2nd edn. Wiesbaden, 1977.

—— "Melodievarianten in Johann Sebastian Bachs Kirchenliedbearbeitungen." In *Das protestantische Kirchenlied im 16. und 17. Jahrhundert*, ed. Alfred Dürr and Walther Killy, 149–63. Wolfenbüttler Forschungen, no. 31. Wiesbaden, 1986.

—— "Zum Choralchorsatz 'Herr Jesu Christ, wahr' Mensch und Gott' BWV 127 (Satz 1) und seiner Umarbeitung." *BJ* 74 (1988): 205–9.

Ehmann, Wilhelm. "Aufführungspraxis der Bachschen Motetten." In *Kongress-Bericht: Gesellschaft für Musikforschung Lüneburg 1950*, ed. H. Albrecht et al., 121–23. Cassel, 1950. Repr. *Musik und Kirche* 21 (1951): 49–67.

Eitner, Robert. "Mitteilungen." *Monatshefte für Musik-Geschichte* 17 (1885): 72 (on BWV Anh. 159).

Engler, Klaus. "Georg Poelchau und seine Musikaliensammlung: Ein Beitrag zur Überlieferung bachscher Musik in der ersten Hälfte des 19. Jahrhunderts." Ph.D. diss., Tübingen, 1984.

Fellerer, Karl Gustav. "J. S. Bachs Bearbeitung der Missa sine nomine von Palestrina." *BJ* 24 (1927): 123–32.

Fock, Gustav. *Der junge Bach in Lüneburg 1700 bis 1702*. Hamburg, 1950.

Forkel, Johann Nikolaus. *Allgemeine Geschichte der Musik*. 2 vols. Leipzig, 1788–1801.

—— *Ueber Johann Sebastian Bachs Leben, Kunst und Kunstwerke*. Leipzig, 1802.

Franke, Erhard, ed. *Johann Christoph Bach: Sämtliche Motetten*. Leipzig, 1982.

Freyse, Conrad, ed. *Aria Eberliniana*, by Johann Christoph Bach. Veröffentlichung der Neuen Bachgesellschaft, no. 39/2. Leipzig, 1940.

Fuhrmann, Martin Heinrich. *Musicalischer-Trichter*. Berlin, 1706.

Geck, Martin. "Zur Datierung, Verwendung und Aufführungspraxis von Bachs Motetten." In *Eine Sammlung von Aufsätze*, ed. Rudolf Eller and Hans-Joachim Schulze. Bach-Studien, no. 5, 63–71. Leipzig, 1975.

Geiringer, Karl and Irene Geiringer. *The Bach Family: Seven Generations of Creative Genius*. New York, 1954.

Gerber, Ernst Ludwig. *Neues historisch-biographisches Lexikon der Tonkünstler*. 4 vols. Leipzig, 1812–14.

Gerber, Rudolf. "Über Formstrukturen in Bachs Motetten." *Die Musikforschung* 3 (1950): 177–89.

Glöckner, Andreas. "Johann Sebastian Bachs Aufführungen zeitgenössicher Passionsmusiken." *BJ* 63 (1977): 75–119.

Grubbs, John W. "Ein Passions-Pasticcio des 18. Jahrhunderts." *BJ* 51 (1965): 10–42.

Grüß, Hans. "Johann Christoph Bachs Hochzeitsstück 'Meine Freundin, du bist schön' aus dem Altbachischen Archiv." In *Johann Sebastian Bachs Traditionsraum*, ed. Reinhard Szeskus. Bach-Studien, no. 9, 78–83. Leipzig, 1986.

Häfner, Klaus. "Der Picander-Jahrgang." *BJ* 61 (1975): 70–113.

Hellmann, Diethard. "Eine Kuhnau-Bearbeitung Joh. Seb. Bachs?" *BJ* 53 (1967): 93–99.

Hill, Robert. "'Der Himmel weiss, wo diese Sachen hingekommen sind': reconstructing the lost keyboard notebooks of the young Bach and Handel." In *Bach, Handel, Scarlatti: Tercentenary Essays*, ed. Peter Williams, 161–72. Cambridge, 1985.

—— "The Möller Manuscript and the Andreas Bach Book: Two Keyboard Anthologies from the Circle of the Young Johann Sebastian Bach." Ph.D. diss., Harvard University, 1987.

Hofmann, Klaus. "Zur Echtheit der Motette 'Jauchzet dem Herrn, alle Welt' BWV Anh. 160." In *Bachiana et alia musicologica: Festschrift Alfred Dürr*, ed. Wolfgang Rehm, 126–40. Cassel, 1983.

—— "Alter Stil in Bachs Kirchenmusik. Zu der Choralbearbeitung BWV 28/2." In *Alte Musik als ästhetische Gegenwart: Bach Händel Schütz: Bericht über den internationalen musikwissenschaftlichen Kongreß Stuttgart 1985*. 2 vols. Ed. Dietrich Berke and Dorothee Hanemann, 1:164–69. Cassel, 1987.

——, ed. *Johann Sebastian Bach (?): Jauchzet dem Herrn, alle Welt BWV Anh. 160*. Neuhausen-Stuttgart, 1978.

Horn, Wolfgang. *Die Dresdner Hofkirchenmusik 1720–1745*. Cassel and Stuttgart, 1987.

Junghans, W. "Johann Sebastian Bach als Schüler der Partikularschule zu St. Michaelis in Lüneburg oder Lüneburg eine Pflegstätte kirchlicher Musik." In *Programm des Johanneums zu Lüneburg: Ostern 1870*.

Karstädt, Georg. *Thematisch-systematisches Verzeichnis der musikalischen Werke von Dietrich Buxtehude. Buxtehude-Werke-Verzeichnis (BuxWV)*. 2nd edn. Wiesbaden, 1985.

Kast, Paul. *Die Bach-Handschriften der Berliner Staatsbibliothek*. Tübinger Bach-Studien, nos. 2/3. Trossingen, 1958.

Kobayashi, Yoshitake. "Zur Chronologie der Spätwerke Johann Sebastian Bachs: Kompositions- und Aufführungstätigkeit von 1736 bis 1750." *BJ* 74 (1988): 7–72.

—— "Zur Teilung des Bachschen Erbes." Typescript, 1988.

Koch, Heinrich Christoph. *Musikalisches Lexikon*. Frankfurt-am-Main, 1802.

Krautwurst, Franz. "Anmerkungen zu den Augsburger Bach-Dokumenten." In *Festschrift Martin Ruhnke*, ed. Institut für Musikwissenschaft der Universität Erlangen-Nürnberg, 176–84. Neuhausen-Stuttgart, 1986.

Krummacher, Friedhelm. *Die Überlieferung der Choralbearbeitungen in der frühen evangelischen Kantate*. Berlin, 1965.

—— "Die Tradition in Bachs vokalen Choralbearbeitungen." In *Bach-Interpretationen: Walter Blankenburg zum 65. Geburtstag*, ed. Martin Geck, 29–56. Göttingen, 1969.

—— "Textauslegung und Satzstruktur in Bachs Motetten." *BJ* 60 (1974): 5–43.

—— "Mehrchörigkeit und thematischer Satz bei Johann Sebastian Bach." *Schütz-Jahrbuch* 1981: 39–50.

Kurtzgefaßtes Musikalisches Lexicon. Chemnitz, 1737.

Landmann, Ortrun. "Das Werk Sebastian Knüpfers im Überblick." Diplomarbeit, Leipzig, 1960.

Leichtentritt, Hugo. *Geschichte der Motette*. Leipzig, 1908.

——, ed. *Ausgewählte Werke von Andreas Hammerschmidt*. DDT 40. Leipzig, 1910.

Lesure, François. *Bibliographie des èditions musicales publiées par Estienne Roger et Michel-Charles Le Cène (Amsterdam 1696–1743)*. Paris, 1969.

Leutge, Wilhelm. "Bachs Motette 'Jesu, meine Freude.'" *Musik und Kirche* 4, no. 3 (1932): 97–113.

Lorenz, Alfred. "Homophone Grossrhythmik in Bachs Polyphonie." *Die Musik* 22, no. 4 (1930): 245–53.

MacCracken, Thomas G. "Die Verwendung der Blechblasinstrumente bei J. S. Bach unter besonderer Berücksichtigung der Tromba da tirarsi." *BJ* 70 (1984): 5989.

Märker, Michael. "Der Stile antico und die frühen Kantaten Johann Sebastian Bachs." In *Johann Sebastian Bachs Traditionsraum*, ed. Reinhard Szeskus. Bach-Studien, no. 9, 72–77. Leipzig, 1986.

Marpurg, Friedrich Wilhelm. *Abhandlung von der Fuge*. 2 vols. Berlin, 1753–54.

Marshall, Robert L. *The Compositional Process of J. S. Bach*. 2 vols. Princeton, 1972.

Mattheson, Johann. *Das neu-eröffnete Orchestre*. Hamburg, 1713.

—— *Das beschützte Orchestre*. Hamburg, 1717.

—— *Critica Musica*. 2 vols. Hamburg, 1722–25.

—— *Der vollkommene Capellmeister*. Hamburg, 1739.

Melamed, Daniel R. "The Authorship of the Motet *Ich lasse dich nicht* (BWV Anh. 159)." *Journal of the American Musicological Society* 41, no. 3 (1988): 491–526.

Meyer, Ulrich. "Zur Einordnung von J. S. Bachs einzeln überlieferten Orgelchorälen." *BJ* 60 (1974): 75–89.

Mizler von Kolof, Lorenz. *Neu-eröffnete musikalische Bibliothek*. 4 vols. Leipzig, 1739–54.

Müller, Joseph. *Die musikalischen Schätze der Königlichen- und Universitäts-Bibliothek zu Königsberg in Preussen*. Bonn, 1870.

Neumann, Werner. *J. S. Bachs Chorfuge*. 2nd edn. Leipzig, 1950.

—— "Welche Handschriften J. S. Bachscher Werke besaß die Berliner Singakademie?" In *Hans Albrecht in Memoriam*, ed. Wilfried Brennecke and Hans Haase, 136–42. Cassel, 1962.

—— "Eine Leipziger Bach-Gedenkstätte: Über die Beziehungen der Familien Bach und Bose." *BJ* 56 (1970): 19–31.

——, ed. *Sämtliche von Johann Sebastian Bach vertonte Texte*. Leipzig, 1974.

Newman, S. T. M. "Bach's motet: 'Singet dem Herrn.'" *Proceedings of the Royal Musical Association* 1937–38, 97–129.

Niedt, Friedrich Erhard. *Musicalische Handleitung Dritter Theil*. Ed. Johann Mattheson. Hamburg, 1717.

Noack, Elizabeth. "Die Bibliothek der Michaeliskirche zu Erfurt." *Archiv für Musikwissenschaft* 7 (1925): 65–116.

Petzoldt, Martin. "Überlegungen zur theologischen und geistigen Integration Bachs in Leipzig 1723." *Beiträge zur Bachforschung* 1 (1982): 46–52.

—— "J. S. Bach's Bearbeitungen des Liedes 'Jesu, meine Freude' von Johann Franck." *Musik und Kirche* 55, no. 5 (1985): 213–25.

Platen, Emil. "Untersuchungen zur Struktur der chorischen Choralbearbeitung Johann Sebastian Bachs." Ph.D. diss., Bonn, 1959.

—— "Eine Pergolesi-Bearbeitung Bachs." *BJ* 48 (1961): 35–51.

Prinz, Ulrich. "Studien zum Instrumentarium Johann Sebastian Bachs mit besonderer Berücksichtigung der Kantaten." Ph.D. diss., Tübingen, 1979.

Richter, Bernhard Friedrich. "Eine Abhandlung Joh. Kuhnau's." *Monatshefte für Musik-Geschichte* 34, no. 9 (1902): 147–54.

—— "Zur Geschichte der Passionsaufführungen in Leipzig." *BJ* 8 (1911): 50–59.

—— "Über die Motetten Seb. Bachs." *BJ* 9 (1912): 1–32.

Riemer, Otto. "Erhard Bodenschatz und sein Florilegium Portense." Ph.D. diss., Halle-Wittenberg, 1927.

Rifkin, Joshua. "Sounds like Bach." BBC radio broadcast script. Unpublished, 1993.

Rochlitz, Johann Friedrich. "Über den Geschmack an Sebastian Bachs Kompositionen, besonders für das Klavier." *Allgemeine musikalische Zeitung* 5, no. 31 (27 April 1803): 509–22.

—— *Für Freunde der Tonkunst.* Leipzig, 1824; 2nd edn. 1830.

Rubin, Norman. "'Fugue' as a delimiting concept in Bach's choruses: a gloss on Werner Neumann's 'J. S. Bachs Chorfuge.'" In *Studies in Renaissance and Baroque Music in Honor of Arthur Mendel*, ed. Robert L. Marshall, 195–208. Hackensack, 1974.

Scheibe, Johann Adolph. *Compendium Musices.* Manuscript. Transcribed in Peter Benary, *Die deutsche Kompositionslehre des 18. Jahrhunderts.* Jenaer Beiträge zur Musikforschung, no. 3. Leipzig, 1961.

—— *Critischer Musikus.* 2nd edn. Leipzig, 1745.

Scheibel, Gottfried Ephraim. *Zufällige Gedanken von der Kirchenmusik, wie sie heutiges Tages beschaffen.* Frankfurt and Leipzig, 1722.

Scheide, William. "Johann Sebastian Bachs Sammlung von Kantaten seines Vetters Johann Ludwig Bach." Part I. *BJ* 46 (1959): 52–94.

—— "'Nun ist das Heil und die Kraft' BWV 50: Doppelchörigkeit, Datierung und Bestimmung." *BJ* 68 (1982): 81–96.

Schering, Arnold. "Die alte Chorbibliothek der Thomasschule in Leipzig." *Archiv für Musikwissenschaft* 1 (1918–19): 275–88.

—— "Über Bachs Parodieverfahren." *BJ* 18 (1921): 49–95.

—— *Musikgeschichte Leipzigs.* Vol. ii. Leipzig, 1926.

—— *Johann Sebastian Bachs Leipziger Kirchenmusik.* 2nd edn. Leipzig, 1954.

——, ed. *Sebastian Knüpfer, Johann Schelle, Johann Kuhnau: Ausgewählte Kirchenkantaten.* DDT 58/59. Leipzig, 1918.

Schicht, Johann Gottfried. *Versteigerungs-Katalog der von dem verstorbenen Herrn J. G. Schicht . . . hinterlassenen Musikaliensammlung.* Leipzig, [1832].

Schmieder, Wolfgang. *Thematisch-systematisches Verzeichnis der musikalischen Werke von Johann Sebastian Bach. Bach-Werke-Verzeichnis (BWV).* Leipzig, 1950.

Schneider, Herbert. *Chronologisch-thematisches Verzeichnis sämtlicher Werke von Jean-Baptiste Lully (LWV).* Tutzing, 1981.

Schneider, Max. *Altbachisches Archiv.* 2 vols. EDM 1/2. Leipzig, 1935.

Schulze, Hans-Joachim. "Marginalien zu einigen Bach-Dokumenten." *BJ* 48 (1961): 79–99.

—— "Frühe Schriftzeugnisse der beiden jüngsten Bach-Söhne." *BJ* 50 (1963/64): 61–69.

—— "'150 Stück von den Bachischen Erben': Zur Überlieferung der vierstimmigen Choräle Johann Sebastian Bachs." *BJ* 69 (1983): 81–100.

—— *Studien zur Bach-Überlieferung im 18. Jahrhundert.* Leipzig, 1984.

Schulze, Hans-Joachim and Christoph Wolff. *Bach Compendium.* Leipzig, 1985– .

Schünemann, Georg. "Die Bachpflege der Berliner Singakademie." *BJ* 25 (1928): 138–71.

—— *Die Singakademie zu Berlin 1791–1941.* Regensburg, 1941.

Seiffert, Max. "Die Chorbibliothek der St. Michaelisschule in Lüneburg zu Seb. Bach's Zeit." *Sammelbände der Internationalen Musik-Gesellschaft* 9, no. 4 (1908): 593–621.

Serauky, Walter. *Musikgeschichte der Stadt Halle.* Vol. ii, part 2. Halle, 1942.

Siegele, Ulrich. "Bemerkungen zu Bachs Motetten." *BJ* 49 (1962): 33–57.

Sing-Akademie zu Berlin. *Zur Geschichte der Sing-Akademie in Berlin nebst . . . einem alphabetischen Verzeichniss aller Personen, die ihr als Mitglieder angehört haben.* Berlin, 1843. (Exemplar SBB.)

Smend, Friederich. "Bach's Matthäus-Passion." *BJ* 25 (1928): 1–95.

Snyder, Kerala. *Dieterich Buxtehude: Organist in Lübeck*. New York, 1987.

Speer, Daniel. *Grundrichtiger Unterricht der musikalischen Kunst*. 2nd edn. Ulm, 1697.

Spitta, Philipp. *Johann Sebastian Bach*. 2 vols. Leipzig, 1873–80.

Terry, Charles Sanford. *Joh. Seb. Bach: Cantata Texts Sacred and Secular*. London, 1926.

Tielke, Martin. "Die Erwerbung der Bach-Autographen durch die Königliche Bibliothek / Preussische Staatsbibliothek in Berlin." Thesis, Bibliothekar-Lehrinstitut des Landes Nordrhein-Westfalen, Cologne, 1980.

Walther, Johann Gottfried. *Musicalisches Lexicon*. Leipzig, 1732.

Welter, Friedrich. "Die Musikbibliothek der Sing-Akademie zu Berlin." In *Sing-Akademie zu Berlin: Festschrift zu 175jährigen Bestehen*, ed. Werner Bollert, 33–47. Berlin, 1966.

Williams, Peter. *The Organ Music of J. S. Bach*. Vol. ii. Cambridge, 1983.

Wolff, Christoph. *Der Stile antico in der Musik Johann Sebastian Bachs*. Beihefte zum Archiv für Musikwissenschaft, no. 6. Wiesbaden, 1968.

—— "Bachs doppelchörige Motetten." *Bachfest-Buch* 44: 96–98. Heidelberg, 1969.

—— "Bachs Leipziger Kantoratsprobe und die Aufführungsgeschichte der Kantate 'Du wahrer Gott und Davids Sohn' BWV 23." *BJ* 64 (1978): 78–94.

—— *The Neumeister Collection of Chorale Preludes from the Bach Circle*. New Haven, 1986.

Zelter, Carl Friedrich. *Catalog musikalisch – literarischer und practischer Werke aus dem Nachlasse der Königl: Professors Dr. Zelter*. Manuscript. SBB N. Mus. ms. theor. 30.

Index of J. S. Bach's works

Includes spurious works. Page numbers in italics refer to music examples.

Oratorios and Latin works

Index of manuscript music sources

Surviving sources only; for lost sources of the Altbachisches Archiv, see table 11–1. Page numbers in italics refer to figures.

General index

Page numbers in italics refer to figures and music examples.

Printed in the United States
44577LVS00003B/85-94